INFECTIOUS DISEASES

HEALTH AND DISEASE IN SOCIETY

INFECTIOUS DISEASES

EDITED BY KARA ROGERS, SENIOR EDITOR, BIOMEDICAL SCIENCES

Educational Publishing

IN ASSOCIATION WITH

EDUCATIONAL SERVICES

Published in 2011 by Britannica Educational Publishing
(a trademark of Encyclopædia Britannica, Inc.)
in association with Rosen Educational Services, LLC
29 East 21st Street, New York, NY 10010.

Distributed exclusively by Rosen Educational Services.
For a listing of additional Britannica Educational Publishing titles, call toll free (800) 237-9932.

First Edition

Britannica Educational Publishing
Michael I. Levy: Executive Editor
J.E. Luebering: Senior Manager
Marilyn L. Barton: Senior Coordinator, Production Control
Steven Bosco: Director, Editorial Technologies
Lisa S. Braucher: Senior Producer and Data Editor
Yvette Charboneau: Senior Copy Editor
Kathy Nakamura: Manager, Media Acquisition
Kara Rogers: Senior Editor, Biomedical Sciences

Rosen Educational Services
Heather M. Moore Niver: Editor
Nelson Sá: Art Director
Cindy Reiman: Photography Manager
Matthew Cauli: Designer, Cover Design
Introduction by Chris Paddock

Library of Congress Cataloging-in-Publication Data

Infectious diseases / edited by Kara Rogers. — 1st ed.
    p. cm. — (Health and disease in society)
"In association with Britannica Educational Publishing, Rosen Educational Services."
Includes bibliographical references and index.
ISBN 978-1-61530-341-0 (library binding)
1. Communicable diseases—Popular works. I. Rogers, Kara.
RA643.I49 2011
616.9—dc22

                                                                2010034056

Manufactured in the United States of America

On the Cover: Shutterstock.com

On pages 1, 27, 45, 76, 96, 115, 131, 150, 164, 181: Contact with dermatophytic fungi can
cause hair, skin, and nail infections. *CDC/Dr. Libero Ajello*

CONTENTS

67

71

73

97

105

119

145

154

167

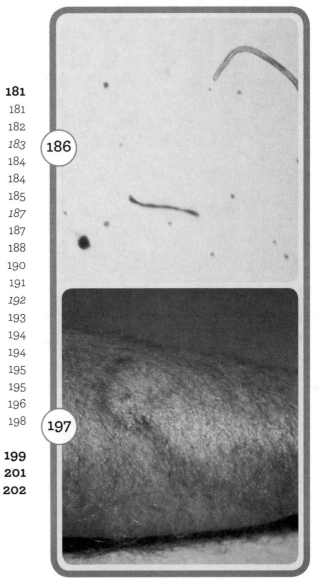

186

197

As humans, we sometimes forget about all the life around us, those organisms that we cannot readily see with the naked eye. Microorganisms, like bacteria, are everywhere in the human environment. They are in the air we breathe, the water we drink, the soil we tread upon. Many even live inside us and can only survive inside of us. Many also perform functions essential to human survival, such as reconditioning nutrients in the soil or purifying water. But there are a certain percentage of these microbes that, should they gain entrance into the body, can be quite dangerous. Infectious agents—certain bacteria, viruses, and protozoans—interact with the human body in all the same ways that more-helpful microbes do. Once they enter a human host, or, rather, invade, they can do a great deal of harm, and even cause death.

This insightful volume provides an overview of diseases caused by infectious agents, and how they affect human lives. The book covers the various infectious diseases; how they are transmitted; details of the human immune response; treatment; and, for some more notable and devastating diseases, a history of their effect on human society.

The major types of infectious agents are roughly grouped as bacteria, viruses, parasites, worms, and fungi. Each type varies in size and biochemistry, and they interact with the human host in very different ways. Bacteria, for example, are themselves organisms and can usually be viewed under a microscope, whereas viruses are not, technically speaking, living organisms at all and cannot be seen with the aid of simple light microscopes. Viruses exist only by means of replicating themselves within the living cells of host organisms.

Infectious agents are spread in numerous and varying ways, and their survival ultimately depends on a given environment. Humans are often the primary factor in spreading infectious disease, with living conditions and travel historically playing crucial roles in the facilitation of epidemics and pandemics. Crowded home environments brought on by overpopulation can create optimum conditions for disease transmission because of proximity and the potential compromises to hygiene caused by too many people using too few resources. The quality of sanitary and hygiene practices generally devolve with the onslaught of overcrowding. With global travel comes more opportunities—more potential hosts—to carry diseases from one place to another, perhaps exposing an infectious agent to a population that may not have immunity to it.

With any animal organism, there is some degree of natural immunity, or resistance to disease. But immunity can be

Although some microorganisms are helpful, others can cause a great deal of harm and even death. iStockphoto/Thinkstock

acquired as well, generally when humans are exposed to a disease at a young age. This trains antibodies to quickly and effectively respond to the disease. With some diseases, like measles, acquired immunity can last a lifetime, but with others, it could last only months. Vaccines are sometimes used to stimulate an effect similar to prolonged exposure, provoking antibodies to respond and build immunity, ensuring a more controlled method of acquiring immunity.

Leprosy and tuberculosis have particularly long, ignominious histories. They spawn from microbes of the same genus, *Mycobacterium*. Mummified remains suggests that leprosy existed in India as many as 4,000 years ago, and genetic evidence traces back tuberculosis even further, to the ancient Egyptians, approximately 9,000 years ago. These diseases have struck fear in humankind for much of their known existences. Leprosy, which affects the skin and peripheral nerves, was thought to be so contagious that, between the 11th and 13th centuries, its victims were quarantined and their positions inherited by relatives. Today, leprosy is deemed curable and is known to be transmitted only through extended human-to-human contact. Tuberculosis, or "consumption," breaks down respiratory and lung tissue and is also transmitted from human to human, although much more easily than leprosy. This "captain of death" was a leading cause of mortality to adults in their prime in the 19th and 20th centuries. Though it

has stabilized in the Western world, it is still a prevalent disease elsewhere and is increasingly associated with the spread of HIV, which compromises the body's immune function.

Cholera and plague are other bacterial diseases with long histories of devastating humankind. Although these diseases vary in their means of transmission, both are tied to poor living conditions and regarded as highly contagious. Cholera is spread when humans consume feces-tainted water containing the bacterium *Vibrio cholerae*. Populations suffering from sanitation and hygiene issues are particularly vulnerable. The world suffered through seven cholera pandemics in the 19th and 20th centuries, and a recent epidemic appeared in Africa in 2008-09. The plague, with its equally sordid past, is transported by rodents infected by fleas that then turn to human hosts once their rodent hosts die off. Plague pandemics have been recorded since the 6th century CE, wiping out almost a third of Europe's population in the 14th century in what is known as the Black Death. The exact means of transmission weren't properly identified until the turn of the 20th century, and rat-proofing measures have dramatically reduced annual worldwide mortality totals.

Fleas and other arthropods, such as ticks and lice, also transmit some rickettsial diseases. Rickettsial bacteria can only reproduce within animal cells and can cause extremely harmful diseases such as Rocky Mountain spotted fever and epidemic typhus. Typhus, carried by body lice, virtually vanished in the early 20th century, as living conditions improved, but caused severe epidemics in Eastern Europe and other parts of the world during World Wars I and II. It is still prevalent in Asia, Africa, and South America.

Chlamydia organisms cause various different infections, which are grouped together as chlamydial diseases. This group includes an array of sexually transmitted diseases, as well as some, like psittacosis, which is transmitted by birds, and trachoma, one of the oldest known diseases. Trachoma is transmitted by ocular secretion, often by use of a towel, and is found most often in areas where poor sanitation and hygiene prevail.

In addition to these disease groupings, a plethora of bacterial contagions have beleaguered humans for centuries. Anthrax may be more recently known as a biological weapon, but its origin is ancient. It has gained notoriety as a means of terrorism. Botulism is one of the better-known bacterial diseases in the Northern Hemisphere. It is commonly transmitted via improperly sterilized canned foods. Spores of the causative organism, *Clostridium botulinum*, can be killed by exposure to high temperatures, but consumption of contaminated products can lead to paralysis. Lyme disease, a relatively recent discovery among bacterial diseases, is often transmitted by various types of ticks by way of an infected deer or other animal.

Viruses cause diseases familiar to many, including chickenpox. Vaccination has proved to be the most successful method of battling viruses, having all but eliminated debilitating and deadly diseases like polio and smallpox. Pox diseases are often spread by airborne particles and are associated with livestock, such as sheep, cows, and chickens. In humans, pox diseases manifest as skin pustules. Smallpox historically was the most feared of the pox diseases, killing or disfiguring millions of people, particularly children. It became one of the first diseases to be contained by vaccination and was officially declared eradicated in 1980 by the World Health Organization (WHO). Polio, a debilitating disease most often affecting children, strangely only reached true epidemic status among developed countries in the 19th and 20th centuries. Although not yet eradicated, polio is limited to only a few countries, mainly in Africa and South Asia.

Influenza has caused significant outbreaks of disease throughout human history. Flu viruses are incredibly resistant to immunization, rapidly mutating to create new subtypes through a process known as antigenic shift. Influenza strains are tracked globally to aid in the development of new vaccines, which can be manufactured and distributed to prevent infection before a new strain infiltrates a population. Antigenic shifts have produced pandemics about once every 50 years. Four pandemics have taken place over the past century, the most recent being the H1N1 flu in 2009. This pandemic was extremely contagious, and the speed of its outreach was exacerbated by the high volume of passenger travel between continents.

Conversely, viral hemorrhagic fevers are usually much more geographically localized, because they are often transmitted by animal or insect hosts that are found only within a certain geographical area. Hemorrhagic fevers can be dangerous, usually causing considerable external or internal bleeding and high fever. Yellow fever is one of the most common hemorrhagic fevers and the only major fever successfully controlled by vaccine. Less common, but more fatal is the Ebola virus, which comes in multiple strains. SARS (severe acute respiratory syndrome), transmitted through sneezing and coughing, is an example of an acute viral infection. It is also a recent example of how passenger travel can quickly spread infectious disease. The 2002 SARS outbreak started in Hong Kong and advanced to North America and Europe within months.

Among recent epidemics, perhaps no infectious disease provokes more social response than AIDS (acquired immunodeficiency syndrome). AIDS, caused by transmission of human immunodeficiency virus (HIV) via direct transfer of bodily fluids (e.g., blood, semen, or breast milk), is incurable, and it has had devastating affects on populations worldwide. Approximately 70 percent of the more than 33.2 million people infected with

HIV live in sub-Saharan Africa. HIV can mutate and evolve quickly to evade recognition by the immune system. HIV/AIDS awareness is considered the best way to educate people on how to prevent the spread of the disease. Social customs in some parts of the world, however, have hindered the progress awareness and education efforts. Much has been done to raise awareness of AIDS, including the establishment of World AIDS Day and the massive AIDS Memorial Quilt, with panels representing tens of thousands of victims.

Malaria is another major infectious disease. Almost 250 million people worldwide are infected annually, with most of the nearly one million deaths occurring in Africa. Malaria is caused by single-celled protozoans, which are transmitted to humans by mosquitoes. Genetic evidence suggests that malaria could be as old as Egyptian King Tutankhamen, who reigned from 1333 to 1323 BCE. Malaria has felled important historical figures—including Alexander the Great, Dante Alighieri, and the artist Raphael—but discoveries revealing how the disease is transmitted have also yielded three Nobel Prizes. Other protozoal diseases affect impoverished populations beyond the reach of healthcare resources. Among the more destructive neglected protozoal diseases are dysentery, an intestinal ailment caused by parasites transmitted by contaminated food or water, and sleeping sickness, an infection that causes fever and inflamed lymph nodes that is transmitted by the tsetse fly.

Less widespread—but no less destructive—are infectious diseases caused by worms, prions, and fungi. Cestodiasis, or tapeworm, is transmitted by contaminated food or water, but it extracts nutrients from the cell of the host, causing harmful symptoms. Prions, however, are not technically organisms at all, but are instead abnormally formed proteins. These infectious agents enter the brain and multiply, causing the central nervous system to degenerate. Prion diseases include bovine spongiform encephalopathy, otherwise known as mad cow disease, and Creutzfeldt-Jakob disease.

The ensuing chapters provide a deeper understanding of the world of infectious diseases, including how they are classified, how they provoke the human immune system, and the symptoms that result from infection. But readers will also discover their influence on humankind, leaving—in the most devastating instances—a profound social and historical legacy.

CHAPTER 1

INFECTIOUS AGENTS AND THE HUMAN IMMUNE RESPONSE

Infectious diseases are among the most ancient afflictions of humankind. At times throughout human history, they have caused more deaths than war and famine, and as a result, they have been and continue to be the diseases most feared by humans. This element of fear is a reflection of the defining feature of infectious disease—transmissibility. Although it was recognized for many centuries that certain diseases are contagious—capable of being spread from one person to another—the discovery that microorganisms can cause infectious disease in humans is a relatively recent event in the history of science and medicine.

The term *infection* is used to describe the invasion of and replication in the body by any of various agents—including bacteria, viruses, fungi, protozoans, and worms—as well as the reaction of tissues to their presence or to the toxins that they produce. When health is not altered, the process is referred to as a subclinical infection. Thus, a person may be infected but not have an infectious disease. This principle is illustrated by the use of vaccines for the prevention of infectious diseases. For example, a virus that causes disease may be attenuated (weakened) and used as an immunizing agent. The immunization is designed to produce an infection in the recipient but generally causes no discernible alteration in the state of

Our surroundings can contain dangerous microorganisms, not visible to the naked eye, but the human body's immune system works quickly to try to fend off disease and infection.
Kane Skennar/Digital Vision/Thinkstock

health. It produces immunity to disease without producing a clinical illness (an infectious disease).

The most important barriers to invasion of the human host by microorganisms are the skin and mucous membranes (the tissues that line the nose, mouth, and upper respiratory tract). When these tissues have been affected by earlier disease, invasion by microorganisms may occur. These microorganisms may produce a local infectious disease, such as boils, or may invade the bloodstream and be carried throughout the body, producing generalized bloodstream infection (septicemia) or localized infection at a distant site, such as meningitis (an infection of the coverings of the brain and spinal cord). Infectious agents swallowed in food and drink can attack the wall of the intestinal tract and cause local or general disease. The conjunctiva, which covers the front of the eye, may be penetrated by viruses that cause a local inflammation of the eye or that pass into the bloodstream and cause a severe general disease, such as smallpox. Microorganisms can enter the body through the genital tract, causing an acute inflammatory reaction in the genital and pelvic organs, such as that characterizing gonorrhea, or spreading out to attack almost any organ of the body, such as the more chronic and destructive lesions of syphilis. Even before birth, viruses and other infectious agents can pass through the placenta and attack developing cells, so that an infant may be diseased or deformed at birth.

From conception to death, humans are targets for attack by countless infectious agents, all of them competing for a place in the common environment. The air people breathe, the soil they walk on, the waters and vegetation around them, the buildings they inhabit and work in, all can be populated with forms of life that are potentially dangerous. Domestic animals may harbour organisms that are a threat, and wildlife teems with agents of infection that can afflict humans with serious disease. The human body, however, is not without defenses against these threats. Indeed, it is equipped with a comprehensive immune system that reacts quickly and specifically against disease organisms when they attack. Survival throughout the ages has depended largely on these reactions, which today are supplemented and strengthened through the use of drugs and other medicines.

INFECTIOUS AGENTS: CATEGORIES OF ORGANISMS

The agents of infection can be divided into different groups on the basis of their size, biochemical characteristics, or manner in which they interact with the human host. The groups of organisms that cause infectious diseases are categorized as bacteria, viruses, fungi, and parasitic protozoans and worms.

BACTERIA

Bacteria can survive within the body but outside individual cells. Some bacteria, classified as aerobes, require oxygen for growth, whereas others, such as those normally found in the small intestine of healthy persons, grow only in the absence of oxygen and, therefore, are called anaerobes. Most bacteria are surrounded by a capsule that appears to play an important role in their ability to produce disease. Also, a number of bacterial species give off toxins that, in turn, may damage tissues. Bacteria are generally large enough to be seen under a light microscope. Streptococci, the bacteria that cause scarlet fever, are about 0.75 μm (1 μm = 0.000039 inch) in diameter. The spirochetes, which cause syphilis, leptospirosis, and rat-bite fever, are 5 to 15 μm long. Bacterial infections can be treated with antibiotics.

Bacterial infections are commonly caused by pneumococci, staphylococci, and streptococci, all of which are often commensals (organisms living harmlessly on their hosts) in the upper respiratory tract but that can become virulent and cause serious conditions, such

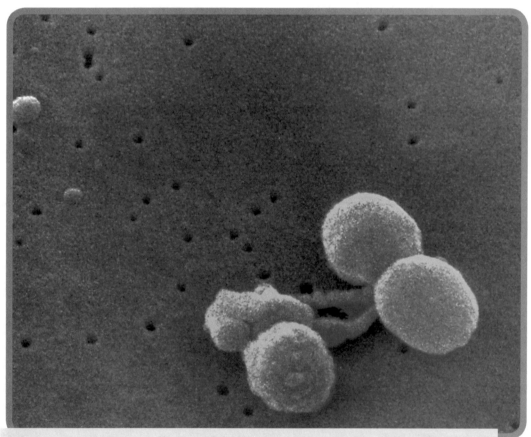

A light microscope is usually powerful enough to view bacteria such as streptococci. CDC/Dr. Richard Facklam. Photo by Janice Carr

as pneumonia, septicemia (blood poisoning), and meningitis. The pneumococcus is the most common cause of lobar pneumonia, a disease in which one or more lobes, or segments, of the lung become solid and airless as a result of inflammation. Staphylococci affect the lungs either in the course of staphylococcal septicemia—when bacteria in the circulating blood cause scattered abscesses in the lungs—or as a complication of a viral infection, commonly influenza—when these organisms invade the damaged lung cells and cause a life-threatening form of pneumonia. Streptococcal pneumonia is the least common of the three and occurs usually as a complication of influenza or other lung disease.

Pneumococci often enter the bloodstream from inflamed lungs and cause septicemia, with continued fever but no other special symptoms. Staphylococci produce a type of septicemia with high, spiking fever. The bacteria reach almost any tissue of the body, including the brain, the bones, and especially the lungs, and destructive abscesses form in the infected areas. Streptococci also cause septicemia with fever, but the organisms tend to cause inflammation of surface lining cells rather than abscesses—for example, pleurisy (inflammation of the chest lining) rather than lung abscess, and peritonitis (inflammation of the membrane lining the abdomen) rather than liver abscess. In the course of either of the last two forms of septicemia, organisms may enter the nervous system and cause streptococcal or staphylococcal

meningitis, but these are rare conditions. Pneumococci, however, often spread directly into the central nervous system, causing one of the common forms of meningitis.

Staphylococci and streptococci are common causes of skin diseases. Boils and impetigo (in which the skin is covered with blisters, pustules, and yellow crusts) may be caused by either. The staphylococcus also can cause a severe skin infection that strips the outer skin layers off the body and leaves the underlayers exposed, as in severe burns, a condition known as toxic epidermal necrolysis. Streptococcal organisms can cause a severe condition known as necrotizing fasciitis, commonly referred to as flesh-eating disease, which causes death in approximately 25 percent of cases. Streptococci can be the cause of the red cellulitis of the skin known as erysipelas.

Some staphylococci produce an intestinal toxin and cause food poisoning. Streptococci settling in the throat produce a reddening toxin that speeds through the bloodstream and produces the symptoms of scarlet fever. Streptococci and staphylococci also can cause toxic shock syndrome. Streptococcal toxic shock syndrome (STSS) is fatal in some 35 percent of cases.

Meningococci are fairly common inhabitants of the throat, in most cases causing no illness at all. As the number of healthy carriers increases in any population, however, there is a tendency for the meningococcus to become more invasive. When an opportunity is presented, it can gain access to the bloodstream, invade the central nervous system, and cause meningococcal meningitis (formerly called cerebrospinal meningitis or spotted fever). Meningococcal meningitis, at one time a dreaded and still a very serious disease, usually responds to treatment with penicillin if diagnosed early enough. When meningococci invade the bloodstream, some gain access to the skin and cause bloodstained spots, or purpura. If the condition is diagnosed early, antibiotics can clear the bloodstream of the bacterium and prevent any from getting far enough to cause meningitis. Sometimes the septicemia takes a mild, chronic, relapsing form with no tendency toward meningitis. This form is curable once it is diagnosed. The meningococcus also can cause one of the most fulminating of all forms of septicemia, meningococcemia, in which the body is rapidly covered with a purple rash, purpura fulminans. In this form the blood pressure becomes dangerously low, the heart and blood vessels are affected by shock, and the infected person dies within a matter of hours. Few are saved, despite treatment with appropriate drugs.

Haemophilus influenzae is a microorganism named for its occurrence in the sputum of patients with influenza—an occurrence so common that it was at one time thought to be the cause of the disease. It is now known to be a common inhabitant of the nose and throat that may invade the bloodstream, producing meningitis, pneumonia, and various other diseases. In children it is the most common cause of acute epiglottitis, an infection in which tissue at the back of the tongue becomes rapidly swollen and obstructs the airway, creating a potentially fatal condition. *H. influenzae* also is the most common cause of meningitis and pneumonia in children younger than age five, and it is known to cause bronchitis in adults. The diagnosis is established by cultures of blood, cerebrospinal fluid, or other tissue from sites of infection. Antibiotic therapy is generally effective, although death from sepsis or meningitis is still common. In developed countries where *H. influenza* vaccine is used, there has been a great decrease in serious infections and deaths.

CHLAMYDIAL ORGANISMS

Chlamydia are intracellular organisms found in many vertebrates, including humans and other mammals. Clinical illnesses are caused by the species *C. trachomatis*, which is a frequent cause of genital infections in women, and, if an infant passes through an infected birth canal, it can produce disease of the eye (conjunctivitis) and pneumonia in the newborn. Young children sometimes develop ear infections, laryngitis, and upper respiratory tract disease from *Chlamydia*. Such infections can be treated with erythromycin.

Another chlamydial organism, *Chlamydophila psittaci*, produces psittacosis, a disease that results from exposure to the discharges of infected birds. The illness is characterized by high fever with chills, a slow heart rate, pneumonia, headache, weakness, fatigue, muscle pains, anorexia, nausea, and vomiting. The diagnosis is usually suspected if the patient has a history of exposure to birds and is confirmed by blood tests. Mortality is rare, and specific antibiotic treatment is available.

RICKETTSIAS

The rickettsias are a family of microorganisms named for American pathologist Howard T. Ricketts, who died of typhus in 1910 while investigating the spread of the disease. The rickettsias, which range in size from 250 nm (1 nm = 3.9 × 10-8 inch) to more than 1 μm and have no cell wall but are surrounded by a cell membrane, cause a group of diseases characterized by fever and a rash. Except for *Coxiella burnetii*, the cause of Q fever, they are intracellular parasites, most of which are transmitted to humans by an arthropod carrier such as a louse or tick. *C. burnetii*, however, can survive in milk, sewage,

Rickettsia akari, *which lives in the body of the ordinary house mouse, causes spotted fever, known as rickettsialpox.* Roel Hoeve/Foto Natura/Minden Pictures/Getty Images

and aerosols and can be transmitted to humans by a tick or by inhalation, causing pneumonia in the latter case. Rickettsial diseases can be treated with antibiotics.

Humans contract most rickettsial diseases only when they break into a cycle in nature in which the rickettsias live. In murine typhus, for example, *Rickettsia mooseri* is a parasite of rats conveyed from rat to rat by the Oriental rat flea, *Xenopsylla cheopis*. The flea bites humans if they intrude into its environment. Scrub typhus is caused by *R. tsutsugamushi*, but it normally parasitizes only rats and mice and other rodents, being carried from one to the other by a small mite, *Leptotrombidium* (previously known as *Trombicula*). This mite is fastidious in matters of temperature, humidity, and food and finds everything suitable in restricted areas, or "mite islands," in South Asia and the western Pacific. It rarely bites humans in their normal environment, but if people invade its territory en masse it will attack, and outbreaks of scrub typhus will follow.

The spotted fevers are caused by rickettsias that spend their normal life cycles in a variety of small animals, spreading from one to the other inside ticks. Infected ticks bite human intruders and cause African, North Asian, and Queensland tick typhus, as well as Rocky Mountain spotted fever. One other spotted fever, rickettsialpox, is caused by *R. akari*, which lives in the body of the ordinary house mouse, *Mus musculus*, and spreads from one to another inside the house mite *Liponyssoides sanguineus*

(formerly *Allodermanyssus sanguineus*). This rickettsia is probably a parasite of wild field mice, and it is perhaps only when cities push out into the countryside that house mice catch the infection.

MYCOPLASMAS AND UREAPLASMAS

Mycoplasmas and ureaplasmas, which range in size from 150 to 850 nanometres, are among the smallest known free-living microorganisms. They are ubiquitous in nature and capable of causing widespread disease, but the illnesses they produce in humans are generally milder than those caused by bacteria. Diseases caused by mycoplasmas and ureaplasmas can be treated with antibiotics.

Mycoplasma pneumoniae is the most important member of its genus. *M. pneumoniae* is associated with 20 percent of all cases of pneumonia in adults and children older than five years of age. Patients have fever, cough, headache, and malaise and, upon physical examination, may be found to have pharyngitis (inflamed throat), enlarged lymph nodes, ear or sinus infection, bronchitis, or croup. Diagnosis is established by chest X-rays and blood tests. Although treatment with erythromycin or tetracycline may shorten the illness, it can last for weeks.

Mycoplasmas may also cause a red, bumpy rash—usually on the trunk or back—that is occasionally vesicular (with blisters). Inflammation of the heart muscle and the covering of the heart (pericardium) is rare but can be caused by mycoplasmas. About one-fourth of the people infected with these organisms experience nausea, vomiting, diarrhea, and cramping abdominal pain. Inflammation of the pancreas (pancreatitis) or the liver (hepatitis) may occur, and infection of the brain and spinal cord is a serious complication.

Ureaplasmas can be recovered frequently from the genital areas of healthy persons. The organism can cause inflammation of the urethra and has been associated with infertility, low birth weight of infants, and repeated stillbirths. In general, however, ureaplasma infections are mild. Tetracycline is the preferred treatment once the organism has been established as the cause of infection by microscopic examination of urethral secretions.

VIRUSES

Viruses are not, strictly speaking, living organisms. Instead, they are nucleic acid fragments packaged within protein coats that require the machinery of living cells to replicate. Viruses are visible by electron microscopy, and they vary in size from about 25 nanometres for poliovirus to 250 nanometres for smallpox virus. Vaccination has been the most successful weapon against viral infection. Some infections may be treated with antiviral drugs or interferon (proteins that interfere with viral proliferation).

Viruses of the Herpesviridae family cause a multiplicity of diseases. Those causing infections in humans are the varicella-zoster virus (VZV),

which causes chickenpox and herpes zoster (shingles); the Epstein-Barr virus, which causes infectious mononucleosis; the cytomegalovirus, which is most often associated with infections of newborn infants and immunocompromised people; and herpes simplex virus, which causes cold sores and herpetic venereal (sexually transmitted) diseases.

There are two serotypes of herpes simplex virus, HSV-1 and HSV-2. HSV-1 is the common cause of cold sores. The primary infection usually occurs in childhood and is without symptoms in 50 to 80 percent of cases. Between 10 and 20 percent of infected individuals have recurrences precipitated by emotional stress or by other illness. HSV-1 can also cause infections of the eye, central nervous system, and skin. Serious infections leading to death may occur in immunocompromised persons. HSV-2 is associated most often with herpetic lesions of the genital area. The involved area includes the vagina, cervix, vulva, and, occasionally, the urethra in females and the head of the penis in males. It may also cause an infection at the site of an abrasion. The disease is usually transmitted by sexual contact. In herpetic sexually transmitted diseases, the lesions are small, red, painful spots that quickly vesiculate, become filled with fluid, and quickly rupture, leaving eroded areas that eventually become scabbed. These primary lesions occur from two to eight days after exposure and may be present for up to three weeks. Viral shedding and pain usually resolve in two weeks. When infections recur, the duration of the pain, lesions, and viral shedding is approximately 10 days.

FUNGI

Fungi are large organisms that usually live on dead and rotting animal and plant matter. They are found mostly in soil, on objects contaminated with soil, on plants and animals, and on skin, and they may also be airborne. Fungi may exist as yeasts or molds and may alternate between the two forms, depending on environmental conditions. Yeasts are simple cells, 3 to 5 μm in diameter. Molds consist of filamentous branching structures (called hyphae), 2 to 10 μm in diameter, that are formed of several cells lying end to end. Fungal diseases in humans, known as mycoses, include disorders such as histoplasmosis, coccidioidomycosis, and blastomycosis. These diseases can be mild, characterized by an upper respiratory infection, or severe, involving the bloodstream and every organ system. Fungi may cause devastating disease in persons whose defenses against infection have been weakened by malnutrition, cancer, or the use of immunosuppressive drugs. Specific types of antibiotics known as antifungals are effective in their treatment.

PARASITES

Among the infectious parasites are the protozoans, unicellular organisms that have no cell wall, that cause diseases such as malaria. The various species of malarial parasites are about 4 μm in diameter. At the other extreme, the tapeworm can grow to several metres in length. Treatment of parasitic infection is designed either to kill the organism or to dislodge it from its host.

The worm *Ascaris lumbricoides* causes ascariasis, one of the most prevalent infections in the world. *Ascaris* lives in the soil, and its eggs are ingested with contaminated food. The eggs hatch in the human intestine, and the worms then travel through the bloodstream to the liver, heart, and lungs. They can cause pneumonia, perforations of the intestine, or blockage of the bile ducts, but infected people usually have no symptoms beyond the passage of worms in the stool. Specific treatment is available and prognosis is excellent.

Infections are also caused by whipworms (genus *Trichuris*) and pinworms (*Enterobius vermicularis*), each popularly named for its shape. The former is parasitic in the human large intestine and may cause chronic diarrhea. The latter can be found throughout the gastrointestinal tract, especially in children, and can cause poor appetite, loss of weight, anemia, and itching in the anal area (where it lays its eggs). Both conditions are easily diagnosed and treated with drugs.

MODES OF AGENT SURVIVAL

Infectious agents have various methods of survival. Some depend on rapid multiplication and rapid spread from one host to another. For example, when the measles virus enters the body, it multiplies for a week or two and then enters the bloodstream and spreads to every organ. For several days before a rash appears, the surface cells of the respiratory tract are bursting with measles virus, and vast quantities are shed every time the infected person coughs or sneezes. A day or two after the rash appears, the amount of antibody (protein produced in response to a pathogen) rises in the bloodstream, neutralizing the virus and stopping further shedding. The patient rapidly becomes noninfectious but already may have spread the virus to others. In this way an epidemic can rapidly occur. Many other infectious agents—for example, influenza virus—survive in this manner. How such viruses exist between epidemics is, in some cases, less clear.

The picture is different in more-chronic infections. In tuberculosis there is neither overwhelming multiplication nor rapid shedding of the tubercle bacillus. Rather, the bacilli remain in the infected person's body for a long period, slowly forming areas of chronic inflammation that may from time to time break down and allow them to escape.

Some organisms form spores, a resting or dormant stage that is resistant to heat, cold, drying, and chemical action. Spore-forming organisms can survive for months or years under the most adverse conditions and may not, in fact, be highly infectious. The bacterium that causes tetanus, *Clostridium tetani*, is present everywhere in the environment—in soil, in dust, on window ledges and floors—and yet tetanus is an uncommon disease, especially in developed countries. The same is true of the anthrax bacterium, *Bacillus anthracis*. Although usually present in abundance in factories in which rawhides and animal wool and hair are handled, it rarely causes anthrax in employees. *Clostridium botulinum*, the cause of botulism, produces one of the most lethal toxins that can afflict humans, and yet the disease is one of the rarest because the microorganism depends for its survival on its resistant spore.

In contrast to these relatively independent organisms, there are others that cannot exist at all outside the human body. The bacteria of syphilis and gonorrhea, for example, depend for survival on their ability to infect and their adaptation to the human environment.

Some organisms have complicated life cycles and depend on more than one host. The malarial parasite must spend a portion of its life cycle inside a mosquito, while the liver fluke *Fasciola hepatica*, an occasional human parasite, spends part of its life in the body of a land animal such as a sheep, part in a water snail, and part in the open air as a cyst attached to grass.

COMMENSAL ORGANISMS

All of the outer surfaces of the human body are covered with microorganisms

FLUKE

A fluke (also called a blood fluke, or trematode) is any member of the invertebrate class Trematoda (phylum Platyhelminthes), a group of parasitic flatworms that probably evolved from free-living forms millions of years ago. There are more than 10,000 species of flukes. They occur worldwide and range in size from about 5 mm (0.2 inch) to several centimetres. Most do not exceed 100 mm (4 inches) in length.

Flukes parasitize members of all vertebrate classes but most commonly parasitize fish, frogs, and turtles. They also parasitize humans, domestic animals, and invertebrates such as mollusks and crustaceans. Some are external parasites (ectoparasites), whereas others attach themselves to internal organs (endoparasites). Some are semi-external, attaching themselves to the lining of the mouth, to the gills, or to the cloaca (the end of the digestive tract). Some attack a single host, whereas others require two or more hosts.

The symmetrical body of a fluke is covered with a noncellular cuticle. Most are flattened and leaflike or ribbonlike, although some are stout and circular in cross section. Muscular suckers on the ventral (bottom) surface, hooks, and spines are used for attachment. The body is solid and filled with a spongy connective tissue (mesenchyme) that surrounds all the body organs. A circulatory system is absent. The digestive system consists of a simple sac with a mouth either at the anterior end or in the middle of the ventral surface. An anus is usually absent, but some species have one or two anal pores. The nervous system consists of a pair of anterior ganglia, or nerve centres, and usually three pairs of lengthwise nerve cords. Most species are hermaphroditic—functional reproductive organs of both sexes occur in the same individual. In some, however, the sexes are separate. Most species pass through egg, larval, and mature stages.

Blood flukes occur in most types of vertebrates. Three species attack humans: the urinary blood fluke (Schistosoma haematobium), the intestinal blood fluke (S. mansoni), and the Oriental blood fluke (S. japonicum). The human diseases caused by them are known as schistosomiasis (bilharziasis). They affect millions of persons, particularly in Africa and East Asia.

The urinary blood fluke (S. haematobium), which lives in the veins of the urinary bladder, occurs mainly in Africa, southern Europe, and the Middle East. Eggs, laid in the veins, break through the vein wall into the bladder and are voided during urination. The larval fluke develops in the body of a snail (chiefly of the genus Bulinus), the intermediate host. The mature larva makes its way into the body of the final host, a human, through the skin or the mouth.

The intestinal blood fluke (S. mansoni), which lives in the veins around the large and small intestines, occurs primarily in Africa and in northern South America. The eggs pass from the host with the feces. The larva enters the body of a snail (any of several genera), the intermediate host, and returns to a human host through the skin.

The Oriental blood fluke, which occurs primarily in China, Japan, Taiwan, the East Indies, and the Philippine Islands, differs from S. mansoni and S. haematobium in that it may attack vertebrates other than humans, including various domestic animals, rats, and mice. Snails of the genus Oncomelania are the intermediate host. The adult occurs in the veins of the small *intestine. Some eggs are carried in the bloodstream to various organs and may cause a variety of symptoms, including enlargement of the liver. Human hosts may die from severe infestations.*

Flukes of detrimental economic significance to humans include the widely occurring giant liver fluke of cattle (Fasciola hepatica) and the Chinese, or Oriental, liver fluke (Opisthorchis sinensis, or Clonorchis sinensis). F. hepatica causes the highly destructive "liver rot" in sheep and other domestic animals. Humans may become infested with this fluke by eating uncooked vegetables.

The Chinese liver fluke infests a variety of mammals, including humans. In addition to the snail as an intermediate host, the Chinese liver fluke infests fish as a second intermediate host before passing to the final host. The cat liver fluke, Opisthorchis felineus, which may also infest humans as the final host, also requires a freshwater snail (Bithynia leachii) and a carp as its secondary intermediate hosts.

that normally do no harm and may, in fact, be beneficial. Those commensal organisms on the skin help to break down dying skin cells or to destroy debris secreted by the many minute glands and pores that open on the skin. Many of the organisms in the intestinal tract break down complex waste products into simple substances, and others help in the manufacture of chemical compounds that are essential to human life.

The gastrointestinal tract is considered in this regard to be one of these "outer" surfaces since it is formed by the intucking, or invagination, of the ectoderm, or outer surface, of the body. The mouth, nose, and sinuses (spaces inside the bones of the face) are also considered to be external structures because of their direct contact with the outside environment. Both the gastrointestinal tract and the mouth, nose, and sinuses are heavily populated with microorganisms, some of which are true commensals—living in humans and deriving their sustenance

from the surface cells of the body without doing any harm—and others of which are indistinguishable from disease germs. The latter may live like true commensals in a particular tract in a human and never cause disease, despite their potential to do so. When the environment is altered, however, they are capable of causing severe illness in their host, or, without harming their host, they may infect another person with a serious disease.

It is not known why, for example, the hemolytic streptococcus bacterium can live for months in the throat without causing harm and then suddenly cause an acute attack of tonsillitis or how an apparently harmless pneumococcus gives rise to pneumonia. Similarly, it is not understood how a person can harmlessly carry *Haemophilus influenzae* type B in the throat but then become ill when the organism invades the body and causes one of the most severe forms of meningitis. It may be that external influences, such as changes in temperature or humidity, are enough to upset the balance between host and parasite or that a new microbial invader enters and, by competing for some element in the environment, forces the original parasite to react more violently with its host. The term *lowered resistance*, often used to describe conditions at the onset of infectious disease, is not specific and simply implies any change in the immune system of the host.

A microorganism's environment can be changed radically, of course. If antibiotics are administered, the body's commensal organisms can be killed, and other, less-innocuous organisms may take their place. In the mouth and throat, penicillin may eradicate pneumococci, streptococci, and other bacteria that are sensitive to the drug, while microorganisms that are insensitive, such as *Candida albicans*, may then proliferate and cause thrush (an inflammatory condition of the mouth and throat). In the intestinal tract, an antibiotic may kill most of the microorganisms that are normally present and allow dangerous organisms, such as *Pseudomonas aeruginosa*, to multiply and perhaps to invade the bloodstream and the tissues of the body. If an infectious agent—for example, *Salmonella*—reaches the intestinal tract, treatment with an antibiotic may have an effect that differs from what was intended. Instead of attacking and destroying the salmonella, it may kill the normal inhabitants of the bowel and allow the salmonella to flourish and persist in the absence of competition from other microorganisms.

ENVIRONMENT AND THE SPREAD OF INFECTIOUS AGENTS

The spread of infectious agents through human populations is determined by multiple factors, ranging from population density within homes and cities to temperature and humidity to occupational exposures. Overcrowding, lack of hygiene and effective sanitary practices, and the movement of people from one place to another are among the major factors facilitating the spread of infectious organisms.

FAMILY PATTERNS

Humans are social animals. As a result, human social habits and circumstances influence the spread of infectious agents. Crowded family living conditions facilitate the passage of disease-causing organisms from one person to another. This is true whether the germs pass through the air from one respiratory tract to another or whether they are bowel organisms that depend for their passage on close personal hand-to-mouth contact or on lapses of sanitation and hygiene.

The composition of the family unit is also important. Infection spreads readily through families with infants and preschool children. This is because young children are both more susceptible to infection and, because of their undeveloped hygiene habits, more likely to share their microbes with other family

Young children and infants, who are more vulnerable to infection, are inexperienced in their hygiene habits and thus more apt to pass along microbes to their families. iStockphoto/ Thinkstock

members. Because of this close and confined contact, infectious agents are spread more rapidly.

Distinction must be made between disease and infection. The virus of polio, for example, spreads easily in conditions of close contact (infection), but it usually causes no active disease. When it does cause active disease, it attacks older people much more severely than the young. Children in more-crowded homes, for example, are likely to be infected at an early age and, if illness results, it is usually mild. In less-crowded conditions, young children are exposed less often to infection. Thus, when they first encounter the virus at an older age, they tend to suffer more severely. The difference between infection and disease is seen even more rapidly in early childhood, when infection leads more often to immunity than to illness. Under high standards of hygiene, young children are exposed less frequently, and fewer develop immunity in early life, with the result that paralytic illness, a rarity under the former conditions, is seen frequently in older children and adults. The pattern of infection and disease, however, can be changed. In the case of the polio virus, only immunization can abolish both infection and disease.

POPULATION DENSITY

Density of population does not of itself determine the ease with which infection spreads through a population. Problems tend to arise primarily when populations become so dense as to cause overcrowding. Overcrowding is often associated with decreases in quality of living conditions and sanitation, and hence the rate of agent transmission is typically very high in such areas. Thus, overcrowded cities or densely populated areas of cities can potentially serve as breeding grounds for infectious agents, which may facilitate their evolution, particularly in the case of viruses and bacteria. Rapid cycling between humans and other hosts, such as rats or mice, can result in the emergence of new strains capable of causing serious disease.

SOCIAL HABITS

The vampire bats of Brazil, which transmit paralytic rabies, bite cattle but not ranchers, presumably because ranchers are few but cattle are plentiful on the plains of Brazil. Bat-transmitted rabies, however, does occur in humans in Trinidad, where herdsmen sleep in shacks near their animals. The mechanism of infection is the same in Brazil and Trinidad, but the difference in social habits affects the incidence of the disease.

During the early 20th century in Malta, goats were milked at the customers' doors, and a *Brucella* species in the milk caused a disease that was common enough to be called Malta fever. When the pasteurization of milk became compulsory, Malta fever almost disappeared from the island. (It continued to occur in rural areas where people still drank their milk raw and were in daily contact with their infected animals.)

Important alterations in environment also occur when children in a modern community first go to school. Colds, coughs, sore throats, and swollen neck glands can occur one after the other. In a nursery school, with young children whose hygiene habits are undeveloped, outbreaks of dysentery and other bowel infections may occur, and among children who take their midday meal at school, foodborne infection caused by a breakdown in hygiene can sweep through entire classes of students. These are dangers against which the children are protected to some extent at home but against which they have no defense when they move to the school environment.

Changing food habits among the general population also affect the environment for humans and microbes. Meals served in restaurants, for example, offer a greater danger of food poisoning if the standard of hygiene for food preparation is flawed. The purchase and preparation of poultry—which is often heavily infected with *Salmonella*—present a particular danger. If chickens are bought fresh from a farm or shop and cooked in an oven at home, food poisoning from eating them is rare. If poultry is purchased while it is deep-frozen and then not fully thawed before it is cooked, there is a good chance that insufficient heat penetration will allow the *Salmonella*—which thrive in the cold—to survive in the meat's centre and infect the people who eat it.

TEMPERATURE AND HUMIDITY

At a social gathering, the human density per square yard may be much greater than in any home, and humidity and temperature may rise to levels uncomfortable for humans but ideal for microbes. Virus-containing droplets pass easily from one person to another, and an outbreak of the common cold may result.

In contrast, members of scientific expeditions have spent whole winters in

As evidence that viruses, rather than cold temperatures, cause colds, members of polar expeditions may spend whole winters in a cold climate, only to become sick when they are later exposed to new people. Shutterstock.com

the Arctic or Antarctic without any respiratory illness, only to catch severe colds upon the arrival of a supply ship in the early summer. This is because viruses, not cold temperatures, cause colds. During polar expeditions, the members rapidly develop immunity to the viruses they bring with them, and, throughout the long winter, they encounter no new ones. Their colds in the summer are caused by viruses imported by the crew of the supply ship. When the members of the expedition return on the ship to temperate zones, they again come down with colds, this time caught from friends and relatives who have spent the winter at home.

MOVEMENT

Movement into a new environment often is followed by an outbreak of infectious disease. On pilgrimages and in wars, improvised feeding and sanitation lead to outbreaks of intestinal infections, such as dysentery, cholera, and typhoid fever, and sometimes more have died in war from these diseases than have been killed in the fighting.

People entering isolated communities may carry a disease such as measles with them, and the disease may then spread with astonishing rapidity and often with enhanced virulence. A traveler from Copenhagen carried measles virus with him to the Faroe Islands in 1846, and 6,000 of the 8,000 inhabitants caught the disease. Most of those who escaped were old enough to have acquired immunity during a measles outbreak 65 years earlier. In Fiji a disastrous epidemic of measles in 1875 killed one-fourth of the population. In these cases, the change of environment favoured the virus. Nearly every person in such "virgin" populations is susceptible to infection, so that a virus can multiply and spread unhindered. In a modern city population, by contrast, measles virus mainly affects susceptible young children. When it has run through them, the epidemic must die down because of a lack of susceptible people, and the virus does not spread again until a new generation of children is on hand. With the use of measles vaccine, the supply of susceptible young children is reduced, and the virus cannot spread and multiply and must die out.

An innocent change in environment such as that experienced during camping can lead to infection if it brings a person into contact with sources of infection that are absent at home. Picnicking in a wood, a person may be bitten by a tick carrying the virus of one of several forms of encephalitis. As the person swims in a canal or river, his or her skin may be penetrated by the organisms that cause leptospirosis. The individual may come upon some watercress growing wild in the damp corner of a field and may swallow with the cress almost invisible specks of life that will grow into liver flukes in the body, giving the person fascioliasis, an illness that is common in cattle and sheep but that can spread to humans when circumstances are in its favour.

OCCUPATION AND COMMERCE

In occupational and commercial undertakings, people often manipulate their environment and, in so doing, expose themselves to infection. A farmer in his fields is exposed to damp conditions in which disease microorganisms flourish. While clearing out a ditch, he may be infected with leptospires passed into the water in rats' urine. In his barns he may be exposed to brucellosis if his herd of cattle is infected or to salmonellosis or Q fever. Slaughterhouse workers run similar risks, as do veterinarians. A worker in a dock or tannery may get anthrax from imported hides. An upholsterer may get the disease from wool and hair. A worker mending sacks that have contained bone meal may contract the disease from germs still clinging to the sack.

Workers in packing plants and shops often are infected from the raw meat that they handle. They are sometimes regarded as carriers and causes of outbreaks of *Salmonella* food poisoning, but as often as not they are victims rather than causes. Workers in poultry plants can contract salmonellosis, more rarely psittacosis or a viral infection of the eye, from the birds that they handle. Forestry workers who enter a reserve may upset the balance of nature of the area and expose themselves to attack from the undergrowth or the trees by insect vectors of disease that, if undisturbed, would never come into contact with humans. Whenever people manipulate the environment—by herding animals, importing goods from abroad, draining a lake, or laying a pipe through swampy land, and in many other seemingly innocent ways—they run the chance of interfering with microbial life and attracting into their own environment agents of disease that they might not otherwise ever encounter.

THE INANIMATE ENVIRONMENT

Dust cannot cause infectious disease unless it contains the living agents of the infection. Yet the term *inanimate* is a convenient one to use when infectious disease arises from contact with an environment in which there is no obvious direct living contact between the source and the victim of an infection. A pencil is an inanimate object, but if it is sucked by a child with scarlet fever and then by a second child, the organisms causing the disease can be conveyed to the second child. Many such objects—a handkerchief or a towel, for example—may convey infection under favourable conditions, and, when they do so, they are known as fomites.

Dust is perhaps one of the most common inanimate elements capable of conveying disease. Organisms present in dust may get on food and be swallowed, settle on the skin and infect it, or be breathed into the respiratory passages. Some germs—the causative agents of anthrax and tetanus, of Q fever, brucellosis, and psittacosis, for example—can live for long periods dried in dust. Under certain conditions all may be dangerous, but under different conditions there may be no danger. The germ that causes tetanus, *Clostridium tetani*, is one of the most common germs in dust, but the incidence of tetanus varies greatly in different parts of the world. In many countries it is rare, in others common, and the difference may be related to slight differences in human behaviour or custom. The wearing of shoes in temperate climates protects the wearer against many wounds, while the barefoot child in the tropics sustains many puncture wounds of the feet that, although minor, may yet carry tetanus spores into the tissues of the foot, where conditions may be ideal for germination and the production of toxin. Obstetrical practices in some parts of the world can lead to infection of the newborn child. Other, more subtle influences, such as changes of temperature or humidity, may affect the spread of diseases by dust. A long wet winter followed by a dry summer may encourage the growth of molds in hay, and the dust, when the hay is disturbed, may lead to infection of the farmer's lungs.

Water is not a favourable medium for the growth and multiplication of microorganisms, and yet many can survive in it long enough to carry infection to humans. Cholera and typhoid fever are both waterborne diseases, and the virus of hepatitis A also can survive in water. But the mere presence of a microorganism in water does not necessarily lead to the spread of disease. People have swum in water polluted with *Salmonella typhi* without getting typhoid fever, while others eating shellfish from the same water have developed the disease. The same may be true of hepatitis. The eating of clams from infected water has often caused the disease, whereas swimming has not proved to be a hazard. Shellfish concentrate germs in their tissues, which is probably why they can transmit diseases.

Water is carried to humans in pipes for drinking, but it is also carried away in pipes as sewage. Defects in these systems may permit water to pass from one to the other, and microorganisms from sewage may get into drinking water. Wells and other water sources can be contaminated by badly sited septic tanks, manure heaps, or garbage dumps. Properly treated, such water is safe to drink. If drunk untreated, however, disease may follow.

The soil of gardens and farmlands can harbour disease organisms, as can food. Smoke, fog, and tobacco can affect the human respiratory tract and render it more vulnerable to disease. Air is probably the most common source of infectious agents. The whole of the environment is, in fact, filled with organisms and objects that can transmit infectious agents to humans.

IMMUNE RESPONSE TO INFECTION

When a pathogenic (disease-causing) microorganism invades the body for the first time, the clinical (observable) response may range from nothing at all, through various degrees of nonspecific reactions, to specific infectious disease.

Immunologically, however, there is always a response, the purpose of which is defense. If the defense is completely successful, there is no obvious bodily reaction. If it is partially successful, the affected person exhibits symptoms but recovers from an infectious disease. If it is unsuccessful, the person may be overwhelmed by the infectious process and die.

The two responses—the clinical and the immunologic—can be illustrated by the natural history of the disease polio. When the virus of this disease enters the body for the first time, it multiplies in the throat and in the intestinal tract. In some people, it gets no farther—virus is shed to the outside from the throat and the bowel for a few weeks, and then the shedding ceases and the infection is over. The host, however, has responded and has developed circulating antibodies to a type of poliovirus. These antibodies are specific antipoliovirus proteins in the blood and body fluids that subsequently prevent disease should the poliovirus again be encountered. In addition, the infected individual develops an antipoliovirus response in a subset of white blood cells known as T cells. Antipoliovirus T cells persist throughout the individual's lifetime.

In other people, the same process occurs but some virus also gets into the bloodstream, where it circulates for a short time before being eliminated. In a few individuals, the virus passes from the bloodstream into the central nervous system, where it circulates for a short time before being eliminated. Finally, in some individuals, the virus passes from the bloodstream into the central nervous system, where it may enter and destroy some of the nerve cells that control movement in the body and so cause paralysis. Such paralysis is the least-common result of infection with poliovirus. Most infected persons have no symptoms at all. Those whose bloodstream contains virus often have a mild illness, consisting of no more than malaise, slight headache, and possibly a sore throat. This so-called minor illness of polio is unlikely to be recognized except by those in close contact with someone later paralyzed by the disease.

If the nervous system becomes invaded by the virus, the infected person has a severe headache and other symptoms suggesting meningitis. Such persons are acutely ill, but most recover their normal health after about one week. Only a few of those with this type of infection have paralysis. Of all the people infected with poliovirus, not more than 1 in 100, possibly as few as 1 in 1,000, has paralysis, though paralysis is the dominant feature of the fully developed clinical picture of polio. This polio is actually an uncommon complication of poliovirus infection.

This wide range of response to the poliovirus is characteristic of most infections, though the proportions may vary. Influenza virus, for example, may cause symptoms ranging from a mild cold to a feverish illness, severe laryngitis (inflammation of the larynx, or voice box) or bronchitis, or an overwhelming and fatal pneumonia. The proportions of a population with these differing outcomes may vary from one epidemic to another. There is perhaps more uniformity of pattern in the operation of the defense mechanisms of the body, called the immune response.

NATURAL AND ACQUIRED IMMUNITY

Every animal species possesses some natural resistance to disease. Humans have a high degree of resistance to foot-and-mouth disease, for example, while the cattle and sheep with which they may be in close contact suffer in the thousands from it. Rats are highly resistant to diphtheria, whereas unimmunized children readily contract the disease.

What such resistance depends on is not always well understood. In the case of many viruses, resistance is related to the presence on the cell surface of protein receptors that bind to the virus, allowing it to gain entry into the cell and thus cause infection. Presumably, most causes of absolute resistance are genetically determined. It is possible, for example, to produce by selective breeding two strains of rabbits, one highly susceptible to tuberculosis, the other highly resistant. In humans there may be apparent racial differences, but it is always important to disentangle factors such as climate, nutrition, and economics from those that might be genetically determined. In some tropical and subtropical countries,

for example, polio is a rare clinical disease, though a common infection, but unimmunized visitors to such countries often contract serious clinical forms of the disease. The absence of serious disease in the residents is caused not by natural resistance, however, but by resistance acquired after repeated exposure to poliovirus from infancy onward. Unimmunized visitors from other countries, with perhaps stricter standards of hygiene, are protected from such immunizing exposures and have no acquired resistance to the virus when they encounter it as adults.

Natural resistance, in contrast to acquired immunity, does not depend upon such exposures. The human skin obviously has great inherent powers of resistance to infection. For example, most cuts and abrasions heal quickly, though often they are smothered with potentially pathogenic microorganisms. If an equal number of typhoid bacteria are spread on a person's skin and on a glass plate, those on the skin die much more quickly than do those on the plate, suggesting that the skin has some bactericidal property against typhoid germs. The skin also varies in its resistance to infectious organisms at different ages: impetigo is a common bacterial infection of children's skin but is rarer in adults, and acne is a common infection of the skin of adolescents but is uncommon in childhood or in older adults. The phenomenon of natural immunity can be illustrated equally well with examples from the respiratory, intestinal, or genital tracts, where large surface areas are exposed to potentially infective agents and yet infection does not occur.

If an organism causes local infection or gains entry into the bloodstream, a complicated series of events ensues. These events can be summarized as follows: special types of white blood cells called polymorphonuclear leukocytes or granulocytes, which are normally manufactured in the bone marrow and circulate in the blood, move to the site of the infection. Some of these cells reach the site by chance, in a process called random migration, because almost every body site is supplied constantly with the blood in which these cells circulate. Additional granulocytes are attracted and directed to the sites of infection in a process called directed migration, or chemotaxis.

When a granulocyte reaches the invading organism, it attempts to ingest the invader. Ingestion of bacteria may require the help of still other components of the blood, called opsonins, which act to coat the bacterial cell wall and prepare it for ingestion. An opsonin generally is a protein substance, such as one of the circulating immunoglobulins or complement components.

Once a prepared bacterium has been taken inside the white blood cell, a complex series of biochemical events occurs. A bacterium-containing vacuole (phagosome) may combine with another vacuole that contains bacterial-degrading proteins (lysozymes). The bacterium may be killed, but its products pass into the bloodstream, where they come in contact with other circulating white blood cells called lymphocytes. Two general types of lymphocytes—T cells and B cells—are of great importance in protecting the human host. When a T cell encounters bacterial products, either directly or via presentation by a special antigen-presenting cell, it is sensitized to recognize the material as foreign, and, once sensitized, it possesses an immunologic memory. If the T cell encounters the same bacterial product again, it immediately recognizes it and sets up an appropriate defense more rapidly than it did on the first encounter. The ability of a T cell to function normally, providing what is generally referred to as cellular immunity, is dependent on the thymus gland. The lack of a thymus, therefore, impairs the body's ability to defend itself against various types of infections.

After a T cell has encountered and responded to a foreign bacterium, it interacts with B cells, which are responsible for producing circulating proteins called immunoglobulins or antibodies. There are various types of B cells, each of which can produce only one of the five known forms of immunoglobulin (Ig). The first immunoglobulin to be produced is IgM. Later, during recovery from infection, the immunoglobulin IgG, which can specifically kill the invading microorganism, is produced. If the same microorganism invades the host again, the B cell immediately responds with a dramatic production of IgG specific for that organism, rapidly killing it and preventing disease.

In many cases, acquired immunity is lifelong, as with measles or rubella. In other instances, it can be short-lived, lasting not more than a few months. The persistence of acquired immunity is related not only to the level of circulating antibody but also to sensitized T cells (cell-mediated immunity). Although both cell-mediated immunity and humoral (B-cell) immunity are important, their relative significance in protecting a person against disease varies with particular microorganisms. For example, antibody is of great importance in protection against common bacterial infections such as pneumococcal pneumonia or streptococcal disease and against bacterial toxins, whereas cell-mediated immunity is of greater importance in protection against viruses such as measles or against the bacteria that cause tuberculosis.

IMMUNIZATION

Antibodies are produced in the body in response to either infection with an organism or, through vaccination, the administration of a live or inactivated organism or its toxin by mouth or by injection. When given alive, the organisms are weakened, or attenuated, by some laboratory means so that they still stimulate antibodies but do not produce their characteristic disease. However stimulated, the antibody-producing cells of the body remain sensitized to the infectious agent and can respond to it again, pouring out more antibody. One attack of a disease, therefore, often renders a person immune to a second attack, providing the theoretical basis for active immunization by vaccines.

Antibody can be passed from one person to another, conferring protection on the antibody recipient. In such a case, however, the antibody has not been produced in the body of the second person, nor have the antibody-producing cells been stimulated. The antibody is then a foreign substance and is eventually eliminated from the body, and protection is short-lived. The most common form of this type of passive immunity is the transference of antibodies from a mother through the placenta to her unborn child. This is why a disease such as measles is uncommon in babies younger than one year. After that age, the infant has lost all of its maternal antibody and becomes susceptible to the disease unless protective measures, such as measles vaccination, are taken. Sometimes antibody is extracted in the form of immunoglobulin from blood taken from immune persons and is injected into susceptible persons to give them temporary protection against a disease, such as measles or hepatitis A.

Generally, active immunization is offered before the anticipated time of exposure to an infectious disease. When unvaccinated people are exposed to an infectious disease, two alternatives are available: active immunization may be initiated immediately in the expectation

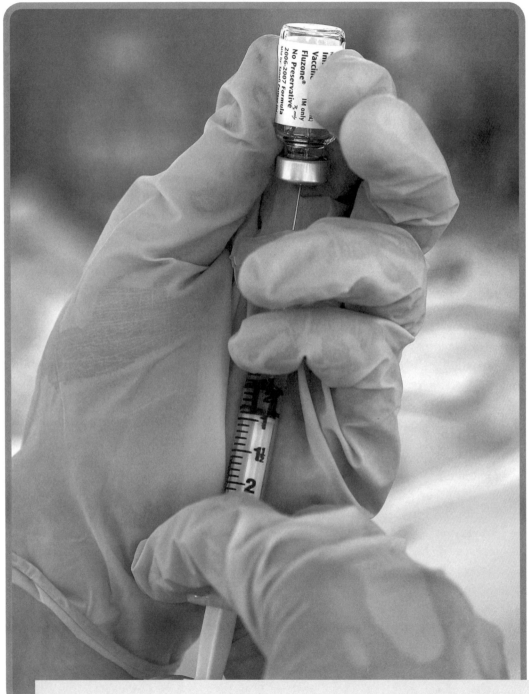

Vaccination is one way to stimulate the body to produce antibodies. David McNew/ Getty Images

that immunity can be developed during the incubation period of the disease, or passive immunity can be provided for the interim period and then active immunization given at an appropriate time. The antigens (foreign substances in the body that stimulate the immune defense system) introduced in the process of active immunization can be live attenuated viruses or bacteria, killed microorganisms or inactivated toxins (toxoids), or purified cell wall products (polysaccharide capsules, protein antigens).

There are five basic requirements for an ideal vaccine. The agents used for immunization should not in themselves produce disease. The immunizing agent should induce long-lasting, ideally permanent, immunity. The agent used for immunization should not be transmissible to susceptible contacts of the person being vaccinated. The vaccine should be easy to produce, its potency easy to assess, and the antibody response to it measurable with common and inexpensive techniques. Finally, the agent in the vaccine should be free of contaminating substances. It is also recognized, however, that vaccine transmissibility can be helpful (e.g., in the case of live polio vaccine, which can be spread from vaccinated children to others who have not been vaccinated).

The route by which an antigen is administered frequently determines the type and duration of antibody response. For example, intramuscular injection of inactivated poliovirus (Salk vaccine) generates less production of serum antibody and induces only a temporary systemic immunity. It may not produce substantial local gastrointestinal immunity and, therefore, may not prevent the carrying of the virus in the gastrointestinal tract. Live, attenuated, oral poliovirus (Sabin vaccine) induces both local gastrointestinal and systemic antibody production. Thus, immunization by mouth is preferred.

The schedule by which a vaccine is given depends upon the epidemiology of the naturally occurring disease, the duration of immunity that can be induced, the immunologic status of the host, and, in some cases, the availability of the patient. Measles, for example, is present in many communities and poses a potential threat to many children older than 5 months of age. A substantial number of infants, however, are born with measles antibody from their mothers, and this maternal antibody interferes with an adequate antibody response until they are between 12 and 15 months of age. Generally, the immunization of infants after the age of 15 months benefits the community at large. In measles outbreaks, however, it may be advisable to alter this schedule and immunize all infants between 6 and 15 months of age.

CHAPTER 2

BACTERIAL DISEASES: LEPROSY AND TUBERCULOSIS

Bacterial organisms of the genus *Mycobacterium* are responsible for several important diseases. The two best-characterized of these are leprosy and tuberculosis, both of which are chronic conditions associated with the progressive deterioration of affected tissues. Leprosy and tuberculosis are diseases that have been known since ancient times, with evidence for both coming from human remains dating back thousands of years and with conditions resembling each having been described in the writings of ancient Indian and Greek physicians.

Today, scientists have an extensive understanding of these diseases, and various diagnostic techniques and drug therapies have been developed for each. But despite the depth of knowledge and technologies available, there remain many questions about mycobacterial diseases. For example, at the centre of ongoing scientific investigations into these afflictions lie important questions about basic infectious processes, such as the mechanisms by which *Mycobacterium* organisms are transmitted to give rise to leprosy and the processes they use to continually evade drug therapies for tuberculosis.

LEPROSY

Leprosy, also called Hansen disease, is a chronic infectious disease that affects the skin, the peripheral nerves (nerves

When leprosy bacillus destroys peripheral nerves, a lack of sensation and tissue degeneration lead to deformed and eroded extremities. Alison Wright/National Geographic Image Collection/Getty Images

outside the brain and spinal cord), and the mucous membranes of the nose, throat, and eyes. It is caused by the leprosy bacillus, *Mycobacterium leprae*. Destruction of the peripheral nerves by the bacillus leads to a loss of sensation, which, together with progressive tissue degeneration, may result in the extremities' becoming deformed and eroded.

In almost all cultures throughout history, leprosy has aroused dread and loathing about the prospect of incurable disease and a lifetime of progressive disfigurement. At one time "lepers," as those with the disease were long called, were ostracized as unclean and were gathered into isolated "leper colonies" to keep them out of sight, to control their contagiousness, and to offer them what little treatment was available. In reality, the leprosy bacillus is not highly infectious, in most cases passing from one person to another only after prolonged and close contact (as, for instance, among family members). In addition, thanks to modern therapy with a number of effective drugs, the disease is now entirely curable, and the term *leper*, connoting somebody who has had and always will have the disease, thus no longer has meaning and in fact is considered to be offensive because of the social stigma long associated with the disease. Health care officials today do not consider a cured former leprosy patient to be any more "leprous" than a cured former cancer patient is "cancerous."

Since the early 1990s, the prevalence rate of leprosy has decreased by 90 percent. Thus, whereas millions of cases of the disease were known in the 1980s, newly reported cases dropped to about 763,200 by 2001 and to some 249,000 in 2008. The disease has disappeared from most temperate countries, but it still occurs in some areas of Africa and southern Asia. The dramatic decline in leprosy prevalence was attributed to a resolution passed in 1991 by the World Health Assembly (the governing body of the World Health Organization) that was designed to eliminate the disease by 2000. Disease elimination was defined as a reduction of prevalence to less than 1 case per 10,000 persons. Of the 122 countries targeted for leprosy elimination, 119 have achieved this goal.

Mysteries of the Disease

Mycobacterium leprae, the organism responsible for leprosy, is a relative of *M. tuberculosis*, the bacillus that causes tuberculosis. (A bacillus is a rod-shaped bacterium.) Scientists theorize that the leprosy bacillus enters the body through a break in the skin or through the mucous membranes of the nose. The disease can be transmitted from person to person by prolonged close contact, but even today scientists are uncertain of the exact mechanism. In fact, much about leprosy remains mysterious. At least in part this is because the bacillus has never been grown in a test tube, and the only tools for studying its transmission have been a limited number of animal models, chiefly armadillo and mouse models.

The geographic distribution of the leprosy bacillus is another mystery. Some scientists suspect that the organism exists in the soil in many parts of the world, but again, because it cannot be grown in a laboratory culture, the only evidence of its presence in a given region is the appearance of the disease itself in humans or other animals that are susceptible to it. Besides humans, the only animals known to develop leprosy in nature are New World armadillos and African primates. For experimental purposes scientists have been able to grow the bacillus in the footpads of laboratory mice.

Given that the organism that causes leprosy is widely distributed and the disease is contagious, it seems logical to ask why leprosy is not a great deal more prevalent than it is. The answer is that the infection apparently is quite difficult to contract. The vast majority of people (95 percent or so) simply are not susceptible to the bacillus and, even under repeated exposure, will never develop the disease. Among the few individuals who do contract the disease, in most cases it will be self-limiting and disappear before any symptoms become evident. Even in cases where early symptoms of leprosy develop, most patients will self-heal. This rather unusual pattern of infection, along with a three- to five-year incubation period (the time that elapses between contact with the bacillus and the onset of symptoms), makes the epidemiology of leprosy particularly difficult to study.

Transmission

In the many centuries since leprosy was first described, a number of theories have been proposed to explain how the bacillus is transmitted. In the 19th century leprosy was believed to be a hereditary ailment. This made sense, as it frequently occurred in households among individuals who were members of a single family. In 1873, however, G.H. Armauer Hansen, a physician working in a leprosy hospital in Bergen, Norway, discovered the leprosy bacillus in a sample of tissue from one of his patients. Hansen was able to identify the organism under the microscope because its propensity to collect iron caused it to appear brownish in colour compared with the tissue itself. His discovery demonstrated that leprosy is an infectious disease propagated by a specific microorganism.

The route of transmission of leprosy remained a matter of debate. The prevailing opinion for many years was that the illness spread via prolonged skin-to-skin contact. Then the theory of respiratory transmission became popular. This theory posited that the bacillus entered the human body through the lining of the nose. For a time scientists even entertained the possibility of transmission by insect bites. Later, experiments with a mouse model of the disease showed that transmission is indeed possible through the intact lining of the nose and through breaks in the skin but not via the mouth, lungs, or digestive tract or through unbroken skin. And, although leprosy can be produced in mice by exposing them to the bacillus, the disease cannot be transmitted from an infected to an uninfected mouse.

Course of Disease

The body's first reaction to the leprosy bacillus takes place in the deep layers of the skin in one of two ways. In one type of reaction, immune cells crowd into the area in an attempt to seal off the bacterium, and in these areas very few bacilli can be found. This gives rise to a form of leprosy known as tuberculoid leprosy because of the hard nodules, or tubercles, that form in the skin. The intense cellular reaction involves all of the thicknesses of the skin and the tissues under it, the sweat glands, the hair follicles, and the nerve fibres that end in the skin. This reaction manifests on the infected person's skin as a firm, dry patch in which there is no sense of heat, cold, or touch. The cellular reaction continues to spread into the main trunk of the involved nerve, so that nerve impulses cannot be transmitted, which thereby causes loss of sensation and decreased circulation in the affected part. This is most commonly seen in the forearm or lower leg, and it leads to claw hand and gross deformity of the foot. Paralysis of muscles of the face, eye, and neck may also occur. The patient is unable to feel pain, and minor injuries remain unnoticed. Large eroding ulcers can form, causing loss of fingers and toes. Sometimes the condition of the limb is so bad that amputation is necessary. It is ironic that this form of leprosy occurs in people whose tissues resist the disease, for the intense cellular response is a reaction of resistance—successful insofar as it prevents local multiplication of the leprosy bacillus and its spread throughout the body but unsuccessful in that it destroys vital tissues in the invaded areas.

In the second type of reaction, giving rise to what is called lepromatous leprosy, there is very little cellular response, and the bacilli can multiply freely. The organisms are found in enormous numbers in the deep layers of the affected skin, and they spread widely through the skin's lymphatic channels. The disease spreads via the nerves but does not adhere to them as in the tuberculoid form. Often it spreads to the skin of the face, where it causes thickening and corrugation of the skin and a typical leonine appearance. Soft nodules appear on the ears, nose, and cheeks and sometimes erode into discharging sores. The nose often is teeming with bacilli, and this sometimes leads to destruction of the septum of the nose and the palate.

The progress of leprosy is slow. It may be years before a child infected by a parent shows the first sign of disease, frequently a vague, scarcely noticed patch on the skin. Often the child has grown to an adult before the disease is recognized. Persons with leprosy have occasional bouts of fever, but the course of the disease is mainly one of increasing disability and disfigurement, slowly progressing through the years even though it does not usually cut life short.

THERAPY

The current treatment of leprosy is extremely effective, halting the progress of the disease. The bacilli can be killed rapidly, and multidrug therapy—the use of two or more antileprosy drugs in combination—prevents the development of drug-resistant strains. Indeed, multidrug therapy—a practice widely adopted in the treatment of tuberculosis and AIDS—was first proposed after scientists observed that some cases of leprosy were becoming resistant to sulfones, the earliest class of antileprosy drugs. A multidrug regimen developed by the World Health Organization (WHO) is the current standard of treatment.

For patients with localized forms of leprosy and relatively few leprosy bacilli in their bodies, two drugs, dapsone and rifampicin, are given for a total of six months. For patients with more widespread disease and relatively large numbers of bacilli, three drugs—dapsone, clofazimine, and rifampicin—are given for

24 months. Most patients are able to tolerate the drugs well, but a few experience undesirable side effects or even exacerbations of the symptoms. Relapses, in general, are rare, occurring in fewer than 1 per 1,000 treated patients. Occasionally the infection persists despite continued therapy.

Killing the bacillus has no effect on body tissues that have already been damaged or destroyed. Up to a point, nerve function can be restored by antileprosy drugs, but once the disease has progressed beyond that point, the loss of function is permanent. Nerve impairment—of which leprosy is the leading cause worldwide—leads to paralysis, loss of sensation, and changes in the individual's physical appearance. About 7 percent of newly diagnosed leprosy patients today have visible deformity or damage to their hands or feet or impaired vision. These disabilities can interfere with their ability to earn a living and otherwise lead a normal life. If the damage is unsightly, and it frequently is, then they also must cope with loss of social acceptance.

LEPROSY THROUGH HISTORY

People tend to think of leprosy as a tropical disease because most cases today are found in less-developed countries, which are mainly in the tropics. This has not always been the case. In 1200 CE an estimated 19,000 leprosy hospitals existed all over Europe. The disease is much older than that, however, and it is believed to have originated on the Indian subcontinent. Indeed, the most ancient evidence of leprosy comes from a 4,000-year-old human skeleton uncovered in India in 2009. The skeleton was found to have erosion patterns similar to those found in skeletons of lepers in Europe dating to the Middle Ages. Thus, there is evidence that leprosy existed in India by 2000 BCE, and this coincides with what is suspected to be the first textual reference to leprosy—in an ancient Sanskrit sacred work known as the Atharvaveda.

There are many difficulties in interpreting ancient medical writings, and the descriptive terms used by ancient authors for clinical conditions are often misleading. An illness that fits the description of leprosy almost certainly appears in the *Sushruta-samhita*, a medical work from India that dates to about 600 BCE. A similar ailment is described in a Chinese medical text from 400 BCE. Several Greek writers, including Galen (2nd–3rd century CE), described a disease that may have been leprosy, though the Greeks did not apply to this disease the term *lepra* ("scaly"), from which the modern term *leprosy* is derived. Instead, they referred to it as *elephantiasis græcorum*. In a similar vein, the "leprosy" referred to in the Bible—both the *tzaraath* of the Hebrew Bible and the *lepra* of the Greek New Testament—is not described in a clinically recognizable manner and probably was any of a number of severe chronic skin diseases.

Tradition has it that members of the army of Alexander the Great contracted the illness when they invaded India in the 4th century BCE and carried it into the Middle East and then throughout the eastern Mediterranean upon their return home. It is also traditionally believed that Roman soldiers in the army of Pompey took the disease from Egypt to Italy in the 1st century BCE and that Roman legionnaires later took the disease as far as the British Isles. Conversely, genetic analysis of the leprosy bacillus indicates that *Mycobacterium leprae* may have evolved some 100,000 years ago in eastern Africa or southwestern Asia. From there it seems to have migrated eastward and westward, developing one distinct subtype in Asia and another subtype in Europe and North Africa. Leprosy appears to have been introduced by Europeans or North Africans into western Africa, where the bacillus evolved yet another distinct subtype. The disease was brought to the Americas by European colonists and western African slaves.

Between the 11th and 13th centuries CE, leprosy spread along trade routes in Europe and also in places in the Holy Land occupied by European Crusaders and pilgrims—its most prominent victim being Baldwin IV, the "leper king" of Jerusalem. So acute was the suffering of those infected by leprosy that the disease was thought to be highly contagious. Persons with leprosy not wealthy enough to live at home in isolation were segregated in what came to be called lazarets or leprosaria. Outside these hospices they were feared and ostracized, frequently condemned to wander the roads

wearing signs and ringing bells to warn healthy people of their approach. Leprosy came to be referred to as the "living death," and often its victims were treated as if they had already died. Funeral services were conducted to declare those living with the disease "dead" to society, and relatives were allowed to claim their inheritance. Like many diseases, leprosy was considered to be a form of divine punishment for worldly sins, and the outward signs of the disease were taken as proof that leprosy victims were utterly embroiled in sin. Special laws required the use of separate seats in churches, separate holy water fonts, and in some cases a "lepers' window" or slot in the church wall through which the afflicted could view the mass without contaminating the congregation or the ceremony.

Rather abruptly and for unknown reasons, the incidence of leprosy began to decline in Europe—with the exception of Scandinavia—between 1200 and 1300. In Norway the disease persisted until the 20th century but has now disappeared. It was taken to what is now Louisiana, in the southern United States, by French Canadians (Acadians) who were expelled from Canada in 1755. Another immigrant group known to include people with leprosy moved to the United States from Scandinavia, mainly Norway, in the middle of the 19th century and settled principally in Minnesota. The disease was transmitted and has persisted in Louisiana, where occasional new cases appear even today among people of Acadian descent, but the disease was not transmitted in Minnesota and has completely disappeared there.

It was in Norway that Hansen identified the leprosy bacillus in 1873. (At that time leprosy affected about 2.5 percent of the population of Bergen, where Hansen did his work.) This great discovery made possible the modern era of treating the disease itself, rather than merely containing it or treating the symptoms. Even into the 20th century, the only effective control applied to prevent the spread of the disease was compulsory segregation of the patient, frequently in large "leper colonies." Perhaps the most famous colony was at Kalaupapa, on the island of Molokai, Hawaii, where the Belgian priest Father Damien served leprosy patients who had been forcibly relocated to the isolated community. In 1894 the Louisiana Leper Home was established near Carville, Louisiana, on the Mississippi River near New Orleans. Early in the 20th century, the Carville home was transferred to U.S. federal control and became officially known as the Gillis W. Long Hansen's Disease Center. The new name Hansen's disease was part of a determined effort by health authorities to rid leprosy of its old social stigma and to focus attention on the fact that leprosy was finally becoming a treatable disease.

For centuries an oil derived from the seeds of the chaulmoogra tree (genus *Hydnocarpus*) had been used to treat leprosy and other skin conditions in India and China. In 1854 Frederic John Mouat,

an English doctor working in Calcutta (Kolkata), reported the possible utility of chaulmoogra oil in treating leprosy, and by the 1920s the oil or derivatives of the oil were the principal medication available. However, the drug was ineffective when applied locally to affected areas, produced nausea when taken orally, and caused pain upon injection. Its real value was never fully accepted by authorities, and it was finally abandoned upon introduction of the sulfones, the first truly effective leprosy drug, in the 1940s.

Diaminodiphenyl sulfone, or DDS, was synthesized in Germany in 1908, but it was not until the 1930s that researchers began to investigate its possible antibacterial properties. In 1941 doctors at Carville began to test a derivative of the compound, called promin, on patients. Promin had drawbacks—it had to be given intravenously, on a regular schedule, and for a long period of time—but it reversed the course of the disease in enough cases to be heralded as the "miracle at Carville." Over the following decade researchers produced sulfone drugs that could be taken orally. The most effective one was a medicinal form of DDS called dapsone, which quickly replaced chaulmoogra oil as the standard medication for leprosy.

The sulfones are bacteriostatic; that is, they interfere with the growth of *Mycobacterium leprae* by preventing it from synthesizing the essential vitamin folic acid. In the 1960s rifampicin, a truly bactericidal (i.e., bacteria-killing) drug, was shown to be extremely effective against the leprosy bacillus. About the same time, clofazimine, another bacteriostatic drug that also had anti-inflammatory properties, was introduced. With these drugs it was possible to treat people with leprosy as outpatients and to cease the practice of isolating them from the general population.

No sooner was leprosy finally treatable than the problem of drug resistance arose. Resistance to the sulfones was first described in the mid-1960s and resistance to rifampicin in the early 1970s. When some strains of M. leprae were shown in the laboratory to be resistant to both the sulfones and rifampicin, the spectre was raised of a return to untreatable leprosy. In the early 1980s experts assembled by WHO issued the recommendation that all leprosy patients receive combination multidrug therapy and that all leprosy treatment be strictly limited in duration. Patients with localized leprosy would be treated for only six months, and the most advanced cases would receive treatment for only two years. Initially, these methods were highly controversial, but, as they were shown to be successful, they became the standard of treatment.

The prospect of improved treatment led public health authorities to embrace the slogan "Leprosy is curable." Leprosy patients who completed multidrug-therapy regimens were counted as cured and were taken off the lists of those with the disease. This had the effect of reducing the official numbers of people with leprosy from millions to only hundreds of thousands. Such was the situation when WHO, in the 1990s, launched an ambitious campaign to eliminate leprosy worldwide by the year 2000.

TUBERCULOSIS

Tuberculosis is an infectious disease that is caused by the tubercle bacillus, *Mycobacterium tuberculosis*. In most forms of the disease, the bacillus spreads slowly and widely in the lungs, causing the formation of hard nodules (tubercles) or large cheeselike masses that break down the respiratory tissues and form cavities in the lungs. Blood vessels also can be eroded by the advancing disease, causing the infected person to cough up bright red blood.

During the 18th and 19th centuries, tuberculosis reached near-epidemic proportions in the rapidly urbanizing and industrializing societies of Europe and North America. Indeed, "consumption," as it was then known, was the leading cause of death for all age groups in the Western world from that period until the early 20th century, at which time improved health and hygiene brought about a steady decline in its mortality rates. Since the 1940s, antibiotic drugs have reduced the span of treatment to months instead of years, and drug therapy has done away with the old TB sanatoriums where patients at one time were nursed for years while the defensive properties of their bodies dealt with the disease.

Before antibiotic drugs and drug therapy, tuberculosis patients spent years convalescing in sanatoriums. William Vandivert/Time & Life Pictures/Getty Images

Today, in less-developed countries where population is dense and hygienic standards poor, tuberculosis remains a major fatal disease. The prevalence of the disease has increased in association with the HIV/AIDS epidemic. An estimated one out of every four deaths from tuberculosis involves an individual coinfected with HIV. In addition, the successful elimination of tuberculosis as a major threat to public health in the world has been complicated by the rise of new strains of the tubercle bacillus that are resistant to conventional antibiotics. Infections with these strains are often difficult to treat and require the use of combination drug therapies, sometimes involving the use of five different agents.

THE COURSE OF TUBERCULOSIS

The tubercle bacillus is a small, rod-shaped bacterium that is extremely hardy. It can survive for months in a state of dryness and can also resist the action of mild disinfectants. Infection spreads primarily by the respiratory route directly from an infected person who discharges live bacilli into the air. Minute droplets ejected by sneezing, coughing, and even talking can contain hundreds of tubercle bacilli that may be inhaled by a healthy person. There the bacilli become trapped in the tissues of the body, are surrounded by immune cells, and finally are sealed up in hard, nodular tubercles. A tubercle usually consists of a centre of dead cells and tissues, cheeselike (caseous) in appearance, in which can be found many bacilli. This centre is surrounded by radially arranged phagocytic (scavenger) cells and a periphery containing connective tissue cells. The tubercle thus forms as a result of the body's defensive reaction to the bacilli. Individual tubercles are microscopic in size, but most of the visible manifestations of tuberculosis, from barely visible nodules to large tuberculous masses, are conglomerations of tubercles.

In otherwise healthy children and adults, the primary infection often heals without causing symptoms. The bacilli are quickly sequestered in the tissues, and the infected person acquires a lifelong immunity to the disease. A skin test taken at any later time may reveal the earlier infection and the immunity, and a small scar in the lung may be visible by X-ray. In this condition, sometimes called latent tuberculosis, the affected person is not contagious. In some cases, however, sometimes after periods of time that can reach 40 years or more, the original tubercles break down, releasing viable bacilli into the bloodstream. From the blood the bacilli create new tissue infections elsewhere in the body, most commonly in the upper portion of one or both lungs. This causes a condition known as pulmonary tuberculosis, a highly infectious stage of the disease. In some cases the infection may break into the pleural space between the lung and the chest wall, causing a pleural effusion, or collection of fluid outside the lung. Particularly among infants, the elderly, and immunocompromised adults (organ transplant recipients or AIDS patients, for example), the primary infection may spread through the body, causing miliary tuberculosis, a highly fatal form if not adequately treated. In fact, once the bacilli enter the bloodstream, they can travel to almost any organ of the body, including the lymph nodes, bones and joints, skin, intestines, genital organs, kidneys, and bladder. An infection of the meninges that cover the brain causes tuberculous meningitis. Before the advent of specific drugs, this disease was always fatal, though most affected people now recover.

The onset of pulmonary tuberculosis is usually insidious, with lack of energy, weight loss, and persistent cough. These symptoms do not subside, and the general health of the patient deteriorates. Eventually, the cough increases, the patient may have chest pain from pleurisy, and there may be blood in the sputum, an alarming symptom. Fever develops, usually with drenching night sweats. In the lung, the lesion consists of a collection of dead cells in which tubercle bacilli may be seen. This lesion may erode a neighbouring bronchus or blood vessel, causing the patient to cough up blood (hemoptysis). Tubercular lesions may spread extensively in the lung, causing large areas of destruction, cavities, and scarring. The amount of lung tissue available for the exchange of gases in respiration decreases, and if untreated the patient will die from failure of ventilation and general toxemia and exhaustion.

DIAGNOSIS AND TREATMENT

The diagnosis of pulmonary tuberculosis depends on finding tubercle bacilli in the sputum, in the urine, in gastric washings, or in the cerebrospinal fluid. The primary method used to confirm the presence of bacilli is a sputum smear, in which a sputum specimen is smeared onto a slide, stained with a compound that penetrates the organism's cell wall, and examined under a microscope. If bacilli are present, the sputum specimen is cultured on a special medium to determine whether the bacilli are *M. tuberculosis*. An X-ray of the lungs may show typical shadows caused by tubercular nodules or lesions. The prevention of tuberculosis depends on good hygienic and nutritional conditions and on the identification of infected patients and their early treatment. A vaccine, known as BCG vaccine, is composed of specially weakened tubercle bacilli. Injected into the skin, it causes a local reaction, which confers some immunity to infection by *M. tuberculosis* for several years. It has been widely used in some countries with success. Its use in young children in particular has helped to control infection in the developing world. The main hope of ultimate control, however, lies in preventing exposure to infection, and this means treating infectious patients quickly, possibly in isolation until they are noninfectious. In many developed countries, individuals at risk for tuberculosis, such as health care workers, are regularly given a skin test, known as a tuberculin test, to show whether they have had a primary infection with the bacillus.

Today, the treatment of tuberculosis consists of drug therapy and methods to prevent the spread of infectious bacilli. Historically, treatment of tuberculosis consisted of long periods, often years, of bed rest and surgical removal of useless lung tissue. In the 1940s and '50s several antimicrobial drugs were discovered that revolutionized the treatment of patients with tuberculosis. As a result, with early drug treatment, surgery is rarely needed. The most commonly used antituberculosis drugs are isoniazid and rifampicin (rifampin). These drugs are often used in various combinations with other agents, such as ethambutol, pyrazinamide, or rifapentine, to avoid the development of drug-resistant bacilli. Patients with strongly suspected or confirmed tuberculosis undergo an initial treatment period that lasts two months and consists of combination therapy with isoniazid, rifampicin, ethambutol, and pyrazinamide. These drugs may be given daily or two times per week. The patient is usually made noninfectious quite quickly, but complete cure requires continuous treatment for another four to nine months. The length of the continuous treatment period depends on the results of chest X-rays and sputum smears taken at the end of the two-month period of initial therapy. Continuous treatment may consist of once daily or twice weekly doses of isoniazid and rifampicin or isoniazid and rifapentine.

If a patient does not continue treatment for the required time or is treated with only one drug, bacilli will become resistant and multiply, making the patient sick again. If subsequent treatment is also incomplete, the surviving bacilli will become resistant to several drugs. Multidrug-resistant tuberculosis (MDR TB) is a form of the disease in which bacilli have become resistant to isoniazid and rifampicin. MDR TB is treatable but is extremely difficult to cure, typically requiring two years of treatment with agents known to have more severe side effects than isoniazid or rifampicin. Extensively drug-resistant tuberculosis (XDR TB) is a rare form of MDR TB. XDR TB is characterized by resistance to not only isoniazid and rifampin but also a group of bactericidal drugs known as fluoroquinolones and at least one aminoglycoside antibiotic, such as kanamycin, amikacin, or capreomycin. Aggressive treatment using five different drugs, which are selected based on the drug sensitivity of the specific strain of bacilli in a patient, has been shown to be effective in reducing mortality in roughly 50 percent of XDR TB patients. In addition, aggressive treatment can help prevent the spread of strains of XDR TB bacilli.

In 1995, in part to prevent the development and spread of MDR TB, the World Health Organization began encouraging countries to implement a compliance program called directly observed therapy (DOT). Instead of taking daily medication on their own, patients are directly observed by a clinician or responsible family member while taking larger doses twice a week. Although some patients consider DOT invasive, it has proved successful in controlling tuberculosis.

Tuberculosis Through History

Evidence that *M. tuberculosis* and humans have long coexisted comes primarily from studies of bone samples collected from a Neolithic human settlement in the eastern Mediterranean. Genetic evidence gathered from these studies indicates that roughly 9,000 years ago there existed a strain of *M. tuberculosis* similar to strains present in the 21st century. Evidence of mycobacterial infection has also been found in the mummified remains of ancient Egyptians, and references to *phthisis*, or "wasting," occur in the writings of the Greek physician Hippocrates. In the medical writings of Europe through the Middle Ages and well into the industrial age, tuberculosis was referred to as phthisis, the "white plague," or consumption—all in reference to the progressive wasting of the victim's health and vitality as the disease took its inexorable course. The cause was assumed to be mainly constitutional, either the result of an inherited disposition or of unhealthy or dissolute living. In the first edition of *Encyclopædia Britannica* (1768), it was reported that a tendency to develop "consumption of the lungs" could tragically be expected in people who were fine, delicate, and precocious:

This is known from a view of the tender and fine vessels, and of the slender make of the whole body, a long neck, a flat and narrow thorax, depressed scapulæ; the blood of a bright red, thin, sharp, and hot; the skin transparent, very white and fair, with a blooming red in the cheeks; the wit quick, subtle, and early ripe with regard to the age, and a merry chearful disposition.

Based on the stage of the disease, treatments included regular bloodletting, administration of expectorants and purgatives, healthful diet, exercise such as vigorous horseback riding, and, in the grim final stages, opiates. The view that tuberculosis might be a contagious disease also had its adherents, but it was not until 1865 that Jean Antoine Villemin, an army doctor in Paris, showed that it could be transmitted from tuberculous animals to healthy animals by inoculation. The actual infectious agent, the tubercle bacillus, was discovered and identified in 1882 by the German physician Robert Koch. By that time the cultural status of the disease was assured. As summarized by Dr. J.O. Affleck of the University of Edinburgh, Scotland, in the ninth edition of *Encyclopædia Britannica* (1885), "Few diseases possess such sad interest for humanity as consumption, both on account of its widespread prevalence and its destructive effects, particularly among the young." Causing as much as one-quarter of all deaths in Europe, arising with particular frequency among young adults between the ages of 18 and 35, and bringing on a lingering, melancholy decline characterized by loss of body weight, skin pallor, and sunken yet luminous eyes, tuberculosis was enshrined in literature as the "captain of death," the slow killer of youth, promise, and genius. Prominent artists who died of consumption in the 19th century included the English poet John Keats, the Polish composer Frédéric Chopin, and all of the Brontë sisters (Charlotte, Emily, and Anne); in the early 20th century they were followed by the Russian playwright Anton Chekhov, the Italian painter Amedeo Modigliani, and the German writer Franz Kafka. Without a clear understanding of the bacterium that caused the disease, little could be done for its victims except to isolate them in sanitariums, where cleanliness and fresh air were thought to help the body's natural defenses to stop or at least slow the progress of the disease.

Preventive inoculation against tuberculosis, in which live but attenuated tubercle bacilli are used as a vaccine, was introduced in France in 1921 by bacteriologists Albert Calmette and Camille Guérin. The strain designated BCG (Bacillus Calmette-Guérin), of bovine origin, became attenuated while growing on culture media containing bile. After its introduction by Calmette, large numbers of children were vaccinated in France, elsewhere in Europe, and in South America; after 1930 the vaccine was used on an extensive scale. In 1943–44 the Ukrainian-born microbiologist Selman A. Waksman and his associates, working at Rutgers University, New Jersey, U.S., discovered the potent antimicrobial agent streptomycin in the growth medium of the soil microorganism *Streptomyces griseus*. In 1944–45 veterinarian W.H. Feldman and physician H.C. Hinshaw, working at the Mayo Clinic in Minnesota, demonstrated its specific effect in inhibiting tuberculosis in both animals and people. Wide clinical use of streptomycin promptly followed, eventually in combination with other drugs to attack resistant bacilli.

In 1952 a great advance was made with the successful testing of isoniazid in the United States and Germany. Isoniazid is the most important drug in the history of chemotherapy for tuberculosis. Other drugs were brought out in following years, including pyrazinamide in 1954, ethambutol in 1962, and rifampicin in 1963. By this time the industrialized countries were already seeing the health benefits of economic improvement, better sanitation, more widespread education, and particularly the establishment of public health practice, including specific measures for tuberculosis control. The rate of deaths from tuberculosis in England and Wales dropped from 190 per 100,000 population in 1900 to 7 per 100,000 in the early 1960s. In the United States during the same time period, it dropped from 194 per 100,000 to approximately 6 per

WORLD TB DAY

World TB Day is an annual observance held on March 24 that is intended to increase global awareness of tuberculosis. This date coincides with German physician and bacteriologist Robert Koch's announcement in 1882 of his discovery of Mycobacterium tuberculosis, the bacillus that causes the disease. The first World TB Day was held one century later—in 1982.

In the 1980s the incidence of tuberculosis was on the rise worldwide. This increase came after nearly 20 years of the disease's being at an all-time low in developed countries, such as the United States and the United Kingdom. Its return to those countries was attributed to several factors, including global increases in travel and migration and in the incidence of HIV/AIDS, as well as local decreases in concern about the risk of infection among public health agencies. This prompted the World Health Organization (WHO) to establish World TB Day. An annual observance would serve to draw the attention of researchers, funding agencies, and the public to the global fight against tuberculosis. World TB Day was initially sponsored by WHO in conjunction with support from other groups, such as the International Union Against Tuberculosis and Lung Disease.

However, the initial efforts by WHO and supporting organizations were not able to stop the spread of tuberculosis in developing regions of the world. The disease was a desperate problem in those areas, especially in countries in Africa, where the number of cases increased annually throughout the 1990s. In response, WHO and supporting groups stepped up their efforts and called on other national and international agencies to assist in raising awareness and increasing financial resources devoted to stopping the spread of tuberculosis. As a result, the global incidence of new cases of the disease stabilized in the early 2000s. However, despite case stabilization, between 1.5 and 2 million people worldwide were dying annually from tuberculosis during this period. Today the emergence of drug-resistant strains of tuberculosis bacilli has raised concern among researchers and health agencies in all countries affected by the disease. Infection with resistant strains requires treatment with multiple drugs, which can be prohibitively expensive for impoverished health care systems. Thus, today World TB Day continues to be an important means of connecting researchers and funding organizations with health care workers and the public in countries in need.

Today the Stop TB Partnership, originally known as the Stop TB Initiative, is the primary international sponsor of World TB Day. The Stop TB Partnership is made up of a network of international and national health agencies and organizations. The common goals of the partnership include raising global awareness of tuberculosis and supporting efforts aimed at preventing and developing a cure for the disease. The Stop TB Partnership is supported in its efforts primarily by WHO, but other organizations, including the U.S. Centers for Disease Control and Prevention, play important supporting roles as well. In preparation for World TB Day, those organizations work to assemble materials and information that can be released to the press and the public.

On World TB Day, workshops for the media, meetings between international organizations, and gatherings of scientists involved in tuberculosis research enable the sharing and dissemination of information on current issues relating to the disease. Efforts also are made to deliver information on the development of new treatments and tools for diagnosis to doctors and health care facilities in countries worldwide. Raising public awareness of tuberculosis on World TB Day is facilitated by charity and other fundraising events, memorial services, and various educational programs and activities.

100,000. In the popular mind, tuberculosis was then a disease of the past, of the indigent, and of the Third World.

However, in the mid-1980s the number of deaths caused by tuberculosis began to rise again in developed countries. The disease's resurgence was attributed in part to complacent health care systems, increased immigration of people from regions where tuberculosis was prevalent, and the spread of HIV. In addition, throughout the 1990s the number of cases of tuberculosis increased in Africa. Global programs such as the Stop TB Partnership, which was established in 2000, have worked to increase awareness of tuberculosis and to make new and existing treatments available to people living in developing countries most affected by the disease. In the early 2000s, as a result of the rapid implementation of global efforts to combat the disease, the epidemic in Africa slowed and incidence rates stabilized. Despite a leveling off of per capita incidence of tuberculosis, the global number of new cases continued to rise, due to population growth, especially in regions of Africa, Southeast Asia, and the eastern Mediterranean. The mortality rate from tuberculosis remains between 1.6 million and 2 million deaths per year.

OTHER MYCOBACTERIAL INFECTIONS

In addition to the leprosy and tuberculosis *Mycobacterium* organisms, several other species are also capable of causing disease. A species known as *M. bovis* is the cause of bovine tuberculosis. *M. bovis* is transmitted among cattle and some wild animals through the respiratory route, and it is also excreted in milk. If the milk is ingested raw, *M. bovis* readily infects humans. The bovine bacillus may be caught in the tonsils and may spread from there to the lymph nodes of the neck, where it causes caseation of the node tissue (a condition formerly known as scrofula). The node swells under the skin of the neck, finally eroding through the skin as a chronic discharging ulcer. From the gastrointestinal tract, *M. bovis* may spread into the bloodstream and reach any part of the body. It shows, however, a great preference for bones and joints, where it causes destruction of tissue and eventually gross deformity. Tuberculosis of the spine, or Pott disease, is characterized by softening and collapse of the vertebrae, often resulting in a hunchback deformity. Pasteurization of milk kills tubercle bacilli, and this, along with the systematic identification and destruction of infected cattle, has led to the disappearance of bovine tuberculosis in humans in many countries.

The AIDS epidemic has given prominence to a group of infectious agents known variously as nontuberculosis mycobacteria, atypical mycobacteria, and mycobacteria other than tuberculosis (MOTT). This group includes the *Mycobacterium* species *M. avium* (or *M. avium-intracellulare*), *M. kansasii, M. marinum,* and *M. ulcerans.* These bacilli have long been known to infect humans and other animals, but they cause dangerous illnesses of the lungs, lymph nodes, and other organs only in people whose immune systems have been weakened. Among AIDS patients, atypical mycobacterial illnesses are common complications of HIV infection. Treatment is attempted with various drugs, but the prognosis is usually poor owing to the AIDS patient's overall condition.

CHAPTER 3

BACTERIAL DISEASES: CHOLERA AND PLAGUE

Cholera and plague are two bacterial illnesses that have devastated human societies repeatedly throughout history. Both diseases are caused by bacteria, and both can be highly contagious. They are unique, however, in their mechanisms of transmission, in the tissues they affect, and in their response to drug therapies. These differences are due to the fact that the diseases are caused by different types of bacterial organisms. Whereas cholera is caused by bacteria of the genus *Vibrio*, which has an affinity for cells of the gastrointestinal tract, plague is caused by bacteria of the genus *Yersinia*, which can infect different tissues but are attracted particularly to the lymph nodes or lungs.

Measures to eliminate plague in countries worldwide have proven much more successful than those aimed at the elimination of cholera. This is largely because the cholera bacterium is spread through contaminated food and water, and its control is heavily dependent on good personal hygiene as well as effective sanitation of water supplies—measures notoriously difficult to implement and maintain in overcrowded or impoverished regions of the world. In contrast, in the case of plague, the elimination of rats, a necessary host in the infectious bacterium's life cycle, has proven much simpler. Thus, whereas cases of plague have decreased substantially, many people continue to suffer severely from cholera.

CHOLERA

Cholera is an acute infection of the small intestine caused by the bacterium *Vibrio cholerae* and characterized by extreme diarrhea with rapid and severe depletion of body fluids and salts. Cholera has often risen to epidemic proportions in sub-Saharan Africa and South Asia, particularly in India and Bangladesh. In the past two centuries, seven pandemics (global epidemics) of cholera have carried the disease to countries around the world.

Cholera is a disease that can incite populations to panic. Its reputation as a fierce and unrelenting killer is a deserved one. Cholera has been responsible for the deaths of millions, for economic losses of immense magnitude, and for the disruption of the very fabric of society in all parts of the world. In spite of the chaos that it continues to generate, cholera is perhaps the best understood of the modern plagues. The organism that causes it has been studied extensively for well over a century, and its modes of transmission have been identified. Safe, effective, and inexpensive interventions for both preventing infection and treating clinical illness have been developed.

THE CHOLERA BACTERIUM AND TOXIN

Vibrio cholerae is a member of the family Vibrionaceae, which includes three medically important genera of water-dwelling bacteria. It is a short, gram-negative, rod-shaped bacterium that appears curved when isolated. There are more than 200 different serogroups of *V. cholerae*, which are distinguished based on the structure of a protein called the O antigen in the bacterium's cell wall. Several of these serogroups are pathogenic in humans. However, only two serogroups of *V. cholerae*—O1 and O139 (sometimes called the Bengal serogroup)—are known to cause cholera. Pathogenic O1 and O139 *V. cholerae* have the ability to produce cholera toxin, a type of enterotoxin that affects intestinal cells. Pathogenic organisms in the O1 serogroup have caused the majority of cholera outbreaks and are subdivided into two biotypes: classical and El Tor. These two biotypes each contain two serotypes, called Inaba and Ogawa (some classifications recognize a third serotype, Hikojima), which are differentiated based on their biochemical properties, namely their expression of type-specific antigens. Inaba and Ogawa serotypes both express a common cholera antigen known simply as A. However, only Ogawa expresses cholera antigen B, and only Inaba expresses cholera antigen C. There also exist multiple strains of Inaba and Ogawa serotypes.

The classical biotype was responsible for most, if not all, of the six great cholera pandemics that swept through the world in the 19th and early 20th centuries. The seventh pandemic, which began in the mid-20th century, was caused by the El Tor biotype. This biotype possesses two characteristics that are of great epidemiological significance. First, it is a much hardier organism than the classical biotype, and it can survive for long periods of time in aquatic environments. Second, many people infected with the El Tor biotype experience only mild symptoms or no symptoms at all. Seriously ill patients are highly effective transmitters of cholera, but persons with mild or no symptoms are more likely to travel, thereby also playing a crucial role in the spread of the disease. As barriers to commerce and to personal travel disappear, the potential for diseases to be transmitted rapidly from one continent to another increases.

Cholera is an intestinal disease that is the archetype of waterborne illnesses. It spreads by the fecal–oral route: infection spreads through a population when feces containing the bacterium contaminate water that is then ingested by individuals. Transmission of the disease can also occur with food that has been irrigated, washed, or cooked with contaminated water. Foods that have the greatest potential to transmit the disease include shellfish and seafoods, especially if eaten raw; fruits and vegetables grown in soil that has been either fertilized with human excrement (night soil) or irrigated with raw sewage; and foods packed in contaminated ice.

Once the bacterium infects the intestine, it secretes the enterotoxin from its external coating. The enterotoxin binds to a receptor on the cells of the lining of the small intestine. Part of the toxin then enters the intestinal cells. The toxin increases the activity of an enzyme that regulates a cellular pumping mechanism that controls the movement of water and electrolytes between the intestine and the circulatory system. This pump effectively becomes locked in the "on" position, causing the outflow of enormous quantities of fluid—up to one litre (about one quart) per hour—into the intestinal tract. All of the clinical manifestations of cholera can be attributed to the extreme loss of water and salts.

SYMPTOMS AND TREATMENT

Cholera is marked by the sudden onset of profuse, watery diarrhea, typically after an incubation period of 12 to 28 hours. The fluid stools, commonly referred to as "rice water" stools, often contain flecks of mucus. The diarrhea is frequently accompanied by vomiting, and the patient rapidly becomes dehydrated. The patient is very thirsty and has a dry tongue. The blood pressure falls, the pulse becomes faint, and muscular cramps may become severe. The patient's eyes become hollow and sunken, and the skin becomes wrinkled, giving the hands the appearance of "washerwoman's hands." Children may also experience fever, lethargy, and seizures as a result of the extreme dehydration. The disease ordinarily runs its course in two to seven days.

The rapid loss of fluid from the bowel can, if untreated, lead to death—sometimes within hours—in more than 50 percent of those stricken. However, with proper modern treatment, mortality can essentially be prevented, with rates kept to less than 1 percent of those requiring therapy. This treatment consists largely of replacing lost fluid and salts with the oral or intravenous administration of an alkaline solution of sodium chloride. For oral rehydration the solution is made by using oral rehydration salts (ORS)—a measured mixture of glucose, sodium chloride, potassium chloride, and trisodium citrate. The mixture can be prepackaged and administered by non-medical personnel, allowing cholera to be treated even under the most adverse conditions. ORS can generally be used to treat all but the most severely dehydrated patients, who require intravenous rehydration.

The administration of antibiotics such as tetracycline during the first day of treatment usually shortens the period of diarrhea and decreases the amount of fluid replacement required. It is also important for patients to resume eating as soon as they are able in order to avoid malnutrition or to prevent existing malnutrition from becoming worse.

PREVENTION

A safe and clean supply of water is the key to cholera prevention. Adequate chlorination of public water supplies and, in some cases, the distribution of chlorine tablets to households with instructions for their proper use are often effective measures. If chemical disinfection is not possible, people can be instructed to boil water before drinking it, but this may be difficult to accomplish, especially in poor countries where fuel may be expensive or unavailable. Sometimes even simpler methods can be effective. For example, in Calcutta (Kolkata), where it is common for people to store water at home, cholera transmission was substantially reduced by replacing open containers, which allowed water to become easily contaminated, with narrow-necked jugs.

Another important intervention is the hygienic disposal of human waste. In areas lacking modern sewerage systems, the use of latrines can substantially lower the risk of infection. Ensuring the safety of food is yet another important control measure. During an epidemic of cholera, it is important that all food—including leftovers—be thoroughly cooked (to a core temperature of 70 °C [158 °F]) and that it be eaten before it cools. It is also important that stored food be covered to avoid contamination and that people always wash their hands after defecation and prior to food preparation. Foods sold by street vendors have been repeatedly implicated as sources of infection and should therefore be avoided by travelers to areas where cholera is endemic.

Vaccines have been developed against cholera, but they have not been considered effective for the prevention of cholera in large populations or during epidemics. Their usefulness is generally restricted to providing short-term protection for travelers visiting areas where cholera is endemic. Public health officials in some countries do not recommend

One key to cholera prevention is clean water, which is made possible through chlorination of public water supplies, boiling, or safe storage. Jupiterimages/Creatas/Thinkstock

cholera vaccination for any reason. Restrictions on travel and on food imports are among the measures that have at times been perceived as important for the prevention of cholera but have been shown to have relatively little benefit.

CHOLERA THROUGH HISTORY

The recorded history of cholera is relatively short and remarkable. Although the ancient Greek physicians Hippocrates (5th–4th century BCE) and Galen (2nd–3rd century CE) referred to an illness that may well have been cholera, and there are numerous hints that a cholera-like malady has been well known in the fertile delta plains of the Ganges River since antiquity, most of what is known about the disease comes from the modern era. Gaspar Correa, a Portuguese historian and the author of *Legendary India*, gave one of the first detailed accounts of the clinical aspects of an epidemic of "moryxy" in India in 1843: "The very worst of poison seemed there to take effect, as proved by vomiting, with drought of water accompanying it, as if the stomach were parched up, and cramps that fixed in the sinews of the joints."

SEVEN PANDEMICS

Cholera became a disease of global importance in 1817. In that year a particularly lethal outbreak occurred in Jessore, India, midway between Calcutta and Dhaka (now in Bangladesh), and then spread throughout most of India, Burma (now Myanmar), and Ceylon (now Sri Lanka). By 1820 epidemics had been reported in Siam (Thailand), in Indonesia (where more than 100,000 people succumbed on the island of Java alone), and as far away as the Philippines. At Basra, Iraq, as many as 18,000 people died during a three-week period in 1821. The pandemic spread through Turkey and reached the threshold of Europe. The disease also spread along trade routes from Arabia to the eastern African and Mediterranean coasts. Over the next few years, cholera disappeared from most of the world except for its "home base" around the Bay of Bengal.

The second cholera pandemic, which was the first to reach into Europe and the Americas, began in 1829. The disease arrived in Moscow and St. Petersburg in 1830, continuing into Finland and Poland. Carried by tradesmen along shipping routes, it rapidly spread to the port of Hamburg in northern Germany and made its first appearance in England, in Sunderland, in 1831. In 1832 it arrived in the Western Hemisphere, and in June more than 1,000 deaths were documented in Quebec. From Canada the disease moved quickly to the United States, disrupting life in most of the large cities along the eastern seaboard and striking hardest in New Orleans, Louisiana, where 5,000 residents died. In 1833 the pandemic reached Mexico and Cuba.

The third pandemic is generally considered to have been the most deadly.

It is thought to have erupted in 1852 in India. From there it spread rapidly through Persia (present-day Iran) to Europe, the United States, and then the rest of the world. Africa was severely affected, with the disease spreading from its eastern coast into Ethiopia and Uganda. Perhaps the worst single year of cholera was 1854, when 23,000 people died in Great Britain alone.

The fourth and fifth cholera pandemics (beginning in 1863 and 1881, respectively) are generally considered to have been less severe than the previous ones. However, in some areas extraordinarily lethal outbreaks were documented: more than 5,000 inhabitants of Naples died in 1884, 60,000 in the provinces of Valencia and Murcia in Spain in 1885, and perhaps as many as 200,000 in Russia in 1893–94. In Hamburg, repeatedly one of the cities in Europe most severely affected by cholera, almost 1.5 percent of the population perished during the cholera outbreak of 1892. The last quarter of the 19th century saw widespread infection in China and particularly in Japan, where more than 150,000 cases and 90,000 deaths were recorded between 1877 and 1879. The disease spread throughout South America in the early 1890s.

The sixth pandemic lasted from 1899 to 1923 and was especially lethal in India, in Arabia, and along the North African coast. More than 34,000 people perished in Egypt in a three-month period, and some 4,000 Muslim pilgrims were estimated to have died in Mecca in 1902.

(Mecca has been called a "relay station" for cholera in its progress from East to West; 27 epidemics were recorded during pilgrimages from the 19th century to 1930, and more than 20,000 pilgrims died of cholera during the 1907–08 hajj.) Russia was also struck severely by the sixth pandemic, with more than 500,000 people dying of cholera during the first quarter of the 20th century. The pandemic failed to reach the Americas and caused only small outbreaks in some ports of western Europe. Even so, extensive areas of Italy, Greece, Turkey, and the Balkans were severely affected. After 1923 cholera receded from most of the world, though endemic cases continued in the Indian subcontinent.

Cholera did not spread widely again until 1961, the beginning of the seventh pandemic. Unlike earlier pandemics, which began in the general area of the delta region of the Ganges River, this pandemic began on the island of Celebes in Indonesia. The seventh pandemic spread throughout Asia during the 1960s. During the next decade it spread westward to the Middle East and reached Africa, where cholera had not appeared for 70 years. The African continent is believed to have been struck harder at this time than ever before and in 1990 was the origin of more than 90 percent of all cholera cases reported to the World Health Organization (WHO). In 1991, 19 African nations reported nearly 140,000 cases in total. A particularly large outbreak occurred in 1994 among the many hundreds of thousands who fled widespread killing in Rwanda and occupied refugee camps near the city of Goma, Zaire (now Democratic Republic of the Congo). Tens of thousands perished from cholera during the first four weeks following their flight.

In 1991 cholera appeared unexpectedly and without explanation in Peru, on the western coast of South America, where it had been absent for 100 years. Cholera caused 3,000 deaths in Peru the first year, and it soon infected Ecuador, Colombia, Brazil, and Chile and leaped northward to Central America and Mexico. By 2005 cholera had been reported in nearly 120 countries. Although the seventh pandemic continued in many parts of the world, the more-industrialized countries of the world were largely spared. As the disparity between industrialized and less-developed countries grew, cholera, which previously had been a global disease, seemed to have become yet another burden to be borne by impoverished nations of the Third World. Moreover, experts predicted that this time cholera would not go away but would become endemic to many parts of the world, much as it has been for centuries to the Ganges delta.

Some health officials who monitor cholera epidemics believed that *V. cholerae* O139 might eventually produce an eighth pandemic. However, the ability of the O139 serogroup to spread in areas affected by the O1 serogroup in the ongoing seventh pandemic appeared limited, and O139 remained confined to India and Bangladesh.

MODERN EPIDEMICS

While the incidence of cholera in developed countries decreased significantly in the late 1990s, the disease remained prevalent in Africa. In 1995, out of some 209,000 total cholera cases worldwide, roughly 72,000 cases occurred in Africa and 86,000 in South and North America. However, in 1998, out of about 293,000 total cases worldwide, there were roughly 212,000 cases in Africa but only 57,000 in the Americas. In the early 2000s many countries within Africa, such as Mozambique, the Democratic Republic of the Congo, and Tanzania, experienced outbreaks that often involved more than 20,000 cases and several hundred deaths. During that time the disparity in the incidence of cholera in Africa relative to other parts of the world continued to grow. The persistence of the disease was attributed to poor water quality, poor hygiene, and poor sanitation—factors that stemmed from the lack of organized sanitation programs—and the lack of access to health care in many regions of Africa.

Zimbabwe, located in southern Africa, experienced a severe epidemic of cholera from 2008 to 2009. The outbreak, which was fueled by the fragmented infrastructure of Zimbabwe's health care system and by the unavailability of food and of clean drinking water, started in August 2008 in a district located south of the country's capital city, Harare. Between August and December 2008 the disease spread quickly, reaching Harare and several surrounding districts and spreading throughout the east, west, and central Mashonaland provinces, the Midlands province, and the Manicaland province. By late April 2009 the epidemic affected over 95 percent of the country's districts, and some 96,700 cases and 4,200 deaths were reported. A small epidemic that occurred in districts near Harare from January to April 2008 possibly caused the epidemic that emerged in August, since inadequate health care services could have enabled undetected transmission of the bacteria to persist.

Economic collapse within Zimbabwe compounded the cholera epidemic of 2008–2009. Economic inflation forced several hospitals to close in late November 2008. They could not afford to buy medicine to refill their stocks. By early December stocks of water-purification chemicals had run out, so people relied on unclean water. While the sanitary conditions declined in many affected areas, conditions were dreadful in Harare, where the failed sewage systems led to raw sewage flowing into streets and rivers; collapsing sanitary regulations meant that refuse accumulated in public places. On Dec. 4, 2008, the Zimbabwean government declared a national state of emergency and sought international aid. WHO, the International Committee of the Red Cross, and other organizations improved disease surveillance, provided medical supplies, and enlisted doctors and sanitary engineers. These organizations also provided shipments of crucial water and water-purification chemicals.

By late December 2008, despite relief organization efforts, cholera had spread to every Zimbabwe province. Risk of infection and death from cholera was exacerbated by severe food shortages and the closure of numerous hospitals and clinics. The cholera fatality rate soared to 5.7 percent in Zimbabwe—surpassing considerably the 1 percent fatality rate typically associated with large-scale cholera epidemics. Fatality rates inflated to 50 percent in rural areas of Zimbabwe where medical services were lacking. In March 2009, 30 different strains of cholera were isolated from water samples collected across the country.

With the spread of cholera in Zimbabwe, the disease reached nearby countries, including Zambia, South Africa, Botswana, and Mozambique. By late January 2009 some 6,000 cases of cholera had been reported in South Africa, nearly half of which occurred in Limpopo province.

On Oct. 21, 2010, a cholera outbreak was confirmed in Haiti following a devastating earthquake that struck the country earlier that year. Haiti, which was still recovering from tropical storms that made landfall there in 2008, suffered from poor water, sanitation, and hygiene conditions as a result of the 2010 earthquake. Cholera erupted, although the disease had not been documented in Haiti in years.

STUDY OF THE DISEASE

Credit for the discovery of the cholera bacterium is usually accorded to Robert Koch, the German bacteriologist who first enunciated the principles of modern germ theory. In June 1883, during the fifth pandemic, Koch and a team of scientists traveled first to Egypt and then to Calcutta to study outbreaks of cholera. By employing a technique he invented of inoculating sterilized gelatin-coated glass plates with fecal material from patients, he was able to grow and describe the bacterium. He was then able to show that its presence in a person's intestine led to the development of cholera in that person. While in Calcutta Koch also made valuable observations on the role played by water in the transmission of the bacterium.

Koch's findings, however, were not original. Rather, they were rediscoveries of work that had been previously done by others. The Italian microbiologist Filippo Pacini had already seen the bacterium and named it "cholerigenic vibrios" in 1854 (a fact of which Koch is assumed not to have been aware). The principal mode of cholera transmission, contaminated water, had also been described previously—by the British anesthesiologist John Snow in 1849. Snow's work, however, was not totally accepted at the time, because other theories of disease causation were prevalent, most notably that of "miasmatism," which claimed that cholera was contracted by breathing air contaminated by disease-containing "clouds."

Biotype El Tor was first described by the German physician E. Gotschlich in 1905, during the sixth pandemic, at a quarantine station at El Tor in the Sinai Desert. The station had been established to study cholera in victims returning from pilgrimages to Mecca. *V. cholerae* O139 was identified in 1992 during a cholera outbreak on the eastern coast of India.

DEVELOPMENT OF TREATMENTS

Little is known about the treatment of cholera prior to its arrival in Europe. One of the early recorded advances was made by the chemist R. Hermann, a German working at the Institute of Artificial Mineral Waters in Moscow during the 1831 outbreak. Hermann believed that water should be injected into the victims' veins to replace lost fluids. William Brooke O'Shaughnessy, a young British physician, reported in *The Lancet* (1831) that, on the basis of his studies, he "would not hesitate to inject some ounces of warm water into the veins. I would also, without apprehension, dissolve in that water the mild innocuous salts which nature herself is accustomed to combine with the human blood, and which in Cholera are deficient." His ideas were put into practice by a Scotsman, Thomas Latta, as early as 1832, with surprisingly good results, but few physicians followed Latta's example. Conventional treatment consisted of enemas, castor oil, calomel (mercurous chloride; a purgative), gastric washing, venesection (bloodletting), opium, brandy, and plugging of the anus to prevent fluid from escaping. Mortality resulting from cholera remained high throughout the 19th century.

The search for an adequate treatment was renewed at the beginning of the 20th century. Among the leading investigators were Sir Leonard Rogers, an Englishman at Calcutta Medical College, and Andrew Sellards, an American in Manila. Rogers developed a replacement fluid that contained a much higher salt content than had previously been used and that resulted in a halving of cholera deaths—from a 60 percent mortality rate down to 30 percent. Sellards suggested that sodium bicarbonate be added to intravenous solutions in addition to sodium chloride, an idea that Rogers then adopted and that resulted in further reductions in mortality—to 20 percent.

The next round of major advances in cholera treatment did not occur until 1958, when Robert A. Phillips, a U.S. Navy physician, identified a solution that proved to be even more effective. Further refinements of Phillips's solution and the methods of administering treatment occurred in Bangkok (Thailand), Taiwan, Manila, and Dhaka. By the mid-1960s, mortality rates in those areas were less than 1 percent.

The next step in the conquest of cholera was to develop a rehydration fluid that could be administered orally. This method would obviate the need for distilled water, needles, and intravenous tubing and theoretically would make simple and effective treatment available to all cholera victims. Oral rehydration therapy was brought to reality by a medical breakthrough sometimes hailed as one of the most important of the 20th century—the discovery that the small intestine's absorption of sodium, the principal ion lost during an acute cholera attack, is linked to the absorption of glucose. It became clear that a solution of sodium, glucose, and water in the intestine would overcome the losses caused by the cholera enterotoxin and would maintain the hydration of the patient.

Early application of oral rehydration solutions was implemented by Ruth R. Darrow in the United States for dehydrated infants and by N.H. Chatterjee in Calcutta for successfully treating patients with mild cholera. Clinical studies carried out simultaneously by physicians Norbert Hirschhorn in Dhaka and Nathaniel F. Pierce in Calcutta helped define the optimal composition of an oral solution. In 1968 researchers David A. Nalin and Richard A. Cash, working in East Pakistan (now Bangladesh), developed an oral glucose-electrolyte solution that was suitable for cholera patients of all ages with all severities of illness. In mild cases the solution was effective as the sole treatment. Finally, in a controlled trial in a refugee camp in West Bengal, India, during the Bangladeshi struggle for independence in 1971, physician Dilip Mahalanabis and his colleagues showed that case-fatality rates in cholera patients treated with oral rehydration salts (ORS) could be kept substantially lower than in patients who were treated with what was, at the time, conventional therapy. Today ORS is the mainstay of treatment not only for cholera but for all diarrheal illnesses.

PLAGUE

Plague is an infectious fever caused by *Yersinia pestis*, a bacterium transmitted from rodents to humans by the bite of infected fleas. Plague was the cause of some of the most devastating epidemics in history. It was the disease behind the Black Death of the 14th century, when as much as one-third of Europe's population died. Huge pandemics also arose in Asia in the late 19th and early 20th centuries, eventually spreading around the world and causing millions of deaths. Today, thanks to strict public health measures and modern antibiotics, plague no longer strikes great numbers of people, nor is it as deadly for those whom it strikes. Nevertheless, it still persists in some parts of the world where large populations of wild or domestic rodents harbour the fleas and occasionally pass them to humans.

NATURE OF THE DISEASE

Plague is primarily a disease of rodents, and humans enter only accidentally into the usual cycle. This cycle, rodent–flea–rodent, as a rule is enzootic—that is, present in an animal community at all times but affecting only small numbers of animals. However, under certain environmental conditions the cycle reaches epizootic proportions (affecting many animals in a region at the same time). Spread of the infection among wild or domestic rodents in the vicinity of human habitations creates conditions favourable for outbreaks of human plague, for when an epizootic outbreak kills off the rodents, fleas from the dead animals fail to find another rodent host and thus begin to infest humans. Today most human cases are sporadic, occurring in rural areas by infection from wild rodents such as ground squirrels, but in the past huge numbers of persons were infected in crowded cities by fleas from domestic rodents such as the black rat.

The virulence of the plague bacillus—its ability to multiply in the tissues of its host and cause death—is remarkably stable and vigorous. Once ingested by a flea, it multiplies until the insect's digestive tract is blocked. When the flea bites another rodent or a human, bacilli are regurgitated into the new host and migrate through the lymphatic system to lymph nodes. There they are able produce proteins that disrupt the normal inflammatory response and that prevent their digestion by infection-fighting macrophages. With the host's immune response thus weakened, the bacilli quickly colonize the lymph nodes, producing a painful swelling and, eventually, destroying the tissue. On occasion they enter the bloodstream either directly or from the lymph nodes, bringing on a general septicemia, or blood poisoning. On postmortem examination they are found in great abundance in the lymph nodes, spleen, bone marrow, and liver.

The disease in humans has three clinical forms: bubonic, pneumonic, and septicemic. Bubonic plague is the best-known form in popular lore, and indeed it constitutes about three-fourths of plague cases. It is also the least dangerous form of plague, accounting today for virtually no deaths and in the past killing only half of its victims (at a time when contracting the other forms of plague brought almost certain death). Typically, bubonic plague starts two to six days after *Yersinia* infection with shivering, then vomiting, headache, giddiness, and intolerance to light; pain in the back and limbs; and sleeplessness, apathy, or delirium. The most characteristic sign, however, is the subsequent appearance of one or more tender, swollen lymph nodes, or buboes, which are usually distributed in the groin and armpits. The temperature rises rapidly to 40 °C (104 °F) or higher and frequently falls slightly on the second or third day, with marked fatigue. Bubonic plague is not directly infectious from person to person; the bacillus is carried from rodent to person or from person to person by infected fleas.

In pneumonic plague the lungs are extensively invaded by bacilli. The physical signs are those of a severe pneumonia (fever, weakness, and shortness of breath). Edema (filling with fluid) of the lungs soon follows, and death will almost certainly occur in three or four days if treatment is not offered. Other manifestations are insomnia, stupor, staggering gait, speech disorder, and loss of memory. Pneumonic plague is highly infectious, as the bacillus can be passed to other people in droplets expelled by coughing or sneezing. The disease can also develop as a complication of bubonic plague.

In septicemic plague the bloodstream is so invaded by *Yersinia* that, in untreated cases, death can ensue even before the bubonic or pneumonic forms have had time to appear. It is marked by fatigue, fever, and internal bleeding. Septicemic plague can arise as a complication of bubonic plague or directly by infection from a flea bite.

Plague is diagnosed first by its symptoms and by a history of possible exposure to rodents. Because the symptoms may be similar to those seen in other fevers such as tularemia, dengue, or pneumonia, positive diagnosis must await the identification of *Yersinia* in a laboratory test of the patient's blood, lymph, or sputum. Antibiotic therapy must be given promptly to protect the patient's life. Treatment is primarily with streptomycin or, if unavailable, gentamicin. Modern therapy has reduced the global fatality rate of plague from its historical level of 50–90 percent to less than 15 percent. The fatality rate is even lower in cases of bubonic plague and in areas where modern health care is available.

Hygienic measures and elimination of rats from human habitations have virtually ended urban epidemics of plague in the developed world. Because it is impossible to eliminate rodents from the wild, the disease will always be present, but its occurrence in humans can be controlled by limiting people's exposure to infested animals. A vaccine specific for plague has been used in the past in endemic areas for people likely to be exposed to rodents and their fleas. Owing to its limited effectiveness, it is not generally available.

PLAGUE THROUGH HISTORY

Plague is an ancient disease that was described during classical times as occurring in North Africa and the Middle East. It is sometimes presumed to be the disease behind several historic epidemics, such as the pestilence described as striking the Philistines in the biblical book of 1 Samuel, but it is impossible to verify the true nature of these outbreaks. The first great plague pandemic to be reliably reported occurred during the reign of the Byzantine emperor Justinian I in the 6th century CE. According to the historian Procopius and others, the outbreak began in Egypt and moved along maritime trade routes, striking Constantinople in 542. There it killed residents by the tens of thousands, the dead falling so quickly that authorities had trouble disposing of them. Judging by descriptions of the symptoms and mode of transmission of the disease, it is likely that all forms of plague were present. Over the next half-century, the pandemic spread westward to port cities of the Mediterranean and eastward into Persia. Christian writers such as John of Ephesus ascribed the plague to the wrath of God against a sinful world, but modern researchers conclude that it was spread by domestic rats, which traveled in seagoing vessels and proliferated in the crowded, unhygienic cities of the era.

The next great plague pandemic is believed to have been the dreaded Black Death of Europe in the 14th century. By this time a highly efficient plague reservoir, the black rat (*Rattus rattus*), was firmly established in Europe, and the disease is supposed to have been brought along trade routes from Central Asia. The number of deaths was enormous, reaching two-thirds or three-fourths of the population in various parts of Europe. It has been calculated that one-fourth to one-third of the total population of Europe, or 25 million persons, died during the Black Death. For the next three centuries outbreaks of plague occurred frequently throughout the continent and the British Isles. The Great Plague of London of 1664–66 caused more than 70,000 deaths in a population estimated at 460,000. Plague raged in Cologne and on the Rhine from 1666 to 1670 and in the Netherlands from 1667 to 1669, but after that it seems to have subsided in western Europe. Between 1675 and 1684 a new outbreak appeared in North Africa, Turkey, Poland, Hungary, Austria, and Germany, progressing northward. Malta lost 11,000 persons in 1675, Vienna at least 76,000 in 1679, and Prague 83,000 in 1681. Many northern German cities also suffered during this time, but in 1683 plague disappeared from Germany. France saw the last of plague in 1668, until it reappeared in 1720 in the port city of Marseille, where it killed as many as 40,000 people. After these last outbreaks, plague seems to have disappeared from Europe. Various explanations have been offered: progress in sanitation, hospitalization, and cleanliness; a change in domestic housing that excluded rats from human dwellings; abandonment of old trade routes; and a natural quiescent phase in the normal rise and decline of epidemic diseases. Such possibilities would have been lost on Europeans at the time, as the very concept of an infectious organism was unknown. As late as 1768 the first edition of *Encyclopædia Britannica* repeated the commonly held scientific notion that plague was a "pestilential fever" arising from a "poisonous miasma," or vapour, that had been brought "from eastern countries" and was "swallowed in with the air."

The pestilential poison disturbs all the functions of the body; for unless it be expelled to the external parts, it is certainly fatal.

Expulsion of the poison was thought to be best accomplished by either natural rupture of the buboes or, if necessary, lancing and draining them. Other recommended means were bloodletting, sweating, induction of vomiting, and loosening of the bowels.

During the 18th and early part of the 19th century, plague continued to prevail in Turkey, North Africa, Egypt, Syria, and Greece. Once it was a maxim that plague never appeared east of the Indus River, but during the 19th century it afflicted more than one district of India: in 1815 Gujarāt, in 1815 Sind, in 1823 the Himalayan foothills, and in 1836 Rājasthān. These

outbreaks merely set the stage for the third great plague pandemic, which is thought to have gained momentum in Yunnan Province, southwestern China, in the 1850s and finally reached Guangzhou (Canton) and Hong Kong in 1894. These port cities became plague distribution centres, and between 1894 and 1922 the disease spread throughout the whole world, more widely than in any preceding pandemic, resulting in more than 10 million deaths. Among the many points infected were Bombay in 1896, Calcutta in 1898, Cape Town and San Francisco in 1900, Bangkok in 1904, Guayaquil (Ecuador) in 1908, Colombo (Sri Lanka) in 1914, and Pensacola (Florida) in 1922. Almost all the European ports were struck, but of all the areas affected, India suffered the most.

The third plague pandemic was the last, for it coincided with (and in some cases motivated) a series of achievements in the scientific understanding of the disease. By the end of the 19th century the germ theory of disease had been put on a sound empirical basis by the work of the great European scientists Louis Pasteur, Joseph Lister, and Robert Koch. In 1894, during the epidemic in Hong Kong, the organism that causes plague was isolated independently by two bacteriologists, the Frenchman Alexandre Yersin, working for the Pasteur Institute, and the Japanese Kitasato Shibasaburo, a former associate of Koch. Both men found bacteria in fluid samples taken from plague victims, then injected them into animals and observed that the animals died quickly

BLACK DEATH

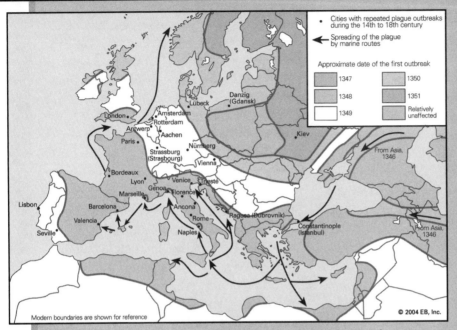

The second pandemic of the Black Death in Europe (1347–51)

The Black Death was a pandemic that ravaged Europe between 1347 and 1351, taking a proportionately greater toll on life than any other known epidemic or war up to that time. The Black Death is widely believed to have been the result of plague, caused by infection with the bacterium *Yersinia pestis*. However, modern scientific evidence has indicated that the pandemic may have been viral in origin.

Originating in China and Inner Asia, the plague was transmitted to Europeans (1347) when a Kipchak army, besieging a Genoese trading post in the Crimea, catapulted plague-infested corpses into the town. The disease spread from the Mediterranean ports, affecting Sicily (1347); North Africa, mainland Italy, Spain, England, and France (1348); Austria, Hungary, Switzerland, Germany, and the Low Countries (1349); and Scandinavia and the Baltic lands (1350). There were recurrences of the plague in 1361–63, 1369–71, 1374–75, 1390, and 1400.

The rate of mortality from the Black Death varied from place to place: whereas some districts, such as the duchy of Milan, Flanders, and Béarn, seem to have escaped comparatively lightly, others, such as Tuscany, Aragon, Catalonia, and Languedoc, were very hard hit. Towns, where the danger of contagion was greater, were more affected than the countryside, and within the towns the monastic communities provided the highest incidence of victims. Even the great and powerful, who were more capable of flight, were struck down: among royalty, Eleanor, queen of Peter IV of Aragon, and King Alfonso XI of Castile succumbed, and Joan, daughter of the English king Edward III, died at Bordeaux on the way to her wedding with Alfonso's son. Canterbury lost two successive archbishops, John de Stratford and Thomas Bradwardine. Petrarch lost not only Laura, who inspired so many of his poems, but also his patron, Giovanni Cardinal Colonna. The papal court at Avignon was reduced by one-fourth. Whole communities and families were sometimes annihilated.

The study of contemporary archives suggests a mortality varying in the different regions between one-eighth and two-thirds of the population, and the French chronicler Jean Froissart's *statement that about one-third of Europe's population died in the epidemic may be fairly accurate. The population in England in 1400 was perhaps half what it had been 100 years earlier. In that country alone, the Black Death certainly caused the depopulation or total disappearance of about 1,000 villages. A rough estimate is that 25 million people in Europe died from plague during the Black Death. The population of western Europe did not again reach its pre-1348 level until the beginning of the 16th century.*

The consequences of this violent catastrophe were many. A cessation of wars and a sudden slump in trade immediately followed but were only of short duration. A more lasting and serious consequence was the drastic reduction of the amount of land under cultivation due to the deaths of so many labourers. This proved to be the ruin of many landowners. The shortage of labour compelled them to substitute wages or money rents in place of labour services in an effort to keep their tenants. There was also a general rise in wages for artisans and peasants. These changes brought a new fluidity to the hitherto rigid stratification of society. The psychological effects of the Black Death were reflected north of the Alps (not in Italy) by a preoccupation with death and the afterlife evinced in poetry, sculpture, and painting. The Roman Catholic church lost some of its monopoly over the salvation of souls as people turned to mysticism and sometimes to excesses.

of plague. Yersin named the new bacillus *Pasteurella pestis*, after his mentor, but in 1970 the bacterium was renamed *Yersinia pestis*, in honour of Yersin himself.

It remained to be determined how the bacillus infected humans. It had long been noticed in many epidemic areas that unusual deaths among rats preceded outbreaks of plague among humans, and this link was particularly noted in the outbreaks in India and China. The relationship was so striking that in 1897 Japanese physician Ogata Masanori described an outbreak on Formosa as "ratpest" and showed that rat fleas carried the plague bacillus. The following year Paul-Louis Simond, a French researcher sent by the Pasteur Institute to India, announced the results of experiments demonstrating that Oriental rat fleas (*Xenopsylla cheopis*) carried the plague bacillus between rats. It was

then demonstrated definitively that rat fleas would infest humans and transmit plague through their bites. With that, massive rat-proofing measures were instituted worldwide in maritime vessels and port facilities, and insecticides were used in areas where plague had broken out. Beginning in the 1930s, sulfa drugs and then antibiotics such as streptomycin gave doctors a very effective means of attacking the plague bacillus directly.

The effectiveness of these measures is told in the declining numbers of plague deaths over the following decades. From a maximum of more than one million in 1907, deaths dropped to approximately 170,000 per year in 1919–28, 92,000 in 1929–38, 22,000 in 1939–48, and 4,600 in 1949–53. Plague is no longer an epidemic disease of port cities. It is now mainly of campestral or sylvatic (that is, open-field or woodland) origin, striking

Great Plague of London

The Great Plague of London was an epidemic of plague that ravaged London, Eng., from late 1664 to early 1666, killing perhaps more than 75,000 of a total population estimated at 460,000. The Great Plague was not an isolated event—some 40,000 Londoners had died of the plague in 1625—but it was the last and worst of the epidemics. It began in the late autumn of 1664 in London's suburb of St. Giles-in-the-Fields, and the greatest devastation remained in the city's outskirts, at Stepney, Shoreditch, Clerkenwell, Cripplegate, and Westminster, quarters where the poor were densely crowded. The epidemic was severe in the winter and revived and spread again in May 1665. The king and court fled from London in June and did not return until the following February. (Parliament kept a short session at Oxford.) The total number of deaths from plague in 1665, according to the bills of mortality, was 68,596. But this number is probably an underestimate, since many of the 6,432 deaths attributed to spotted fever were really caused by plague.

In December 1665 the mortality rate fell suddenly and continued down through the winter. In 1666 only 2,000 deaths were recorded. From London the disease spread widely over the country, but from 1667 on there was no epidemic of plague in any part of England, though sporadic cases appeared in bills of mortality up to 1679. This disappearance of plague from London has been attributed to the Great Fire in September 1666, but it also subsided in other cities without such cause. The decline has also been ascribed to quarantine, but effective quarantine was actually not established until 1720. The cessation of plague in England must be regarded as spontaneous.

individuals and occasionally breaking out in villages and rural areas where *Yersinia* is kept in a constant natural reservoir by various types of rodents, including ground squirrels, voles, and field mice. Some 1,000 to 3,000 people worldwide contract plague each year, and some 200 of them die. The main regions of plague are in western North America; the Andes region and Brazil in South America; a broad band across Southwest, Central, and Southeast Asia; and eastern Africa. Most cases today occur in Africa.

With the rise of global terrorism, plague came to be seen as a potential weapon of biological warfare. During World War II, Japan is said to have spread *Yersinia*-infected fleas in selected areas of China, and during the Cold War the United States and the Soviet Union developed means for spreading *Yersinia* directly as an aerosol—a particularly efficient way to infect people with lethal pneumonic plague. Such an attack might cause a high casualty rate in only limited areas, but it might also create panic in the general population. In response, some governments developed plans and stockpiled medications for dealing with emergency outbreaks of plague.

CHAPTER 4

RICKETTSIAL AND CHLAMYDIAL DISEASES

Rickettsial and chlamydial diseases represent important groups of vector-borne and zoonotic diseases—conditions arising from the transmission of infectious agents to humans by the bite of an arthropod (such as a tick) or other animal. Rickettsial bacteria include members of several genera classified in the family Rickettsiaceae. The rickettsiae are rod-shaped or variably spherical bacteria, and most species are gram-negative. They are natural parasites of certain arthropods (notably lice, fleas, mites, and ticks) and can cause serious diseases—usually characterized by acute, self-limiting fevers—in humans and other animals. Examples of rickettsial diseases in humans include typhus, Rocky Mountain spotted fever, and Q fever.

Chlamydial organisms are bacterial parasites that cause several different diseases in humans. The *Chlamydia* genus contains *C. trachomatis*, various strains of which cause trachoma, lymphogranuloma venereum, and conjunctivitis in humans. Related species known to cause serious disease in humans include *Chlamydophila psittaci*, which causes psittacosis, and *Chlamydophila pneumoniae*, which causes respiratory-tract infections.

RICKETTSIAL DISEASES

The rickettsiae range in size from roughly 0.3 to 0.5 µm by 0.8 to 2.0 µm. Virtually all rickettsiae can reproduce only within animal cells. Rickettsiae are usually transmitted to humans by a bite from an arthropod carrier. Because certain species can withstand considerable drying, transmission of rickettsia can also occur when arthropod feces are inhaled or enter the skin through abrasion. Most rickettsiae normally infect animals other than humans, who become involved as dead-end hosts only accidentally. Epidemic typhus and trench fever are exceptions, because humans are the only host of proven importance. The other rickettsial infections occur primarily in animals, which serve as reservoirs from which bloodsucking arthropods acquire the rickettsial bacteria and in turn transmit them to other animals and, occasionally, humans.

The largest rickettsial genus, *Rickettsia*, is generally subdivided into the typhus group, the spotted fever group, and the scrub typhus group. This genus alone is responsible for a number of highly virulent diseases including Rocky Mountain spotted fever, epidemic typhus, Brill-Zinsser disease, scrub typhus, and others.

Protective measures against rickettsial disease agents include the control of arthropod carriers when necessary and immunization. Animals that recover from a rickettsiosis exhibit long-lasting immunity. Artificial immunity, as a preventive, is variably effective, typhus and the spotted fevers being among the easiest to immunize against. The most effective treatment of most rickettsioses includes the timely and prolonged administration of large amounts of broad-spectrum antibiotics such as tetracycline or, if tetracycline cannot be used, chloramphenicol.

BARTONELLOSIS

Bartonellosis is a rickettsial infection limited to South America and caused by the bacterium *Bartonella bacilliformis* of the order Rickettsiales. Bartonellosis is characterized by two distinctive clinical stages: Oroya fever, an acute febrile anemia of rapid onset, bone and joint pains, and a high mortality if untreated, and verruga peruana, a more benign skin eruption characterized by reddish papules and nodules, which usually follows the Oroya fever but may also occur in individuals who have not exhibited previous symptoms. The skin lesions are thought to be an expression of developing immunity in the affected persons. Reinfection is extremely rare.

The disease is transmitted to humans by the night-biting sand fly of the genus *Phlebotomus*, which propagates in the Andes Mountains in parts of Peru, Ecuador, and Colombia. The disease responds well to certain antibiotics. Control measures are directed principally at the insect carrier, with the use of insecticides and insect repellents.

BOUTONNEUSE FEVER

Boutonneuse fever (French: Fièvre Boutonneuse, or Fièvre Exanthématique) is a mild, typhuslike fever caused by the bacterium *Rickettsia conorii*, which

Howard T. Ricketts

(b. Feb. 9, 1871, Findlay, Ohio, U.S.—d. May 3, 1910, Mexico City, Mex.)

American pathologist Howard T. Ricketts discovered the causative organisms and mode of transmission of Rocky Mountain spotted fever and epidemic typhus (known in Mexico, where Ricketts worked for a time and died of typhus, as tabardillo).

Ricketts graduated in medicine from Northwestern University, Chicago, and in 1902 joined the faculty of the University of Chicago. In the spring of 1906 he demonstrated that Rocky Mountain spotted fever could be transmitted to a healthy animal by the bite of a certain tick. Two years later he described the causative microorganism. He found it in the blood of the infected animals and also in the ticks and their eggs.

*In 1909 Ricketts and his assistant, Russel M. Wilder, went to Mexico City to study epidemic typhus. They learned that it was transmitted by the body louse (*Pediculus humanus humanus*), a discovery that had been made the same year by French bacteriologist Charles-Jules-Henri Nicolle. Ricketts and Wilder located the disease-causing organism both in the blood of the victim and in the bodies of the lice. Before he succumbed to typhus later that year, Ricketts showed that the disease could be transmitted to monkeys, which, after recovering, would develop immunity to the disease. In memory of Ricketts, the genus* Rickettsia *was established for the causative organisms that he had identified.*

is transmitted by ticks. The disease is endemic in most of the Mediterranean countries, and it is present in Crimea (southern Ukraine). Available evidence suggests that the diseases described as Kenya typhus and South African tick-bite fever are probably identical with boutonneuse fever although conveyed by a different species of tick.

Primarily, the carrier was found to be a brown dog tick, *Rhipicephalus sanguineus*. Other species of ticks, however, have also been incriminated. The reservoir probably exists in nature in the lower animals, but the dog is apparently a major source of infection. The course of the disease is somewhat similar to Rocky Mountain spotted fever, but it is milder. The case fatality rate is under 3 percent. A primary lesion, or *tâche noire* (French: "black spot"), is often found at the site of the infecting tick bite and, therefore, on any part of the body, but it is usually on a part covered by clothing.

Epidemic Typhus

Typhus is a series of acute infectious diseases that appear with a sudden onset of headache, chills, fever, and general pains, which proceed on the third to fifth day with a rash and toxemia (toxic substances in the blood). Typhus diseases, which generally terminate after two to three weeks, are caused by different species of rickettsia bacteria that are transmitted to humans by lice, fleas, mites, or ticks. The insects are carried person to person or are brought to people by rodents, cattle, and other animals.

Epidemic typhus is an important form of typhus. Epidemic typhus has also been called camp fever, jail fever, and war fever, names that suggest overcrowding, underwashing, and lowered standards of living. It is caused by the bacterium *Rickettsia prowazekii* and is conveyed from person to person by the body louse, *Pediculus humanus humanus*. The louse is infected by feeding with its powerful sucking mouth on a person who has the disease. As the louse sucks the person's blood, rickettsiae pass into the insect's gut, where they invade the intestinal cells. There they multiply until the cells burst, releasing hordes of rickettsiae into the louse's intestinal canal. These either reinfect other cells or are excreted in the louse's feces. The infection kills the louse, but people are commonly infected by scratching a louse bite, thus rubbing the louse's infected feces into the wound by abrasion. (Rickettsiae may remain viable and retain their virulence for many days in dried louse feces.) Lice leave a body when it becomes too hot from fever or too cold from death and crawl to another human host. Also, the clothing of a person heavily infested with typhus is contaminated with louse feces, and careless removal of it may raise a cloud of infected dust in the air and, in this way, spread typhus to others, especially medical professionals.

About 10 days after being bitten, an infected person experiences headache, loss of appetite, malaise, and a rapid rise in temperature with fever, chills, marked prostration, and nausea. Four to six days after onset, a characteristic rash appears over most of the body. The sick person is flushed, and the eyes are bleary. The temperature reaches a maximum range by the end of the first week and is sustained until about the 12th day, when it generally falls rather rapidly, becoming normal in an uncomplicated course about the 14th to 16th day. Depression and weakness may be protracted during the recovery, and the patient's convalescence is slow. If the disease is untreated, circulation becomes sluggish and there may be spots of gangrene on the fingers, genitals, nose, and ears. Signs of pneumonia or kidney failure are common. Prostration is progressive, and delirium and coma follow. Cardiac failure may be the immediate cause of death. Tetracycline and chloramphenicol have a dramatic curative effect, however, and, if treated early enough, few die. The disease can be diagnosed clinically during epidemics and by laboratory tests.

Epidemic typhus has been one of the great disease scourges in human history. It is classically associated with people crowded together in filth, cold, poverty, and hunger; wars and famine; refugees; prisons and jails; concentration camps; and ships. Recognizable descriptions of the disease occur in European literature from the Middle Ages on, and devastating epidemics of typhus continued to

Conditions during the Irish Potato Famine were ripe for epidemic typhus, which flourishes in circumstances including crowding, filth, and starvation, among others. Hulton Archive/ Getty Images

occur intermittently throughout Europe in the 17th, 18th, and 19th centuries. Prominent outbreaks occurred during the Napoleonic Wars and during the Irish Potato Famine of 1845–49. Epidemic typhus was clearly differentiated as a disease entity from typhoid fever in the 19th century.

Major progress in combating the disease began only after 1909, when French physician Charles-Jules-Henri Nicolle demonstrated that typhus is transmitted from person to person by the body louse. (Nicolle later won the Nobel Prize for his efforts.) In the early 20th century typhus decreased and then practically disappeared from western Europe as improvements in living conditions and hygiene occurred. The disease remained intermittently epidemic in eastern Europe, the Middle East, and parts of Africa, however. At the close of World War I the disease caused several million deaths in Russia, Poland, and Romania. During World War II it again caused epidemics, this time among refugees and displaced persons, particularly in German concentration camps. The disease is now almost eliminated from countries of the developed world, but it still appears in the highlands of impoverished countries in South America, Africa, and Asia.

As already noted, epidemic typhus can be quickly and effectively treated by administration of chloramphenicol and tetracyclines. In addition, a vaccine for typhus was developed during World War II. Two doses were given about one month apart, and a third was given after three months. Thereafter, doses at intervals of several months were given to people who had been exposed to the disease. The vaccine provided significant protection against attack and almost complete protection against death. To prevent outbreaks of epidemic typhus, however, the body louse must be eliminated. The development of the powerful and long-lasting pesticide DDT in the mid-20th century provided an effective means of doing so. Since its banning for ecological reasons, its place has been taken by other chemicals such as permethrin and carbaryl. Insecticide is applied directly to the clothing of persons at risk and kills the lice as they hatch on the person's body. Chemical control of the disease has significantly reduced the need for vaccination.

A delayed complication of epidemic typhus is Brill-Zinsser disease, or recrudescent typhus, in which mild symptoms of epidemic louse-borne typhus reappear after a latent period, sometimes of many years, in persons who at one time had contracted epidemic typhus. The disease was first noted when cases of typhus occurred in communities that were free of lice. If treated early with chloramphenicol or a tetracycline drug, most patients with Brill-Zinsser disease recover.

In addition to epidemic typhus, there are also murine, or endemic, typhus (flea-borne); scrub typhus, or tsutsugamushi disease (mite-borne); and tick-borne typhus. Endemic, or murine, typhus, which is caused by *Rickettsia typhi*, has as its principal reservoir of infection the Norway rat. Occasionally, the common house mouse and other species of small rodents have also been found to be infected. The Oriental rat flea *Xenopsylla cheopis* is the principal carrier of the disease, and transmission to humans occurs through the medium of infected flea feces. The frequency of occurrence of human cases is determined by the amount of contact humans have with domestic rodents. The course of the illness is essentially the same as for epidemic typhus, but it is milder, complications are less frequent, and the overall fatality rate is less than 5 percent. Scrub typhus and tick-borne typhus are classed as separate diseases.

Q FEVER

Q fever (also known as rickettsial pneumonia, or Balkan grippe) is an acute, self-limited, systemic disease caused by the rickettsia *Coxiella burnetii*. Q fever spreads rapidly in cows, sheep, and goats, and in humans it tends to occur in localized outbreaks. The clinical symptoms

CHARLES-JULES-HENRI NICOLLE

(b. Sept. 21, 1866, Rouen, France—d. Feb. 28, 1936, Tunis, Tunisia)

French bacteriologist Charles-Jules-Henri Nicolle received the 1928 Nobel Prize for Physiology or Medicine for his discovery (1909) that typhus is transmitted by the body louse.

After obtaining a medical degree in Paris in 1893, Nicolle returned to Rouen, where he became a member of the medical faculty and engaged in bacteriological research. In 1902 he was appointed director of the Pasteur Institute in Tunis, and during his 31 years' tenure in that post, the institute became a distinguished centre for bacteriological research and for the production of serums and vaccines to combat infectious diseases.

In Tunis Nicolle noticed that typhus was extremely contagious outside the hospital, with sufferers of the disease transmitting it to many people who came into contact with them. Once inside the hospital, however, these same patients ceased to be contagious. Nicolle suspected that the key point in this reversal was that of admission to the hospital, when patients were bathed and their clothes were confiscated. The carrier of typhus must be in the patients' clothes or on their skin and could be removed from the body by washing. The obvious candidate for the carrier was the body louse (Pediculus humanus humanus), which Nicolle proved to be the culprit in 1909 in a series of experiments involving monkeys.

Nicolle extended his work on typhus to distinguish between the classical louse-borne form of the disease and murine typhus, which is conveyed to humans by the rat flea. He also made valuable contributions to the knowledge of rinderpest, brucellosis, measles, diphtheria, and tuberculosis.

are those of fever, chills, severe headache, and pneumonia. The disease is usually mild, and complications are rare. Treatment with tetracycline or chloramphenicol shortens the duration of illness.

Q fever was first recognized in 1935 in Queensland, Australia, by Edward Holbrook Derrick. According to Derrick, *Q* stands for *query*, an appellation applied because of the many unanswered questions posed by the new disease at the time of its first description. Because the disease was originally encountered among abattoir (slaughterhouse) workers, cattle ranchers, and dairy farmers in Australia and later among sheep ranchers, it was first thought to be restricted to that continent. Several outbreaks of what was ultimately shown to be Q fever, however, occurred among Axis and Allied troops in the eastern Mediterranean theatre of World War II during the winter of 1944–45. These were the first naturally occurring outbreaks of Q fever recognized outside Australia. The disease thereafter was reported from various parts of the world.

While many species of ticks in various parts of the world have been found to be naturally infected, the role of these arthropods in the dissemination and maintenance of the rickettsiae is unclear. It seems likely that some small mammal, perhaps a rodent, serves as a reservoir of the rickettsiae and that ticks keep the infection alive in nature by spreading the rickettsiae from animal to animal within the host species. Humans and their domestic livestock are not necessary to the survival of the rickettsiae in nature and are infected only accidentally.

Tick-transmitted Q fever appears to be rare in humans and, in some parts of the world, in domestic livestock as well. Because the rickettsiae are found in cows' and goats' milk, the ingestion of infected dairy products may play a role in the infection of humans and livestock. The common mode of infection, however, appears to be inhalation of infected material. The infected animal sheds the rickettsiae through its milk, excreta, and, most importantly, through the placenta and birth fluids. Contamination of the environment leads to airborne dissemination of the rickettsiae and thus to infection of persons in close contact with livestock, contaminated clothing, and other infected sources.

The incubation period of the disease is from two to four weeks, averaging about 18 to 21 days. The onset may be gradual but generally is sudden, and the disease is ushered in by fever, chills or chilly sensations, headache, muscle aches, loss of appetite, disorientation, and profuse sweating. Symptoms in the upper respiratory tract may be present but generally are infrequent and minimal. Pneumonia, even when relatively extensive, may be detectable only by X-ray examination. Although Q fever is, on the whole, a mild disease, it can sometimes result in severe and protracted illness. The outlook for recovery is excellent, and the mortality rate is believed to be less than 1 percent. The disease is amenable to therapy with wide-spectrum antibiotics, which are highly effective. Q fever seems to be in large part an infection associated with particular occupations, and vaccines prepared from killed *C. burnetii* can be used to protect persons whose work makes them likely to be exposed to infection.

ROCKY MOUNTAIN SPOTTED FEVER

Rocky Mountain spotted fever is a form of tick-borne typhus that was first described in the Rocky Mountain section of the United States. It is caused by *Rickettsia rickettsii*. Discovery of the microbe of Rocky Mountain spotted fever in 1906 by Howard T. Ricketts led to the understanding of other rickettsial diseases. Despite its name, Rocky Mountain spotted fever is most common on the eastern coast of the United States and has been found in every state. In fact, it is identical with a disease known as São Paulo fever in Brazil and with the spotted fever of Colombia. It is a disease of the summer and early fall, when ticks are active.

In western North America, the carrier species is the wood tick, *Dermacentor andersoni*, which is widely distributed in

The wood tick is among several kinds of ticks that transmit a form of typhus known as Rocky Mountain spotted fever. CDC/ Dr. Christopher Paddock. Photo by James Gathany

the adult form on large mammals, particularly cattle and sheep. In the eastern and southern United States, the common (or American) dog tick, *Dermacentor variabilis*, which attacks humans, also acts as a carrier. In the southwestern United States, human cases are also traced to the lone star tick, *Amblyomma americanum*. In Brazil the common carrier is *Amblyomma cajennense*.

The illness begins with headache, fever, and chills, soon followed by pains in the bones and joints, weakness, and fatigue. A rash develops in the first week of illness, beginning on the extremities and spreading to the trunk. It is more profuse than the rash of epidemic typhus and affects the face as well as the body. In some people the colour of the rash deepens after a day or two, and in the worst cases it turns purple with blood. By the end of a week in severe cases, the patient shows signs of brain irritation and may be agitated, sleepless, or delirious. Breathing becomes laboured and circulation poor, and areas of gangrene may develop on the hands and feet. In the worst cases, the patient may become comatose and die, but in most cases fever gradually abates and the patient slowly recovers. Convalescence is likely to be slow and may be complicated by visual disturbances, deafness, and mental confusion. Although the patient's recovery may be delayed, it is usually complete. The case-fatality rate, as in typhus, varies directly with age.

Early treatment with antibiotics greatly shortens the disease and decreases the risk of death. Prevention depends primarily upon the exercise of personal care in protection against tick bites. Persons exposed to known infected areas should frequently examine their clothing and body for ticks. Usually the tick does not become attached to its host immediately but crawls about for several hours. The chance of receiving infection from the bite of a tick is directly proportional to the length of time that the tick has fed. The ticks should be removed and the skin area involved swabbed with an antiseptic.

There is a satisfactory vaccination procedure against Rocky Mountain spotted fever: the vaccine is administered in the spring or early summer before the beginning of the tick season and is repeated annually, because the maximum degree of protection conferred is for less than a year. The degree of immunity afforded is relative, but the chance for subsequent infection is lessened, and the risk of death is greatly reduced.

SCRUB TYPHUS

Scrub typhus, also known as tsutsugamushi disease, is an acute infectious disease in humans that is caused by the parasite *Orientia tsutsugamushi* (formerly *Rickettsia tsutsugamushi*). The bacterium is transmitted to humans by the bite of certain kinds of mites, of which two closely related species, *Leptotrombidium (Trombicula) akamushi* and *L. deliens*, serve as the primary carriers of the disease. During their larval stage, these mites acquire the infection from wild rodents or other small animals. The infection is passed to humans when a mite larva bites a person. Scrub typhus occurs in Southeast Asia and its associated archipelagoes and in Japan, in which latter country the disease was first described (1899) and systematically investigated (1906–32). During World War II scrub typhus killed or incapacitated thousands of troops who were stationed in rural or jungle areas in the Pacific theatre.

A person falls ill with scrub typhus about 10 to 12 days after being bitten by an infected mite. A reddish or pinkish lesion appears at the site of the mite bite, and the person begins to experience headache, fever, chills, and general pains, along with swollen lymph glands. About one week after the fever has started, a pinkish rash develops over the skin of the trunk and may extend to the arms and legs. While the course of the fever may end in two weeks, it is not unusual for it to last three or even four weeks. A

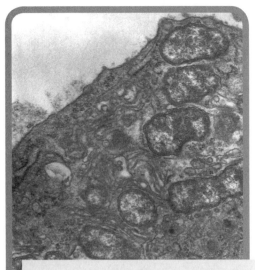

Transmission electron micrograph of a peritoneal mesothelial cell of a mouse infected with Rickettsia tsutsugamushi (Orientia tsutsugamushi). Dr. Ed Ewing/Centers for Disease Control and Prevention (CDC) (Image Number: 8750)

more or less extensive pneumonitis is common, and abnormalities in the heart, lungs, and blood may also arise, leading to impairment of heart function and circulatory failure. When untreated, scrub typhus can be fatal, but the course of the disease can now be arrested by the administration of chloramphenicol or the tetracyclines, upon which recovery is prompt and uneventful.

TRENCH FEVER

Trench fever is an infectious disease characterized by sudden onset with fever, headache, sore muscles, bones, and joints, and outbreaks of skin lesions on the chest and back. It is transmitted from one person to another by a body louse harbouring the causative organism, the rickettsial bacterium *Bartonella quintana* (formerly *Rochalimaeaquintana*). There may be one period of fever, or the fever may recur several times at intervals of four to five days. Most persons recover within about two months. There may be relapses, however, and the disease becomes chronic in about 5 percent of the cases. Treatment with chlortetracycline brings permanent relief of the symptoms, but the patient continues to carry rickettsiae and remains infectious for lice. First recognized in 1915, trench fever was a major medical problem during World War I. It reappeared in epidemic form among German troops on the Eastern front during World War II. The control of body lice is the chief means of prevention.

CHLAMYDIAL DISEASES

Chlamydia organisms can cause a variety of diseases in humans. For example, in addition to causing trachoma and conjunctivitis, *C. trachomatis* also causes a variety of sexually transmitted diseases, chiefly nongonococcal urethritis (infection of the urethra) in males and females and epididymitis (infection of the epididymus) in males. In men, nongonococcal urethritis has symptoms similar to those of gonorrhea. In women, *C. trachomatis* infection ordinarily produces few if any symptoms. If untreated, however,

C. trachomatis can seriously infect the cervix (causing cervicitis), the urethra (causing urethritis), or the fallopian tubes (causing salpingitis), and it can also cause pelvic inflammatory disease. Infection of the fallopian tubes can cause sterility, and a chlamydial infection also leads to a higher risk of premature births, ectopic pregnancies, and postpartum infections. A woman with an infected cervix may give birth to infected newborns who can develop pneumonia or the eye disease known as neonatal conjuctivitis.

The bacterium *Chlamydophila pneumoniae* was identified as a separate chlamydial species in the 1980s. It causes various respiratory-tract infections, most commonly a mild, atypical pneumonia with symptoms of fever, cough, and sore throat. In the diagnosis of chlamydial diseases, doctors often first eliminate gonorrhea as a cause for the symptoms. Specific tests for chlamydia include smears and cultures. The preferred treatment for chlamydial infections is tetracycline. Erythromycin and sulfonamide drugs have also been effective in treating the infections. Appropriate treatment produces a speedy recovery.

PSITTACOSIS

Psittacosis (also known as ornithosis, or parrot fever) is an infectious disease of worldwide distribution caused by a bacterial parasite (*Chlamydophila psittaci*) and transmitted to humans from various birds. The infection has been found in about 70 different species of birds. Parrots and parakeets (Psittacidae, from which the disease is named), pigeons, turkeys, ducks, and geese are the principal sources of human infection.

The association between the human disease and sick parrots was first recognized in Europe in 1879, although a thorough study of the disease was not made until 1929–30, when severe outbreaks, attributed to contact with imported parrots, occurred in 12 countries of Europe and America. During the investigations conducted in Germany, England, and the United States, the causative agent was revealed. Strict regulations followed concerning importation of psittacine birds, which undoubtedly reduced the incidence of the disease but did not prevent the intermittent appearance of cases. The infection was later found in domestic stocks of parakeets and pigeons and subsequently in other species. Infected turkeys, ducks, or geese have caused many cases among poultry handlers or workers in processing plants.

Psittacosis usually causes only mild symptoms of illness in birds, but in humans it can be fatal if untreated. Humans usually contract the disease by inhaling dust particles contaminated with the excrement of infected birds. The bacterial parasite thus gains access to the body and multiplies in the blood and tissues. In humans psittacosis may cause high fever and pneumonia. Other symptoms include chills, weakness, head and body aches, and an elevated respiratory rate. The typical duration of the disease is two to three weeks, and convalescence often is protracted. Before modern antibiotic drugs were available, the case fatality rate was approximately 20 percent, but penicillin and the tetracycline drugs reduced this figure almost to zero.

TRACHOMA

Trachoma is a chronic inflammatory disease of the eye caused by *Chlamydia trachomatis*, a bacterium that grows only within cells of the infected host. The conjunctiva becomes thickened and roughened, and deformation may result. Extension of inflammation to the cornea occurs in varying degree, and resultant scarring can lead to corneal opacity and blindness. Transmission occurs by personal contact with infective ocular secretions or indirectly by common use of a towel.

Trachoma occurs especially under conditions of poverty, overpopulation, or poor sanitation and is often complicated by other eye infections of bacterial origin. One of the oldest diseases known to humans, trachoma is present in most areas of the world and is especially prevalent in Asia and North Africa. In the United States after about mid-20th century, most cases were limited to a few localities, particularly among native Indian populations. A conjunctival infection of newborns (inclusion conjunctivitis) is caused by a similar disease agent found in the birth canal of the mother. Beginning in 1957 with the discovery that the trachoma microorganism could be grown in the laboratory, fundamental studies on the disease agent, as well as development of experimental vaccines, became possible. Sulfonamide drugs, as well as some antibiotics, are curative.

CHAPTER 5

BACTERIAL DISEASES: ANTHRAX TO YAWS

In addition to the mycobacterial, rickettsial, and chlamydial diseases, there are a number of other bacterial afflictions known to humans. Efforts to systematically characterize these diseases is complicated by the extraordinary diversity in the life cycles and pathological nature of the causative organisms. Each of these diseases, however, poses a serious threat to human health, and some, including anthrax and syphilis, historically were feared for the suffering, certain death, and stigmas with which they were associated. Many of these diseases continue to be sources of concern today.

ANTHRAX

Anthrax (also known as malignant pustule, or woolsorters' disease) is an acute, infectious, febrile disease of animals and humans caused by *Bacillus anthracis*, a bacterium that under certain conditions forms highly resistant spores capable of persisting and retaining their virulence for many years. Although anthrax most commonly affects grazing animals such as cattle, sheep, goats, horses, and mules, humans can develop the disease by eating the meat or handling the wool, hair, hides, bones, or carcasses of affected animals. When anthrax—its name derived from the Greek word for coal—attacks a person's skin, a sore with a coal-black centre develops. Anthrax spores can also be produced inexpensively and converted into either a powder or a liquid, allowing anthrax to be used in a variety of weapons systems. Its potential use as a biological weapon has made anthrax a prime concern of countries seeking to control the spread of terrorism.

Anthrax in humans occurs as a cutaneous, pulmonary, or intestinal infection. The most common type, cutaneous anthrax, occurs as a primary localized infection of the skin in the form of a carbuncle. It usually results from handling infected material, lesions occurring mostly on the hands, arms, or neck as a small pimple that develops rapidly into a large vesicle with a black necrotic centre (the malignant pustule). There are also bouts of shivering and chills, but there is little other disability. In more than 90 percent of the cases of anthrax in humans, the bacilli remain within the skin sore. However, the bacilli may escape from the sore and spread via a lymph channel to the nearest lymph node, where their spread is usually halted. Only seldom do the bacilli invade the bloodstream, causing rapidly fatal septicemia (blood poisoning), internal bleeding, and, sometimes, meningitis. The pulmonary form, called inhalation anthrax (woolsorters' disease), affects principally the lungs and pleura and results from inhaling anthrax spores (e.g., in areas where hair and wool are processed). Inhalation anthrax is occasionally transmitted to humans by spore-contaminated brushes or by wearing apparel such as furs and leather goods. This form of the disease usually runs a rapid course and terminates fatally because of the suffocating pneumonia that results. The intestinal form of the disease, which sometimes follows the consumption of contaminated meat, is characterized by an acute inflammation of the intestinal tract, vomiting, and severe diarrhea.

In all forms of anthrax, prompt diagnosis and early treatment are of great importance. Antianthrax serum, arsenicals, and antibiotics (e.g., ciprofloxacin) are used with excellent results. The hazard of infection to industrial workers can be reduced by sterilization of potentially contaminated material before handling, wearing of protective clothing, use of respirators, and sanitizing of facilities. Agricultural workers can be safeguarded by vaccination and by avoiding the skinning or opening of animals that died of the disease.

Farm animals that graze on contaminated pastures are susceptible to anthrax. Outbreaks in swine, dogs, cats, and wild animals held in captivity generally result from consumption of contaminated food. In the acute forms there is a rise in body temperature followed by spasms, respiratory or cardiac distress, trembling, staggering, and convulsions. Bloody discharges sometimes come from the natural body openings, and edematous (serous fluid) swellings may appear on different parts of the body. Death usually occurs within a day or two. Chronic anthrax occurs mostly in swine and dogs and is characterized by marked swelling of the throat, difficult breathing, and a bloodstained frothy discharge from the mouth. Affected animals sometimes die of suffocation. Prophylactic vaccination is extensively used in preventing anthrax in livestock. During outbreaks, strict quarantine measures, disposal of diseased carcasses by burning, fly control, and good sanitation are essential in controlling the disease.

Anthrax is one of the oldest recorded diseases, being mentioned in the biblical book of Exodus and among the Classical authors of Greek and Roman antiquity. Devastating epidemics of the disease were recorded by many medieval and modern writers. In the 16th to 18th century it sometimes spread across the southern part of Europe, taking a heavy toll on human and animal life. The causative agent was identified by French biologist Casimir-Joseph Davaine in 1863 and by German bacteriologist Robert Koch, who isolated the organism in pure culture in 1876. An effective vaccine was demonstrated by French chemist and microbiologist Louis Pasteur in 1881. These discoveries were part of the origin and development of the modern sciences of bacteriology and immunology.

The bacterium that causes anthrax has a number of attributes that, in combination, make it suitable as a biological weapon. In addition to being widely available—located around the world in soil and in diseased animals and their remains—B. anthracis spores are small enough to lodge readily in the lungs of humans. The anthrax bacterium has a short incubation period and is highly lethal, requiring only a small amount to cause a mass casualty effect.

Indeed, aerosolized forms of anthrax sprayed over a large population centre or a massed military force are capable of lethality approaching or exceeding that of a nuclear weapon. Moreover, anthrax can be produced inexpensively, in larger quantities than can other biological warfare agents, and in facilities that are relatively easy to hide. It is more resilient to degradation from ultraviolet light than most other biological agents. Finally, anthrax can be converted into either a powder or a liquid, allowing it to be used in a number of types of weapons systems that use a variety of delivery means, including missiles, bombers, artillery, mortars, or crop dusters and similar aircraft.

Anthrax has been weaponized by a number of states. Before it terminated its offensive biological weapons program in 1969, the United States had a significant anthrax weapons program. The former Soviet Union developed the world's largest biological weapons program, which it clandestinely continued 20 years beyond the date when it signed the Biological Weapons Convention of 1972, which prohibited the development and stockpiling of biological weapons. Iraq, under the rule of Ṣaddām Ḥussein, also developed anthrax and a number of other biological weapons agents but claimed to have destroyed such weapons after the Persian Gulf War of 1990–91. At least 14 other countries were believed to have biological weapons programs.

Terrorists have used anthrax in an attempt to kill and frighten victims in

REWARD
UP TO $2,500,000

For information leading to the arrest and conviction of the individual(s) responsible for the mailing of letters containing anthrax to the New York Post, Tom Brokaw at NBC, Senator Tom Daschle and Senator Patrick Leahy:

AS A RESULT OF EXPOSURE TO ANTHRAX, FIVE (5) PEOPLE HAVE DIED.

The person responsible for these deaths…

- Likely has a scientific background/work history which may include a specific familiarity with anthrax

- Has a level of comfort in and around the Trenton, NJ area due to present or prior association

Anyone having information, contact **America's Most Wanted** at **1-800-CRIME TV** or the **FBI** via e-mail at **amerithrax@fbi.gov**

All information will be held in strict confidence. Reward payment will be made in accordance with the conditions of Postal Service Reward Notice 296, dated February 2000. Source of reward funds: US Postal Service and FBI $2,000,000; ADVO, Inc. $500,000.

In 2001 a terrorist used the U.S. mail to send anthrax, the lethal spores of which are both widely available and inexpensively produced. Getty Images

both Japan and the United States. The AUM Shinrikyo religious sect released anthrax in Tokyo on three separate occasions in 1993, targeting downtown crowds and members of the Japanese legislature. In 2001 a number of anthrax-laced letters were sent through the mail to the offices of two U.S. senators and various media headquarters in New York and Florida, killing five people along the letters' routes and infecting more than a dozen others.

Several effective vaccines have been developed to protect against possible anthrax infection, including Anthrax Vaccine Adsorbed (AVA), the vaccine developed to protect United States military personnel. The anthrax vaccine can provide protection to most recipients, although a small percentage do not acquire complete immunity. However, if vaccinated military personnel were to encounter a massive dose of anthrax, such as might be encountered on a battlefield, even a sensitized immune system can be overwhelmed. A well-fitting mask with fine-grain filters is necessary to provide protection in such instances.

BOTULISM

Botulism is poisoning caused by botulinum toxin, which is produced by *Clostridium botulinum* bacteria. This poisoning results most frequently from the eating of improperly sterilized home-canned foods containing the toxin. Botulism also may result from wound infection. *C. botulinum* bacteria—which cannot survive in the presence of oxygen—normally live in the soil, where they form heat-resistant spores that may contaminate fresh food to be canned. The spores survive if the food is not cooked at 120 °C (248 °F) for a sufficient length of time. This temperature can be achieved with certainty only in commercial canning plants or in a pressure cooker (boiling is not reliable). Then, inside the sealed can, the spores germinate and release the bacteria, and, as the bacteria multiply, they secrete botulinum toxin, a protein that is one of the most potent poisons known. Unlike the clostridial spores, the toxin is readily destroyed by heat. It remains potent only if the contaminated food is not heated to at least 70 °C (158 °F) for two minutes before it is eaten.

Once ingested and absorbed, *C. botulinum* toxin damages the autonomic nervous system by blocking the release of acetylcholine, a neurotransmitter that allows muscle contraction. When the toxin is swallowed in food, it is absorbed rapidly and carried in the bloodstream to nerve endings in muscles. The toxin attacks the fine nerve fibrils and stops the impulse from passing along these fibres. No acetylcholine is released and the muscle cannot contract; it is paralyzed.

The first symptoms of botulism, nausea and vomiting, usually appear six hours or less after the contaminated food is eaten, depending upon the amount of toxin ingested. The poisoned person becomes tired and may complain of headache and dizziness. The muscles of the eyelid may be paralyzed, a sign that may appear within hours of eating the food. The vision is often blurred, and the affected person may see double. Next, the paralysis affects the muscles used for speech. The mucous membranes of the throat may become dry; the affected person may feel a constriction in the throat, soon associated with difficulty in swallowing and speaking; and a general muscle weakness soon occurs. The respiratory muscles become involved. About half the deaths from botulism result from paralysis of the respiratory muscles. The person remains conscious through most of the illness, until suffocation occurs. Death may come within a day, although people less severely poisoned may live for a week. Few who reach the stage of severe paralysis survive, although a person who survives the paralysis will recover completely. Infant botulism, which may result from feeding infants honey contaminated with the clostridial spores, exhibits symptoms such as constipation, poor feeding, and a weak cry. Children under the age of one year should not be given honey because of this risk.

With early diagnosis, the chance of a person's surviving is greatly enhanced by the prompt administration of botulism antitoxins, which contain equine antibodies that neutralize the toxin in the body. *C. botulinum* antitoxin is given in large doses intravenously, but it is doubtful that antitoxin can do anything to dislodge the toxin once it has reached the nerve fibrils. A chemical, guanidine hydrochloride, counteracts the action of *C. botulinum* toxin on nerve endings and

has been used successfully in treatment, but it is itself a toxic substance that should be given only with great care. Paralyzed muscle can recover if the patient can be kept alive, and perhaps the best hope of survival in otherwise desperate cases lies in tube feeding, a tracheotomy (making an opening in the windpipe), and use of an artificial respirator.

DIPHTHERIA

Diphtheria is an acute infectious disease caused by the bacillus *Corynebacterium diphtheriae* and characterized by a primary lesion, usually in the upper respiratory tract, and more generalized symptoms resulting from the spread of the bacterial toxin throughout the body. Diphtheria was a serious contagious disease throughout much of the world until the late 19th century, when its incidence in Europe and North America began to decline and was eventually reduced even further by immunization measures. It still occurs mainly in the temperate regions of the world, being more common during the colder months of the year and most often affecting children under age 10.

The diphtheria bacillus was discovered and identified by German bacteriologists Edwin Klebs and Friedrich Löffler. In most cases the bacillus is transmitted in droplets of respiratory secretions expelled by active cases or carriers during speaking or coughing. The most common portals of entry of the diphtheria bacillus are the tonsils, nose, and throat. The bacillus usually remains and propagates in that region, producing a powerful toxin that spreads throughout the body via the bloodstream and lymph vessels and damages the heart and the nervous system.

The symptoms of diphtheria include moderate fever, fatigue, chills, and a mild sore throat. The propagation of the diphtheria bacilli leads to the formation of a thick, leathery, grayish membrane that is composed of bacteria, dead cells from the mucous membranes, and fibrin (the fibrous protein associated with blood clotting). This membrane firmly adheres to the underlying tissues of the mouth, tonsils, pharynx, or other site of localization. The membrane separates in 7 to 10 days, but toxic complications occur later in severe cases. The heart is affected first, often in the second or third week. The patient develops toxic myocarditis (inflammation of the heart muscle), which can be fatal. If the person survives this dangerous period, the heart will recover completely and the patient will appear to be well. However, this appearance is deceptive and is indeed one of the most treacherous aspects of the disease, because paralysis caused by the action of the toxin on the nervous system often strikes when the patient seems to have recovered. Paralysis of the palate and some eye muscles develops in about the third week, although this is usually transient and not severe. As late as the fifth to eighth week, however, paralysis affecting swallowing and breathing develops in severe cases, and the patient may die after weeks of apparent well-being. Later

still, paralysis of the limbs may occur, though it is not life-threatening. If the patient can be supported through this critical phase, recovery will be complete.

There are several types of diphtheria, depending in large part on the anatomic location of the primary lesion. The membrane appears inside the nostrils in anterior nasal diphtheria. Almost no toxin is absorbed from this site, so there is little danger to life, and complications are rare. In faucial diphtheria, the most common type, the infection is limited mostly to the tonsillar region. Most patients recover if properly treated with diphtheria antitoxin. In the most fatal form, nasopharyngeal diphtheria, the tonsillar infection spreads to the nose and throat structures, sometimes completely covering them with the membrane and causing septicemia (blood poisoning). Laryngeal diphtheria usually results from the spread of the infection downward from the nasopharynx to the larynx. The airway may become blocked and must be restored by inserting a tube or cutting an opening in the trachea (tracheotomy). Cutaneous diphtheria affects parts of the body other than the respiratory tract, notably the skin, following a wound or sore.

In response to the presence of diphtheria exotoxin, the body makes a neutralizing substance called antitoxin, which enables the affected person to recover from the disease if the antitoxin is produced fast enough and in sufficient quantities. The only effective treatment of diphtheria is in fact the prompt administration of this antitoxin, which is obtained from the blood of horses that have been injected with exotoxin and have responded by producing antitoxin. Antitoxin does not neutralize toxin that has already been bound to tissue and that has produced tissue damage. The antitoxin may be lifesaving if given early enough, but the body eventually eliminates it as a foreign substance, and it does not give any permanent protection against the disease. Antibiotics can destroy the diphtheria bacillus in the throat and also are given to every patient.

To prevent diphtheria, the body must produce its own antitoxin in response to active immunization with diphtheria toxin. Active immunization has become a routine measure in many countries through immunization with diphtheria toxoid, a form of the exotoxin that has been rendered nontoxic but that has retained its capacity to induce antitoxin formation once injected into the body. The diphtheria toxoid is usually first given in several successive doses during the first few months of life, with booster doses within one or two years and again at five or six years of age.

LYME DISEASE

Lyme disease is a tick-borne bacterial disease that was first conclusively identified in 1975. It is named for the town in Connecticut, U.S., in which it was first observed. The disease has been identified in every region of the United States and in Europe, Asia, Africa, and Australia.

Lyme disease is caused by the spirochete (corkscrew-shaped bacterium) *Borrelia burgdorferi*. The spirochete is transmitted to the human bloodstream by the bite of various species of ticks. In the northeastern United States, the carrier tick is usually *Ixodes dammini*; in the West, *I. pacificus*; and in Europe, *I. ricinus*. Ticks pick up the spirochete by sucking the blood of deer or other infected animals. *I. dammini* mainly feeds on white-tailed deer and white-footed mice, especially in areas of tall grass, and is most active in summer. The larval and nymphal stages of this tick are more likely to bite humans than are the adult and are therefore more likely to cause human cases of the disease.

In humans the disease progresses in three stages. The first and mildest stage is characterized by a circular rash in a bull's-eye pattern that appears anywhere from a few days to a month after the tick bite. The rash is often accompanied by such flulike symptoms as headache, fatigue, chills, loss of appetite, fever, and aching joints or muscles. The majority of persons who contract Lyme disease experience only these first-stage symptoms and never become seriously ill. A minority, however, will go on to the second stage of the disease, which begins two weeks to three months after infection. This stage is indicated by arthritic pain that migrates from joint to joint and by disturbances of memory, vision, movement, or other neurological symptoms. The third stage of Lyme disease, which generally begins within two years of the

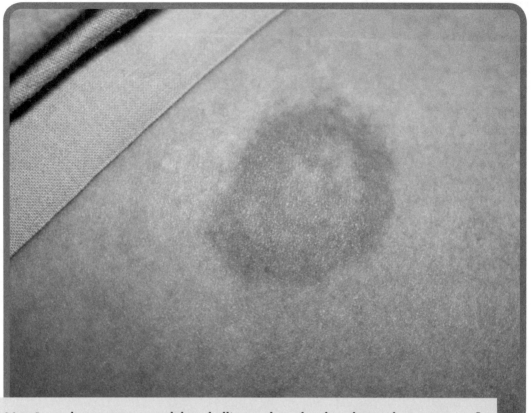

Most Lyme disease patients exhibit a bull's-eye-shaped rash and may also experience flu-like symptoms. Dr. Kenneth Greer/Visuals Unlimited/Getty Images

bite, is marked by crippling arthritis and by neurological symptoms that resemble those of multiple sclerosis. Symptoms vary widely, however, and some persons experience facial paralysis, meningitis, memory loss, mood swings, and an inability to concentrate.

Because Lyme disease often mimics other disorders, its diagnosis is sometimes difficult, especially when there is no record of the distinctive rash. Early treatment of Lyme disease with antibiotics is important in order to prevent progression of the disease to a more serious stage. More powerful antibiotics are used in the latter case, though symptoms may recur periodically thereafter.

RELAPSING FEVER

Relapsing fever is an infectious disease characterized by recurring episodes of fever separated by periods of relative well-being and caused by spirochetes,

TICK

Ticks are invertebrates that make up the suborder Ixodida in the order Parasitiformes (subclass Acari). Ticks are important parasites of large wild and domestic animals and are also significant as carriers of serious diseases. Although no species is primarily a human parasite, some occasionally attack humans.

Hard ticks, such as the common (or American) dog tick (Dermacentor variabilis), attach to their hosts and feed continuously on blood for several days during each life stage. When an adult female has obtained a blood meal, she mates, drops from the host, and finds a suitable site where she lays her eggs in a mass and dies. Six-legged larvae hatch from the eggs, move up on blades of grass, and wait for a suitable host (usually a mammal) to pass by. The odour of butyric acid, emanated by all mammals, stimulates the larvae to drop onto and attach to a host. After filling themselves with the host's blood, the larvae detach and molt, becoming eight-legged nymphs. Nymphs also wait for, and board, a suitable host in the same way as larvae. After they have found a host and engorged themselves, they also fall off, and then they molt into adult males or females. Adults may wait for a host for as long as three years.

Most hard ticks live in fields and woods, but a few, such as the brown dog tick (Rhipicephalus sanguineus), are household pests. Soft ticks differ from hard ticks by feeding intermittently, laying several batches of eggs, passing through several nymphal stages, and carrying on their developmental cycles in the home or nest of the host rather than in fields.

Hard ticks damage the host by drawing large amounts of blood, by secreting neurotoxins (nerve poisons) that sometimes produce paralysis or death, and by transmitting diseases, including Lyme disease, Texas cattle fever, anaplasmosis, Rocky Mountain spotted fever, Q fever, tularemia, hemorrhagic fever, and a form of encephalitis. Soft ticks also are carriers of diseases.

Adults range in size up to 30 mm (slightly more than 1 inch), but most species are 15 mm or less. They may be distinguished from their close relatives, the mites, by the presence of a sensory pit (Haller's organ) on the end segment of the first of four pairs of legs. Eyes may be present or absent.

This group has a worldwide distribution, and all species are assigned to three families: Argasidae, comprising the soft ticks, and Nuttalliellidae and Ixodidae, together comprising the hard ticks. The family Nuttalliellidae is represented by one rare African species.

or spiral-shaped bacteria, of the genus *Borrelia*. The spirochetes are transmitted from one person to another by lice (genus *Pediculus*) and from animals to humans by ticks (genus *Ornithodoros*). The tick-borne disease is frequently contracted by persons visiting wooded campsites or cabins. The louse-borne disease spreads under conditions of crowding, cold weather, and poor hygiene, all of which favour the spread of lice. Epidemics of the disease have occurred during wars, earthquakes, famines, and floods.

After the spirochete has lived about one week in its newly infected host, the person experiences a sudden onset of high fever, chills, headache, and muscle aches. The symptoms persist for about a week in cases contracted from lice and usually for a shorter period in the tick-borne disease. The attack ends in a crisis of profuse sweating, low blood pressure, low temperature, and malaise, after which the patient is fairly well until, about a week later, febrile symptoms return. Additional relapses may follow—rarely more than one or two in the louse-borne disease but up to 12 (usually decreasing in severity) in cases contracted from ticks. The mortality is variable, ranging from nil in some tick-transmitted varieties to 6 percent or as high as 30 percent in some louse-borne epidemics associated with famine conditions. The spirochetes may invade the central nervous system and cause a variety of usually mild neurological symptoms. An enlarged liver or spleen, rashes, and inflammation of the eye and heart also may be noted in patients with relapsing fever.

Borrelia spirochetes were the first microbes to be associated clearly with serious human disease. German bacteriologist Otto Obermeier observed the organisms in the blood of relapsing-fever patients in 1867–68 and published his observations in 1873. They are easily seen in dark-field microscopic preparations of the patient's blood collected during the height of the febrile attack, but they disappear from the blood during the intervals between attacks. These observations, as well as the relapsing symptoms, have been related to changes in the antigenic characteristics of the spirochetes. As the patient develops immunity to the prevailing type and recovers from the attack, a new (mutant) type of the spirochete develops and produces the relapse. Because neither the bite nor the excreta of the louse is infectious, human infections usually result from crushing the louse on the skin while scratching.

A diagnosis of relapsing fever can be made by specific serological tests or by identification of the loosely coiled organism in the patient's blood. Penicillin and other antibiotics have proved effective against the disease. Inadequate therapy commonly results in relapse after treatment, probably because of the persistence of live spirochetes in the brain, where the drug concentration does not reach curative levels. After treatment these protected spirochetes may reinvade the bloodstream. Prevention by the elimination of the vectors that transmit the disease is of the utmost importance.

SYPHILIS

Syphilis is a systemic disease that is caused by the spirochete bacterium *Treponema pallidum*. Syphilis is usually a sexually transmitted disease, but it is occasionally acquired by direct nonsexual contact with an infected person, and it can also be acquired by an unborn fetus through infection in the mother. A related group of infections, collectively known as treponematosis or nonvenereal syphilis, is not spread by sexual contact and is localized in warm parts of the world where crowded conditions and poor health care favour its development.

The causative organism of venereal syphilis is a slender, coiled, flexible bacterium with regular, tightly wound coils. This bacterium, *T. pallidum*, averages 8 to 10 μm in length. The bacterium requires moisture to exist, so continuous moisture is a necessity for the transfer of the microorganism from one person to another. The most common means of such transferal is sexual intercourse. In the body's tissues, the spirochete bacteria reproduce and remain present for the lifetime of the infected person unless destroyed by treatment. Syphilis is effectively treated with penicillin, which kills the spirochetes.

COURSE OF DISEASE

The course of untreated venereal syphilis spans three stages. The primary stage, beginning anywhere from 10 days to 10 weeks following infection, is marked by the appearance of a small, hard, painless swelling, or chancre, at the site of inoculation—usually the genital organs but on occasion the mouth or rectum. The chancre enlarges and often breaks in the centre, leaving a shallow ulcer. The chancre may be so slight in colour as to go unnoticed, but the presence of spirochetes in the chancre serum is diagnostic for syphilis. Even without treatment, this sore heals within 10 to 40 days, leaving no scar.

The secondary stage, evident in about half the persons infected, is characterized by rashes on the skin, particularly on the palms of the hands and the soles of the feet. Other generalized symptoms include fever, sore throat, enlargement of the lymph nodes, and headaches. The secondary stage may begin four to eight weeks after the appearance of the chancre, or it may be delayed for many months. Once initiated, the secondary stage lasts for a variable period up to several months, and the skin lesions disappear spontaneously, usually without scarring. Throughout both the primary and secondary stages of syphilis, the infection can easily be passed to other people who come into contact with the open sores.

Following the secondary stage, a latent period ensues, ranging in length from a few months to a lifetime, during which no outward sign of syphilis is recognizable. Serologic tests, however, remain positive for a long time. Most patients with latent syphilis, even if untreated, do not progress to the final stage—called late, or tertiary, syphilis—but about one in four may be expected to do so. In about half the patients showing tertiary-stage symptoms, the disease is relatively benign, but in the rest it is incapacitating or fatal. Almost any part of the body may be affected by the spirochetes. In cardiovascular syphilis, for example, large numbers of spirochetes attack the aorta (the great trunk artery carrying blood from the heart), destroying elastic tissue, predisposing to aneurysm (localized thinning and swelling), and producing degeneration of the aortic valves. Neurosyphilis mimics other neurologic disorders and can be crippling if not fatal. For example, paresis, a particularly fearsome degeneration into insanity, is caused by widespread destruction of the brain by the spirochetes. Another neurologic disorder, tabes dorsalis, or locomotor ataxia, is produced by degeneration of the posterior columns of the spinal cord. This brings on intense back pain, lack of muscular coordination, and wasting.

Benign late syphilis is indicated by ulcerated lesions, called gummas, of the skin, mucous membranes, bone, and other organs, particularly the liver, testes, and brain. These lesions are not infectious, and the term *benign* is used because they usually do not endanger the patient's life.

Syphilis is transmitted to the fetuses of untreated pregnant women. About one-fourth of these fetuses die and are spontaneously aborted, while another one-fourth die soon after birth. Those infants that survive may be born with rashes, pneumonia, and skeletal abnormalities. If congenital syphilis is not treated, blindness, deafness, perforation of the palate, inflammation of the liver, and involvement of the central nervous system may ensue. On rare occasions a congenitally syphilitic infant may appear normal at birth and show no symptoms until adolescence, when manifestations of late-stage syphilis usually appear.

The nonvenereal syphilis diseases are caused by other *Treponema* bacteria. Some researchers consider them to be subspecies of *T. pallidum*, whereas others classify them as separate species. The illnesses and their agents include: yaws (*T. pertenue*), occurring in equatorial regions around the world; bejel, or endemic syphilis (*T. endemicum*), found mainly in the Middle East and Saharan region; and pinta (*T. carateum*), most common in the Caribbean and Central and South America. These infections are passed by direct contact, usually among children and young adults. They cause early skin and mouth lesions that are indistinguishable from those caused by venereal syphilis, and in some cases bone deformation may follow. However, the nervous and cardiovascular systems rarely become seriously affected, and fatalities are very rare. All of these infections are quickly and effectively treated by penicillin.

DETECTION AND TREATMENT

There are several laboratory procedures for the detection of syphilis. The most common procedures are serologic tests for syphilis, or STS, carried out on a sample of blood serum. The STS are based on their ability to detect syphilis reagin (an antibody-like substance) by initiating its reaction with an antigen to produce visible clumping, or flocculation, within the serum. Various flocculation tests have been designed. The more widely used among them are the RPR (rapid plasma reagin) test and the VDRL (venereal disease research laboratory) test. Both are rapid techniques with a relatively high degree of sensitivity and specificity. However, none of the flocculation tests is fully specific for syphilis, and "false positive" results may be shown owing to reaction with a wide variety of infections, from mononucleosis to malaria and even influenza. For this reason, positive RDR and VDRL tests are routinely followed by other more complicated and expensive blood tests in order to detect *T. pallidum* directly. In addition, the spirochetes can be viewed by examining fluid from the primary chancre or secondary lesions under the microscope.

The prognosis for syphilis varies with the promptness of diagnosis and treatment. Injections of penicillin or other antibiotics such as tetracycline or erythromycin are very effective at killing the spirochetes and stopping the course of the disease at any stage, and for this reason syphilis is no longer the lifelong affliction it once was. However, in curing late-stage syphilis, nothing can repair the neurologic or other damage already caused by the spirochetes. Pregnant women are routinely tested for syphilis and, if they are found to be infected, they are treated to protect their fetuses.

SYPHILIS THROUGH HISTORY

The historical origin of venereal syphilis is obscure. Indisputable reference to it in European literature occurred only after the return of Columbus from the New World. The rapidly spreading scourge was given several names, including "Great Pox" and "French disease," the latter after invading French soldiers either brought the infection to Italy or caught it from the Italians. The modern name was coined in 1530 by the Italian physician and writer Girolamo Fracastoro, who made poetic reference to a mythic Greek shepherd, Syphilus, who was cursed by the god Apollo with a dread disease. The theory of a New World origin has been supported by evidence of treponematosis found in the skeletal remains of pre-Columbian American Indians. On the other hand, "leprosy" in Europe before 1500 was considered highly contagious, was associated with sexual contact, had hereditary features, and was said to respond to mercury therapy. Therefore, it is possible that many cases thought to be leprosy were actually syphilis.

After the post-Columbian outbreak, treatment of syphilitic lesions with mercury was widespread, and in 1836 potassium iodide, less toxic and more effective, was introduced. The first drug to attack the spirochete directly—arsphenamine, an arsenic compound commonly known as Salvarsan or 606—was developed in 1909 by the German bacteriologist Paul Ehrlich. Much was learned about the course of the disease from the infamous Tuskegee syphilis study (1932–72). The use of antibiotics developed in 1943 after the discovery by the American physician John Friend Mahoney and others that penicillin was an effective treatment for nonadvanced cases of syphilis. Since that time the number of syphilis cases has declined considerably, particularly in developed countries.

TETANUS

Tetanus, or lockjaw, is an acute infectious disease of humans and other animals that is caused by toxins produced by the bacillus *Clostridium tetani*. The disease is characterized by rigidity and spasms of the voluntary muscles. The almost constant involvement of the jaw muscles accounts for the popular name of the disease.

Spores of *Clostridium* are distributed widely in nature, especially in soil, and may enter the body through any wound, even a superficial abrasion. Puncture wounds and deep lacerations are particularly dangerous because they provide the oxygen-free environment needed for growth of the microorganism.

Both the occurrence and severity of tetanus are determined by the amount of toxin produced and the resistance of the host. The neurotoxic component, tetanospasmin, is one of the deadliest poisons known. It is believed to act on the synthesis and liberation of acetylcholine, a substance having a key role in the synaptic transmission of nerve impulses throughout the body. Once it has entered the body, the toxin rapidly spreads by way of the bloodstream or directly by a nerve to the central nervous system, where it attacks motor nerve cells and excites them to overactivity. Excessive impulses rush through the nerves to the muscles, which are thrown into severe convulsive spasm. The most common spasms occur in the muscle of the jaw, and the first sign of the illness often is stiffness of the jaw, or trismus. The muscles of the mouth are often affected, pulling the lips out and up over the teeth into a grimace, the mixture of smile and snarl that heralds the onset of the generalized convulsive stage of tetanus. Spasm of the muscles of the throat can make swallowing impossible, whereas the muscles of the larynx or of the chest wall can be thrown into such violent spasm that breathing is impossible and life is threatened. This is a common cause of death if the tetanus is untreated, but there are other effects on the heart, blood pressure, and vital brain centres that may cause death later in the disease.

The incubation period is quite variable in length—from two days to two weeks in most cases but sometimes up to three months. In general, the longer the incubation period, the milder will be the disease. Treatment of tetanus is primarily supportive. Tetanus antitoxin, which contains antibodies derived from the blood of persons who have been immunized against the disease, is given to help neutralize the toxin in the bloodstream, but it has little effect once the toxin has affected the nerve endings. Intravenous penicillin kills the organisms that remain within the wound site. Patients are usually intentionally paralyzed with drugs (such as curare) to prevent muscle spasms caused by the disease. Artificial or mechanical respiration is necessary because the respiratory muscles are paralyzed. After a few weeks, when the disease is curtailed, the curare treatment is stopped and the patient begins to breathe on his or her own again.

Passive protection with tetanus antitoxin should be administered in all cases of injuries that may be contaminated by clostridial spores. Active immunization with tetanus toxoid (prepared by chemical modification of toxin) is a relatively slow process, requiring weeks or months to become effective, and must be renewed every few years (booster doses). A first dose should be given to every accident victim, followed by two more doses several months later. This applies also to persons who have recovered from tetanus, for an attack of the disease does not confer immunity.

TULAREMIA

Tularemia is an acute infectious disease resembling plague, but much less severe. It was described in 1911 among ground squirrels in Tulare county, California (from which the name is derived), and was first reported in humans in the United States in 1914. The causative agent is the gram-negative bacterium *Francisella tularensis*. The disease is primarily one of animals, and human infections are incidental. It occurs naturally in many types of wildlife. In the United States the rabbit, especially the cottontail (*Sylvilagus*), is an important source of human infection, but other mammals, birds, and insects also spread the disease. Human cases in Sweden and Norway have been transmitted by hares. In Russia transmission was found to occur by water rats. *F. tularensis* has been found in some natural water sources, causing incidences of the disease in humans and animals. Tularemia can be spread to humans by the bite of an infected animal, by contact with blood or fine dust from the animal's body during skinning or similar operations, by the ingestion of infected animal products that have not been properly cooked, or by the bite of an insect, most commonly a deerfly, *Chrysops discalis* (the human disease is also called deerfly fever).

Various ticks of the genera *Dermacentor*, *Haemaphysalis*, *Rhipicephalus*, *Amblyomma*, and *Ixodes* may be largely responsible for maintenance of the animal infection. In addition, the infection is transmitted from the adult tick to the egg, and both larvae and nymphs are infectious and form an insect reservoir of infection. No case of human-to-human contamination has been reported.

The most common form of the disease in humans is the ulceroglandular form, in

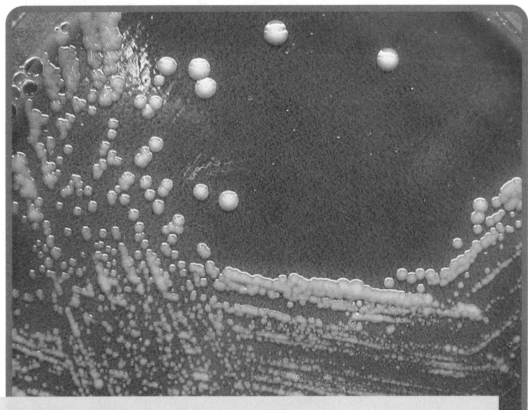

Culture of Francisella tularensis, *the causative agent of tularemia.* Larry Stauffer, Oregon State Public Health Laboratory/Centers for Disease Control and Prevention (CDC) (Image Number: 1910)

which there is a painful sore at the site of the infection and a swelling of the lymph node that drains the area. The sore is often on the finger and the swelling, or bubo, in the armpit. The bubo can break down and discharge pus, but it sometimes remains hard and tender for weeks. Along with these local signs, the infected person has a fever that may persist for two or three weeks, with headache, vomiting, body pains, and general weakness. Infection of the eye is also common, with

swelling of related lymph glands. The fatality rate is very low. Approximately 200 cases of the disease are reported each year in the United States, and the disease has been encountered in all parts of the country except Hawaii, although it is most common in the south-central or western states. Tularemia also occurs in a typhoidal form marked by an exhausting, or feverish, illness and a pneumonic form caused by inhalation of dust contaminated by *F. tularensis*. Mortality is sometimes as high as 5 to 7 percent in the typhoidal and pneumonic forms.

The tetracyclines are reasonably effective in treating the disease. Gentamicin and streptomycin are the most effective antibiotics. Healing usually takes place within 10 days. A live attenuated vaccine has been generally successful in conferring immunity on susceptible hosts, although its use is usually limited to persons at high risk.

WHOOPING COUGH

Whooping cough, or pertussis, is an acute, highly communicable respiratory disease characterized in its typical form by paroxysms of coughing followed by a long-drawn inspiration, or "whoop." The coughing ends with the expulsion of clear, sticky mucus and often with vomiting. Whooping cough is caused by the bacterium *Bordetella pertussis*.

Whooping cough is passed from one person directly to another by inhalation of droplets expelled by coughing or sneezing. Beginning its onset after an incubation period of approximately one week, the illness progresses through three stages—catarrhal, paroxysmal, and convalescent—which together last six to eight weeks. Catarrhal symptoms are those of a cold, with a short dry cough that is worse at night, red eyes, and a low-grade fever. After one to two weeks the catarrhal stage passes into the distinctive paroxysmal period, variable in duration but commonly lasting four to six weeks. In the paroxysmal state, there

is a repetitive series of coughs that are exhausting and often result in vomiting. The infected person may appear blue, with bulging eyes, and be dazed and apathetic, but the periods between coughing paroxysms are comfortable. During the convalescent stage there is gradual recovery. Complications of whooping cough include pneumonia, ear infections, slowed or stopped breathing, and occasionally convulsions and indications of brain damage.

Whooping cough is worldwide in distribution and among the most acute infections of children. The disease was first adequately described in 1578, although it is believed to have existed for a long time before then. About 100 years later, the name *pertussis* (Latin: "intensive cough") was introduced in

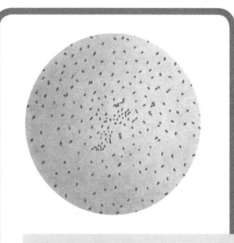

Bordetella pertussis, *the causative agent of whooping cough, isolated and coloured with Gram stain.* Centers for Disease Control and Prevention (CDC) (Image Number: 2121)

England. In 1906 at the Pasteur Institute, the French bacteriologists Jules Bordet and Octave Gengou isolated the bacterium that causes the disease. It was first called the Bordet-Gengou bacillus, later *Haemophilus pertussis*, and still later *Bordetella pertussis*. The first pertussis immunizing agent was introduced in the 1940s and soon led to a drastic decline in the number of cases. Now included in the DPT (diphtheria, tetanus, and pertussis) vaccine, it confers active immunity against whooping cough to children. Immunization is routinely begun at two months of age and requires five shots for maximum protection. A booster dose of pertussis vaccine should be given between 15 and 18 months of age, and another booster is given when the child is between four and six years old. Later vaccinations are in any case thought to be unnecessary, because the disease is much less severe when it occurs in older children, especially if they have been vaccinated in infancy.

The diagnosis of the disease is usually made on the basis of its symptoms and is confirmed by specific cultures. Treatment includes erythromycin, an antibiotic that may help to shorten the duration of illness and the period of communicability. Infants with the disease require careful monitoring because breathing may temporarily stop during coughing spells. Sedatives may be administered to induce rest and sleep, and sometimes the use of an oxygen tent is required to ease breathing.

YAWS

Yaws, also known as frambesia, is a contagious disease occurring in moist tropical regions throughout the world. It is caused by a spirochete, *Treponema pertenue*, that is structurally indistinguishable from *T. pallidum*, which causes syphilis. Some syphilologists contend that yaws is merely a tropical rural form of syphilis, but yaws is not contracted primarily through sexual activity, and later systemic complications from the disease are much rarer than in syphilis. The Wassermann and Kahn tests for syphilis, however, often read positive with yaws, and there is some degree of cross-immunity. The spirochetes of yaws are present in the discharge from lesions on the skin and are transferred by direct contact to the abraded skin of an uninfected person; contaminated clothing; and flies that feed on the sores. The disease is most frequently contracted in early childhood, and considerable immunity to subsequent infection is acquired.

Yaws has three stages. The symptoms are an initial papule on the skin at the site of inoculation, followed by multiple cauliflower eruptions, and later, in some cases, by mutilating destruction of the skin, mucous membranes, and bones. The primary yaws sore is characterized by a wartlike thickening of the epidermis, which becomes fibrous, cracks open, bleeds easily, and discharges a serous fluid.

A month or more later, when the first lesion may have disappeared except for a scar, multiple eruptions of the same type characteristically develop, often at junctions of the skin and mucous membranes, as around the mouth, nose, and anus, or on the skin of the crotch, neck, arms, legs, and buttocks. These lesions, whether initial or secondary, are yellowish-red and look somewhat like a raspberry (hence the name frambesia, latinized from the French *framboise*, meaning "raspberry"). Later, the disease may subside, leaving only superficial scarring, but in some instances there may be deforming tertiary yaws involving the nose, long bones ("boomerang leg" of Australia), and, rarely, the spleen, brain, and great blood vessels.

Penicillin is rapidly effective in killing the spirochete and in curing yaws except in the tertiary stage, when oxophenarsine with bismuth subsalicylate is used. Prevention centres on isolating and promptly treating cases to reduce exposure and on maintaining personal and group hygiene. All abrasions and sores of the skin and mucous membranes should be treated with appropriate antiseptics and covered with clean dressings, and all clothing in contact with yaws lesions should be sterilized or destroyed.

CHAPTER 6

VIRAL DISEASES: POX, POLIO, AND CLASSIC CHILDHOOD INFECTIONS

Each year classic childhood infections—chickenpox, measles, and other viral diseases—cause illness in countless children worldwide. They also cause illness in susceptible adults. Many of these infections have been known for thousands of years, but only beginning in the 18th century did scientists discover that many of them can be prevented through vaccination. Vaccines administered in childhood are vitally important to ensuring individual and community health, because they confer protection during a developmental period when individuals are most susceptible and most likely to spread disease.

The discovery of viruses themselves is fairly recent, having occurred in the late 19th and early 20th centuries. Thus, for most of human history, the causative agents of some of the worst afflictions of children were unknown. And while scientists' understanding of pox diseases, polio, measles, mumps, and rubella advanced rapidly in the 20th and early 21st centuries, prevention remains the primary means of dealing with these diseases. Vaccination programs against smallpox and polio in particular illustrate the significance of prevention—international efforts to eradicate these diseases have resulted in the disappearance of smallpox and the near-complete eradication of polio from the world.

POX DISEASE

Pox diseases are viral diseases in humans and domestic animals that are marked chiefly by eruptions of the skin and mucous membranes. Sheep pox and rabbit pox are spread by airborne infectious particles that are inhaled. Horse pox, fowl pox, and mouse pox usually are spread by skin contact. Cowpox (vaccinia) and pseudocowpox (paravaccinia), localized on the udder and teats of cows, are transmissible to humans by skin contact. Horse pox (contagious pustular stomatitis) is now rare. Swine pox, of two types, is prevalent but rarely fatal. Sheep pox, the most severe pox disease of domestic animals, and goat pox are now confined to parts of southeastern Europe, North Africa, and Asia.

Effective vaccines are available for most pox diseases, though outbreaks have continued. Buffalopox was reported in Maharashtra, India, in the 1990s. Monkeypox, which was first identified in 1958 and found primarily in Africa, was cited in the United States in 2003.

Smallpox was declared eradicated in 1980. In 2000, however, accidental exposure to smallpox vaccine (made from a virus related to smallpox) resulted in an isolated outbreak in Russia. Only two laboratories—in Russia and in the United States—were known to have live samples of smallpox in the 21st century.

CHICKENPOX

Chickenpox, or varicella, is a contagious viral disease characterized by an eruption of vesicles (small blisters) on the skin. The disease usually occurs in epidemics, and the infected persons are generally between two and six years old, although they can be of any age. The incubation period is about two weeks. There are practically no premonitory symptoms, though slight fever for about 24 hours may precede the eruption. A number of raised, itching red papules appear on the back or chest. Within 12 to 24 hours these develop into tense vesicles filled

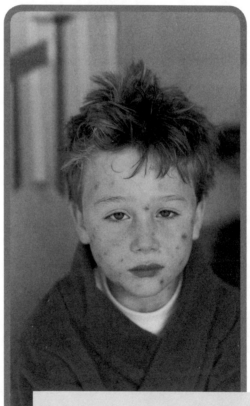

Chickenpox (varicella) usually infects young children (ages two to six years) with an outbreak of little blisters on the skin. Digital Vision/Thinkstock

with a clear fluid, which in another 36 hours or so becomes opalescent. During the fourth day the vesicles shrivel up and become scabs. Eventually the scabs fall off, usually leaving no scar. Fresh spots continue to appear during the first three days, so that at the end of that time they can be seen in all stages of growth and resolution. The eruption is most marked on areas covered by clothing, but it also occurs on the face and limbs and on the mucous membrane of the mouth and palate. The temperature of the infected person rarely rises above 39 °C (102 °F). The disease runs a favourable course in most cases and usually produces permanent immunity.

The illness requires no treatment, but the patient should be isolated at home to prevent infection of others. It is particularly important that the patient avoid contact with persons who have suppressed immune systems, in whom chickenpox can be severe or fatal. The patient also should be prevented from scratching, which could lead to ulceration of the vesicles and scarring. Common antipruritic skin medications such as calamine lotion may be helpful. Complications, although uncommon, include secondary invasion of the skin by bacteria and spread of those bacteria to virtually any organ system in the body.

Chickenpox is caused by the varicella-zoster virus, the same virus that causes herpes zoster (also called zoster, shingles, or zona), a localized eruption of large blisters. Chickenpox is the clinical reaction to a first exposure to the virus. After recovery, the virus may settle in a nerve ganglion and be reactivated many years later. The cause of reactivation is unknown. Upon reactivation, the virus travels along a nerve to the skin and causes herpes zoster. In most cases the lesions of herpes zoster occur in the distribution of a dermatome, an area of skin associated with the branch of a single spinal nerve. For this reason, herpes zoster is usually unilateral (on one side of the body). Severe pain is felt in the area of the blisters, which last from three to five days and then subside on their own. A person with herpes zoster is able to infect another person with varicella-zoster virus, resulting in chickenpox, but the reverse does not occur, because herpes zoster is a result of reactivation of latent virus from a prior varicella infection. Specific antiviral agents may have a role in the treatment of herpes zoster.

Injections of zoster immune globulin (ZIG), a preparation made from the plasma of adults who have recently had herpes zoster, are sometimes given to prevent the development of chickenpox in exposed children. ZIG contains antibodies to varicella-zoster virus and provides temporary protection against the virus. ZIG administration is usually reserved for children with leukemia or immune-deficiency disorders, for whom chickenpox poses significant risks. In 1995 a chickenpox vaccine prepared from a live, attenuated strain of the virus was approved for use in the United States.

SHINGLES

Shingles, or herpes zoster, is an acute viral infection affecting the skin and nerves. It is characterized by groups of small blisters appearing along certain nerve segments. The lesions are most often seen on the back and may be preceded by a dull ache in the affected site. Herpes zoster is caused by the same virus as that of chickenpox. It probably constitutes the response of the partially immune person, resulting from the reactivation of a latent virus, whereas chickenpox is the response of the non-immune host. In most cases, spontaneous recovery occurs within two weeks. However, neuralgia may persist for months or even years after recovery from the infection. Herpes zoster is contagious if blisters have opened and the person with whom the virus comes into contact has not been previously affected by chickenpox (contagious spread causes chickenpox rather than herpes zoster).

COWPOX

Cowpox, or vaccinia, is a mildly eruptive disease of cows that when transmitted to otherwise healthy humans produces immunity to smallpox. The cowpox virus is closely related to variola, the causative virus of smallpox. The word *vaccinia* is sometimes used interchangeably with cowpox to refer to the human form of the disease, sometimes to refer to the causative virus, and sometimes to refer only to the artificially induced human form of cowpox.

Cowpox disease, which is evident from the ulcers on the teats of cows, had been known as a disease of cows for hundreds of years. Human cowpox occurred as a self-contained localized ulcer on the hands or at other sites where scratches or abrasions allowed entry of the virus. The preventive effect of vaccination, or intentional inoculation with the vaccinia virus,

was demonstrated in the late 18th century. During the 1980s, researchers discovered that rodents were also a natural reservoir for the virus and that rodents, not cattle, were responsible for most cowpox infections in humans.

The vaccinia virus used in modern vaccines, though descended from cowpox, differs genetically from the existing cowpox virus. This difference may be a result of documented contamination of earlier vaccine cultures with variola virus, creating a hybrid that still confers immunity to smallpox infection. Vaccinia, by the strictest definition, does not occur in nature but enters the body during vaccination. Although this usually produces a self-limiting, local ulcer like cowpox infection, it can cause a systemic smallpox-like disease in patients whose immunity is compromised, and it has—though rarely—been found to cause encephalitis. With the disappearance of human smallpox, these risks have caused the discontinuation of routine vaccination on a population-wide basis.

SMALLPOX

Smallpox, or variola major, is an acute infectious disease that begins with a high fever, headache, and back pain and then proceeds to an eruption on the skin that leaves the face and limbs covered with cratered pockmarks, or pox. For centuries smallpox was one of the world's most dreaded plagues, killing as many as 30 percent of its victims, most of them children. Those who survived were permanently immune to a second infection, but they faced a lifetime of disfigurement and in some cases blindness. But smallpox was also one of the first diseases to be controlled by a vaccine, particularly following the great experiments of the English physician Edward Jenner in 1796. In 1967 the World Health Organization (WHO) began a global vaccination program against smallpox, and in 1980 the disease was officially declared eradicated.

COURSE OF DISEASE

Each case of smallpox arose from close contact with another case of the disease, usually by inhalation of virus that had been expelled in the breath or saliva droplets of an infected person. Despite the hardiness of the variola virus, smallpox was not a highly infectious disease. Infected persons usually did not infect more than two to five of their closest contacts. The great danger from the disease was that it could cause only a very mild attack in vaccinated persons, yet these persons could unwittingly spread the fatal form of the disease. It was therefore essential in dealing with an outbreak to make thorough enquiry into all possible contacts of patients and to follow these contacts and either ascertain that they had escaped infection or else isolate them at once if they showed any sign of infection.

Once variola major entered the body through the mucous membranes of the respiratory tract, there was a one- to two-week incubation period during which the person showed no signs of infection. The virus multiplied in the lymph nodes, spleen, and bone marrow, then migrated in white blood cells to small blood vessels near the surface of the skin. Illness first became apparent with a sudden high fever of 38.5 to 40.5 °C (101 to 105 °F), severe headache and back pain, and sometimes abdominal pain and vomiting. Two to five days later these flulike symptoms abated. However, they were followed by the appearance of lesions in the mouth and by a rash on the skin that was heaviest on the face and lower part of the limbs, displaying what was called a centrifugal, or centre-fleeing, distribution. The rash might be so profuse as to be confluent, especially on the face, or so scanty that the lesions were missed altogether. The first manifestation of the rash was a flat spot, or macule, which over the next few days changed into a raised papule, then into a clear blister, or vesicle, and finally into an infected pustule. By this time the fever usually returned. In fatal cases, death frequently came after a week or two of illness, brought on by the toxic effects of huge quantities of virus in the blood and the inflammatory response of the body's immune system. In nonfatal cases, the pustules dried up and formed scabs that, upon separation, left multiple pockmarked scars.

In some cases there was a toxic eruption during the initial fever, before the appearance of the true smallpox rash. These toxic rashes might be diffuse blushes on trunk or limbs, somewhat suggestive of scarlet fever or measles. They might be deeper red, however, with small hemorrhages like fleabites or larger blotches in the skin. The first type of rash was clinically unimportant, but the deep red, hemorrhagic rash occurred in the most severe, usually fatal cases of the disease. Frequently, such patients died before the true smallpox rash had time to develop, and the disease was not diagnosed. These cases were not usually sources of infection, however, because smallpox was not infectious until the characteristic focal eruption had come out in the throat and on the skin.

If smallpox vaccine was given within a few days of exposure to the virus, it would act to prevent illness or lessen the degree of symptoms. However, once symptoms appeared, treatment was limited. The patient was kept as clean and comfortable as possible, the fever was treated with analgesics, and pustules were treated with antiseptics to prevent secondary infection.

SMALLPOX THROUGH HISTORY

Smallpox is caused by infection with variola major, a virus of the family Poxviridae. (A less-virulent form of smallpox, called alastrim, is caused by a closely related virus known as variola minor.) There are no natural animal carriers or natural propagation of variola outside the human body. The disease is thought by some scholars to have arisen among settled agricultural populations in Mesopotamia as early as the 5th millennium BCE and in the Nile River valley in the 3rd millennium BCE. The mummified body of the Egyptian pharaoh Ramses V (died c. 1156 BCE) bears evidence of pustules characteristic of smallpox. It is possible that smallpox was behind the great plague of Athens in 430 BCE, recorded by the Greek historian Thucydides, and a devastating plague carried to Italy by a Roman army returning from Mesopotamia around 165 CE. Smallpox is assumed to have been endemic in (localized within) the Ganges River basin in India by the 1st millennium BCE. The earliest likely references to the disease occur in the *Caraka-saṃhitā* and *Suśruta-saṃhitā*, medical works compiled by the first centuries of the Common Era. By the 2nd century CE, smallpox was endemic in the Huang He and Yangtze River valleys of China, the disease being distinctly described by the alchemist Ge Hong around 340. Smallpox appeared in North Africa and southern Europe following the Moorish conquests of the 8th century, and after the Crusades it appeared sporadically throughout Europe. Possibly as early as the 12th century, Arab and Indian traders took the disease to the coast of East Africa, and Muslim caravaners and pilgrims crossing the Sahara Desert took it to West Africa as well.

It is difficult to discern from early writings whether people were able to distinguish smallpox from other diseases. The most reliable early account comes from the Persian physician al-Rāzī, c. 900. Al-Rāzī, known as Rhazes to his European translators, clearly described the symptoms of smallpox and distinguished it from measles. Around 570, Bishop Marius of Avicentum (near Lausanne, Switzerland) had introduced the Latin term *variola* (meaning "pox" or "pustule") to describe diseases that may have included smallpox. The English term *pox* was used to describe various eruptive diseases, including smallpox, but it was not until the 16th century that variola became popularly known as the "small pox," to distinguish it from syphilis (the "Great Pox"). By that time smallpox seems to have succeeded plague as the most feared pestilence in Europe. A huge pandemic reached from Europe to the Middle East in 1614, and epidemics arose regularly in Europe throughout the 17th and 18th centuries. There were frequent outbreaks in the American colonies and in British India as well. Introduced to the Americas by European conquerors and settlers, smallpox decimated native populations from the Plains Indians of Canada and the United States to the Aztecs of Mexico and the Araucanians of Chile. The Australian Aboriginals also suffered large losses from the disease in the 19th century.

Though medical science had not yet grasped the concept of infectious organisms such as viruses, it was understood that smallpox was somehow a contagious disease and that its victims had to be separated from the general populace. Little could be done for the victims. The first edition of *Encyclopædia Britannica* (1768) repeats the general approach of the great 17th-century English physician Thomas Sydenham, which included procedures such as bloodletting, induction of vomiting, and administration of enemas in order to "keep the inflammation of the blood within due bounds." In all parts of the world, smallpox outbreaks brought on desperate pleas by believers for divine assistance in lifting the scourge. Beyond that, the only hope lay in preventing outbreaks from occurring.

In southwestern Asia it had been known for centuries that a healthy person could be made immune to smallpox by being injected with pus taken from the sores of an infected person. Another technique, practiced in China, was to grind the scabs of a smallpox victim and blow the powder through a tube into the nose of a healthy person. People inoculated in this way would suffer a brief illness themselves and would be contagious for a period, and a few would contract a serious infection and die. But the risk of dying was far less than in a smallpox epidemic (roughly 2 percent, compared with 20 to 30 percent), and the benefit of immunity was clear. In the early 18th century several European doctors and, most prominently, Lady Mary Wortley Montagu, the wife of Britain's ambassador to Turkey, began to publicize the value of inoculation (or variolation, as it came to be known), and the practice was soon adopted by royalty and people of means in Europe and America. However, the procedure was expensive and difficult, and it had little influence beyond the well-to-do classes and certain military forces.

A much safer procedure was developed by Edward Jenner, a physician in Gloucestershire, England. In 1796 Jenner deliberately infected a small boy with variolae vaccinae, or cowpox, a bovine version of smallpox. The boy suffered only a mild noncontagious reaction and then showed no reaction to a subsequent inoculation with variola major. The superiority of vaccination, as this technique came to be known, was immediately recognized. During the 19th century, vaccination programs, many of them compulsory, were instituted in many countries. At first vaccine was obtained directly from vaccinated persons, but soon it was being commercially harvested from pustules grown on the skin of inoculated calves. Later in the century it became apparent that the cowpox virus had been supplanted in vaccines by a different strain. It is still not certain whether the new virus, called vaccinia, was a mutation of cowpox virus or a completely

separate strain, but it remains the virus used for vaccine production to this day.

By the beginning of the 20th century, smallpox was no longer endemic in several countries of continental Europe. Endemic smallpox was eradicated from the United Kingdom in 1934, the U.S.S.R. in 1936, Canada in 1946, the United States in 1949, Japan in 1951, and China in 1961. Still, in an age of global travel only an international effort could completely eradicate the disease. In 1967 WHO began to vaccinate entire populations around every reported outbreak of smallpox. The disease was no longer endemic in India by 1975 and in Ethiopia by 1976. The last endemic case of smallpox (actually an infection of variola minor) was recorded in Somalia in 1977. No cases were reported from 1977 to 1980, with the exception of two cases in England in 1978 whose source was in a laboratory, and in 1980 the disease was declared exterminated.

With the disappearance of the global threat, there was less incentive for prevention. In the United States, routine vaccination already had been discontinued in 1971, and production of vaccine was suspended in 1982. Stocks of variola major were kept in only two countries, the United States and Russia, which had cultivated the virus as part of their biological weapons programs during the Cold War. At the beginning of the 21st century, the increasing sophistication and viciousness of international terrorist groups raised concerns that entire populations were now vulnerable to deliberate infestation. In response, many countries began to produce and store fresh stocks of vaccine for use in emergencies.

In 2007 the Food and Drug Administration in the United States approved a new smallpox vaccine, the only new vaccine for smallpox to be approved since 1931. The new vaccine, called ACAM2000, is produced using basic cell-culture techniques that allow it to be made quickly and in sufficient quantity in the event of a national smallpox emergency.

POLIO

Polio (poliomyelitis; also called infantile paralysis) is an acute viral infectious disease of the nervous system that usually begins with general symptoms such as fever, headache, nausea, fatigue, and muscle pains and spasms and is sometimes followed by a more serious and permanent paralysis of muscles in one or more limbs, the throat, or the chest. More than half of all cases of polio occur in children under the age of five. The paralysis so commonly associated with the disease actually affects fewer than 1 percent of persons infected by the poliovirus. Between 5 and 10 percent of infected persons display only the general symptoms outlined above, and more than 90 percent show no signs of illness at all. For those infected by the poliovirus, there is no cure, and in the mid-20th century hundreds of thousands of children were struck by the disease every year. Since the 1960s, thanks to widespread use of polio vaccines, polio has been eliminated from most of the world, and it is now endemic only in several countries of Africa and South Asia. Approximately 1,000–2,000 children are still paralyzed by polio each year, most of them in India.

COURSE OF DISEASE

Poliomyelitis means "gray marrow inflammation," referring to the propensity of the poliovirus to attack certain cells in the spinal cord and brainstem. The poliovirus is a picornavirus (family Picornaviridae), a member of a group known as enteroviruses that inhabits the human digestive tract. (Humans are the only known hosts of the poliovirus.) The virus enters the body most often by the so-called fecal-oral route—that is, from fecal matter taken into the mouth through contaminated food or fingers. It can also enter by ingestion of droplets expelled from the throat of an infected person. New victims may become ill about 7 to 14 days after ingesting the virus. Infected persons may shed the virus from their throats for a week, beginning a day or more before suffering any symptoms themselves, and they may continue to shed the virus in their feces for a month or more after their illness.

After the poliovirus is swallowed, it multiplies in lymph nodes of the intestinal tract and spreads through the body via the bloodstream. In some people the virus gets no farther, causing only a vague flulike illness to develop. The most common early symptoms of polio are mild headache, fever, sore throat, nausea, vomiting, diarrhea, restlessness, and drowsiness. Fever peaks in two to three days and then rapidly subsides, and patients recover within three to four days without the development of paralysis.

In some cases, however, the virus begins an assault on the central nervous system, inflaming and destroying motor cells of the spinal cord and brainstem. In these cases, patients become irritable and develop pain in the back and limbs, muscle tenderness, and stiff neck. Many recover at this stage, but approximately one in 200 persons with polio develops what is known as flaccid paralysis. The motor impulses that normally move along the nerve fibres from the spinal cord to muscles are blocked, and, as a result, muscles become limp and cannot contract. The extent of paralysis depends on where the virus strikes and the number of nerve cells that it destroys. Cells that are not severely injured recover their normal function in time. To the extent that they do recover, a corresponding restoration of muscle function may be

Some polio patients develop flaccid paralysis, a condition in which the motor impulses are prevented from moving to the muscles. When the muscles cannot contract they become limp. Paula Bronstein/Getty Images

expected. Cells that are destroyed, however, are not replaced, because nerve cells cannot regenerate. In this case the paralysis is complete and permanent, with associated progressive atrophy of the unused muscles.

In most cases paralytic polio strikes the limb muscles, particularly the legs. Paralysis does not always involve the limbs, however. The abdominal muscles or the muscles of the back may be paralyzed, affecting posture. The neck muscles may become weak, so that the head cannot be raised. Paralysis of the face muscles may cause twisting of the mouth or drooping eyelids. In some types of spinal polio, the virus damages the upper part of the spinal cord, with resulting difficulties in breathing. In bulbar polio the virus attacks the brainstem, and the nerve centres that control swallowing and talking are damaged. Secretions collect in the throat and may lead to suffocation by blocking the airway. Some 5 to 10 percent of persons afflicted with paralytic polio die, usually of respiratory complications.

There seem to be individual differences in the degree of natural susceptibility to the disease. Many persons have acquired antibodies to the poliovirus in their blood without having had any symptoms of infection. It is generally held that a lasting immunity follows recovery from the disease. However, because there are three different serotypes of poliovirus—commonly called types I, II, and III—second attacks can occur. Persons who recover from an infection caused by

one type of poliovirus are permanently immune to reinfection by that type but not to infection by the other types. For this reason polio vaccines are trivalent—that is, designed to generate antibodies to all three poliovirus types.

Among as many as one-quarter of former polio victims whose condition has been stabilized for years or even decades, a condition called post-polio syndrome has been recognized. Post-polio syndrome manifests itself as increased weakness, muscle atrophy, or other conditions involving the originally affected muscle groups or a different group of muscles. The cause of the syndrome is not known for certain, but it may arise when nerve branches grown by nerve fibres that survived the original infection begin to deteriorate as the former polio victim passes through middle age. There is no cure for post-polio syndrome.

TREATMENT AND VACCINATION

Treatment during the preparalytic stages of polio includes complete bed rest, isolation, and careful observation. If paralysis occurs, passive movement of the limbs can be used to avoid deformities. As muscle strength returns, exercises are increased. Breathing may require mechanical aids such as the positive pressure ventilator, which pumps air into the patient's lungs through an endotracheal tube inserted into the windpipe. Ventilators have largely replaced the "iron lungs" that gave polio such a dreadful image during the 20th century. Formally known as tank respirators, iron lungs were large steel cylinders that enclosed the abdomen or the entire body (except for the head) of a patient lying immobilized on a bed. Through the action of an attached bellows, air pressure inside the cylinder was alternately reduced and restored, forcing the paralyzed patient's lungs to expand and contract.

There are two types of polio vaccine: the inactivated poliovirus vaccine (IPV), also known as the Salk vaccine after its inventor, Jonas Salk; and the oral poliovirus vaccine (OPV), or Sabin vaccine, named for its inventor, Albert Sabin. IPV, based on killed, or inactivated, poliovirus types I, II, and III, was the first vaccine to break the scourge of polio epidemics in the 1950s. It is administered by injection and circulates through the bloodstream, where it causes the generation of antibodies against active, or "wild" (as opposed to vaccine-type), virus. OPV is based on live but weakened, or attenuated, poliovirus. There are two types of OPV: trivalent (tOPV), which contains all three types of live attenuated polioviruses; and monovalent (mOPV), which contains one of the three types of live attenuated polioviruses. Thus, trivalent vaccine is effective against all three types of poliovirus, and monovalent vaccines are effective against a single type of poliovirus. The specificity of mOPVs increases their effectiveness, such that a single dose of mOPV1, which is effective only against poliovirus type I, confers immunity to type I virus in roughly 70 to 80 percent of children, whereas a single dose of tOPV confers immunity to type I virus in about 20 to 40 percent of children.

OPV is administered by drops in the mouth. After the vaccine is swallowed, the attenuated virus multiplies in the small intestine and lymph nodes and causes the generation of antibodies against wild virus. It is also shed through the inoculated person's feces, thus indirectly immunizing other people through the fecal-oral route. OPV became the predominant vaccine after it was introduced in the early 1960s. Both vaccines are given three times, preferably in the first few months of an infant's life and then usually once as a "booster" when the child reaches school age. With these four doses, immunity against polio is almost completely assured.

In rare cases, OPV can give rise to vaccine-derived polioviruses (VDPVs), which are mutated strains of the live attenuated virus contained in the vaccine. There are several different types of VDPVs, including circulating vaccine-derived viruses (cVDPVs), which cause paralysis and occur within populations that have low polio-immunization rates. OPV has also been known to cause rare cases of what is known as vaccine-associated paralytic polio (VAPP) in both vaccine recipients and their contacts. Such cases occur once in every two million or more doses of OPV. VAPP appears to be caused by a reversion mutation of attenuated virus, thereby converting the virus back to an infectious form that subsequently attacks the nervous system. VAPP is more likely to arise in persons whose immune systems are deficient. Because of this risk, OPV was dropped from immunization programs in the United States in 2000 in favour of IPV. However, OPV, particularly mOPV1, which was found to be four times more effective in children than other polio vaccines, continued to be used in countries such as Nigeria, where polio remained a significant problem in the early 21st century.

POLIO THROUGH HISTORY

Polio epidemics did not begin to occur until the latter part of the 19th century, but evidence indicates that it is an ancient disease. A well-known stele from the 18th dynasty of ancient Egypt (1570–1342 BCE) clearly depicts a priest with a telltale paralysis and withering of his lower right leg and foot. The mummy of the pharaoh Siptah from the late 19th dynasty (1342–1197 BCE) shows a similarly characteristic deformity of the left leg and foot. However, owing to the sporadic appearance of the infection, the absence of epidemics until relatively recent times, and the nonspecific nature and infrequency of the acute illness, there is hardly another recognizable trace of the disease until the 18th century. In 1789 a pediatrician in London, Michael Underwood, published the first clear description of paralytic disease of infants in a medical textbook. In the early 19th century, small groups of polio-afflicted patients began to be reported in the medical literature, but still only as sporadic cases.

It is an irony of medical history that the transformation of polio into an epidemic disease occurred only in those industrialized countries in North America and Europe that had experienced significant improvements in hygiene during the 19th and 20th centuries. This has led health experts to conjecture that the infection was common in earlier times but that people were exposed and infected (in typically unhygienic environments) at very young ages, when they were less likely to suffer permanent paralysis as an outcome. As hygiene improved, the certainty of young people of successive generations being exposed to the virus was gradually reduced. In this new situation it was not long before enough susceptible children and adults had accumulated to allow epidemics to break out.

The first epidemics appeared in the form of outbreaks of at least 14 cases near Oslo, Norway, in 1868 and of 13 cases in northern Sweden in 1881. About the same time the idea began to be suggested that the hitherto sporadic cases of infantile paralysis might be contagious. The next significant epidemic, 10 times larger than previous outbreaks, with 132 recognized cases, erupted in the U.S. state of Vermont in 1894. During an epidemic of 1,031 cases in Sweden in 1905, Ivar Wickman recognized that patients with nonparalytic disease could spread the virus, and during an epidemic of 3,840 cases in 1911, Carl Kling and colleagues in Stockholm recovered the virus from healthy carriers as well as paralytic patients. In studying several fatal cases from the same outbreak, Kling found the virus in the victims' throats and also in tissues of their small intestines. During the second decade of the 20th century, it became apparent that far more people were being rendered immune to polio by previous asymptomatic infections than were being immunized by recovery from overt disease. By then polio was well on the way to becoming a widely feared periodic phenomenon. In the 1940s and early 1950s, western Europe and North America lived through summertime terrors brought about by nearly annual polio epidemics. At its peak incidence in the United States, in 1952, approximately 21,000 cases of paralytic polio (a rate of 13.6 cases per 100,000 population) were recorded. As outbreaks were concentrated in the summer and early autumn, children were kept away from swimming pools, movie theatres, and other crowded places where they might be exposed to the dreaded virus. Outbreaks were widely reported in the press, and polio victims encased in iron lungs were often displayed in public places such as department stores in order to encourage donations to efforts to research and combat the disease. In such an environment, it is not surprising that the announcement of an effective vaccine in 1955 was hailed as a mid-20th-century miracle.

The poliovirus itself was discovered in 1908 by a team led by Viennese immunologist and future Nobel Prize winner Karl Landsteiner. The existence of telltale antibodies specific to the virus circulating in the blood of infected persons was discovered only two years later. In 1931 two Australian researchers, Frank Macfarlane Burnet and Jean Macnamara, using immunologic techniques, were able to identify the different serotypes of the poliovirus. (Burnet was to receive a Nobel Prize in 1960.) In 1948 the team of John Enders, Thomas Weller, and Frederick Robbins, working at Harvard Medical School in Massachusetts, showed how the virus could be grown in large amounts in tissue culture (an advance for which they shared a Nobel Prize in 1954). From there it was only a short step to an announcement in 1953 by Jonas Salk at the University of Pittsburgh, Pennsylvania, that he had developed an effective killed-virus vaccine.

Salk's vaccine, known as the inactivated poliovirus vaccine (IPV), was put to a massive nationwide test in 1954–55. Called the Francis Field Trial after Thomas Francis, Jr., a University of Michigan professor who directed it, the test involved 1.8 million children in the first, second, and third grades across the United States. The trial was declared a success on April 12, 1955, and over the next four years more than 450 million doses of the Salk vaccine were distributed. During that time the incidence of paralytic polio in the United States fell from 18 cases per 100,000 population to fewer than 2 per 100,000. In the years 1961–63, approval was given to a new vaccine developed by Albert Sabin at the University of Cincinnati, Ohio. The Sabin vaccine, using live but attenuated virus, could be given in drops through the mouth and therefore became known as the oral poliovirus vaccine (OPV). Soon it became the predominant vaccine used in the United States and most other countries. By the early 1970s the annual incidence of polio in the United States had declined a thousand-fold from prevaccine levels, to an average of 12 cases a year.

This progress was mirrored in other industrialized countries. Canada, having suffered its worst outbreak in 1953 (almost 9,000 cases of all types of polio), quickly began production of the Salk and Sabin vaccines, and in 1965 only three cases of polio were reported. Finland began limited vaccination with the Salk vaccine in 1957 following two major outbreaks in 1954 and 1956. Some 1.5 million persons were vaccinated in a mass campaign in 1960–61, which eliminated the disease altogether in that country. Belgium began using the Salk vaccine in 1958 and the Sabin vaccine in 1963. As a result, polio disappeared as an endemic disease in the late 1960s. Denmark introduced IPV to its population in 1955 and OPV in 1963 and experienced only sporadic cases of the disease after 1962.

Even as the introduction of vaccines led inexorably to the decline and eventual disappearance of polio in the developed countries of the temperate world, only some 5 percent of schoolchildren were being routinely immunized in the less-developed countries of the tropics, where the disease was not considered to be a problem. However, when "lameness surveys" were conducted during the 1970s in several tropical countries, it was learned to considerable surprise that from 5 to 9 of every 1,000 schoolchildren had evidence of lameness due to paralytic polio. Immunization against polio was included in the Expanded Program on Immunization, launched by the World Health Organization (WHO) in 1974, and by 1989 the proportion of children being immunized rose to some 67 percent.

In 1985 the Pan American Health Organization, WHO's regional body for the Americas, announced an initiative to eradicate indigenous transmission of polio from that part of the world by the end of 1990. This followed not only the success of the United States and Canada in eliminating the disease but also successes in Brazil and Cuba, among other countries. Cuba began mass immunizations in 1962 and brought the number of cases down from 214 per year in the 1950s to a total of five cases between 1963 and 1978. Brazil began an immunization campaign in 1980. The reported cases there dropped from an average of 2,330 per year in the late 1970s to 69 cases in 1982. In 1994 all of the Western Hemisphere was declared free of indigenous polio.

Progress in the Americas was a major factor in the decision by WHO's World Health Assembly in 1988 to call for the eradication of polio from the globe by the year 2000. The Global Polio Eradication Initiative was joined by UNICEF, Rotary International, and other organizations, and by 2000 the number of new cases of paralytic polio had been reduced from more than 250,000 per year to approximately 1,000–2,000. Complete elimination of the disease by the target year was not possible, given the complexity of storing and distributing the vaccine, the disruption of record keeping in countries plagued by poverty and conflict, and suspicion and resistance on the part of some local leaders. Nevertheless, polio as an endemic disease had been limited to a handful of countries in Africa and South Asia, though travelers from these countries frequently exported cases to other countries.

MEASLES, MUMPS, AND RUBELLA

Measles, or rubeola, is a contagious viral disease marked by fever, cough, conjunctivitis, and a characteristic rash. Measles is commonest in children but may appear in older persons who have escaped it earlier in life. Infants are immune up to four or five months of age if the mother has had the disease. Immunity to measles following an attack is usually lifelong.

Measles is so highly communicable that the slightest contact with an active case may infect a susceptible person. After an incubation period of about 10 days, the patient develops fever, redness and watering of the eyes, profuse nasal discharge, and congestion of the mucous membranes of the nose and throat—symptoms often mistaken for those of a severe cold. This period of invasion lasts for 48 to 96 hours. The fever increases with appearance of a blotchy rash, and

the temperature may rise as high as 40 °C (about 105 °F) when the rash reaches its maximum. Twenty-four to 36 hours before the rash develops, there appear in the mucous membranes of the mouth typical maculae, called Koplik spots—bluish-white specks surrounded by bright red areas about 0.75 mm ($^1/_{32}$ inch) in diameter. After a day or two the rash becomes a deeper red and gradually fades, the temperature drops rapidly, and the catarrhal symptoms disappear.

No drug is effective against measles. The only treatment required is control of fever, rest in bed, protection of the eyes, care of the bowels, and sometimes steam inhalations to relieve irritation of the bronchial tree. When no complications occur, the illness lasts 10 days. Uncomplicated measles is seldom fatal. Deaths attributed to measles usually result from secondary bronchopneumonia caused by bacterial organisms entering the inflamed bronchial tree. Conversely, complications of measles are frequent and include a superimposed bacterial ear infection or pneumonia or a primary measles lung infection. Encephalitis is a rare occurrence. Measles virus can invade various organ systems and cause hepatitis, appendicitis, and gangrene of the extremities. A large percentage of cases of severe measles are associated with inadequate intake of vitamin A, and there is evidence that treatment with vitamin A may reduce measles complications.

Mortality caused by measles declined steadily in the 20th century as the health of children and infants improved and effective treatment of complications became possible through the use of sulfonamide and antibiotic drugs. The widespread use of measles vaccine, beginning in the late 1960s, raised hopes for the eventual eradication of the disease. But, contrary to expectations, the incidence of measles remains high worldwide. The main problem is that the vaccine is not given to infants before the age of nine months, when the disease is most serious in the less-developed countries. Another problem is that the measles vaccine is a live vaccine, and it rapidly becomes inert if exposed to warm temperatures. Just 10 minutes in sunlight is sufficient to kill it. This sensitivity is a great hindrance to its use in tropical areas. Research is currently directed toward development of a more stable vaccine. In developed countries, a measles vaccine is commonly given at 12 to 15 months of age as part of a combined measles-mumps-rubella (MMR) vaccine.

Measles must be differentiated from other disorders accompanied by an eruption. In roseola infantum, a disease seen in babies, a measleslike rash appears after the child has had a high temperature for two or three days, but there is no fever at the time of the rash. German measles (rubella) can be superficially differentiated from measles by the shorter course of the disease and mildness of the symptoms. Sometimes the rashes of scarlet fever, serum reactions, and other conditions may, on certain parts of the body, look like measles. Drugs that

may produce rashes similar to measles are phenobarbital, diphenylhydantoin, the sulfonamides, phenolphthalein, and penicillin.

On extremely rare occasions, persistent infection with a mutant measles virus can cause a degenerative central nervous system disease called subacute sclerosing panencephalitis (SSPE), in which there is a gradual onset of progressive behavioral and intellectual deterioration. Motor incoordination and impairment of speech and sight subsequently develop. The final stages of stupor, dementia, blindness, and death occur within six to nine months. There is no treatment for SSPE.

Mumps, which is also called epidemic parotitis, is an acute contagious disease caused by a virus and characterized by inflammatory swelling of the salivary glands. It frequently occurs as an epidemic and most commonly affects young persons who are between 5 and 15 years of age.

The incubation period is about 17 to 21 days after contact. Danger of transmission begins one week before symptoms appear and lasts about two weeks. Mumps generally sets in with symptoms of a slightly feverish cold, soon followed by swelling and stiffening in the region of the parotid salivary gland in front of the ear. The swelling rapidly increases and spreads toward the neck and under the jaw, involving the numerous glands there. The condition is often found on both sides of the face. Pain is seldom

MAURICE RALPH HILLEMAN

(b. Aug. 30, 1919, Miles City, Mont., U.S.—d. April 11, 2005, Philadelphia, Pa.)

American microbiologist Maurice Ralph Hilleman developed some 40 vaccines, including those for chickenpox, hepatitis A, hepatitis B, measles, meningitis, mumps, and rubella. His work was credited with having saved tens of millions of lives by making possible the virtual elimination from many countries of once-common deadly childhood diseases and by serving as the basis for public health measures against many other infectious diseases.

Hilleman received a Ph.D. in microbiology from the University of Chicago in 1944. As a researcher at E.R. Squibb & Sons, he developed his first vaccine, which was used to protect U.S. troops in World War II from the Japanese B encephalitis virus. He was chief of respiratory diseases (1949–57) at Walter Reed Army Medical Center, Washington, D.C., where he began research on the influenza virus. In 1957 he joined what became Merck & Co., Inc.

Hilleman's accomplishments included the development of vaccinations that combine vaccines against more than one disease, the discovery of patterns of genetic change in the influenza virus relating to its ability to infect persons, and the discovery or co-discovery of several viruses, including the hepatitis A virus and the rhinoviruses that cause colds. The animal vaccine he developed against Marek disease, which causes a cancer in chickens, became of great economic importance to the poultry industry. Following his retirement (1984) Hilleman was an adviser to public health organizations, notably the World Health Organization.

severe, nor is there much redness or any tendency to discharge pus. There is, however, interference with chewing and swallowing. After four or five days the swelling subsides.

In patients past puberty, there is occasionally swelling and tenderness in other glands, such as the testicles in males (orchitis) and the breasts (mastitis) or ovaries (oophoritis) in females, and, rarely, involvement of the pancreas, but these are of short duration and usually of no serious significance. The testicles may become atrophied, but sterility from this cause is uncommon.

Meningoencephalitis (inflammation of the brain and its membranous covering) is a fairly common concomitant of mumps, but the outlook for recovery is favourable.

Mumps itself requires no special treatment, and a single attack usually confers lifelong immunity. Infection with mumps virus was once common in childhood, but the frequency of infection was drastically reduced with the introduction in 1967 of routine immunization for prevention of the disease with a vaccine made from attenuated (weakened) live mumps virus. This vaccine is administered after the age of about one year, often in combination with measles and rubella vaccines.

Rubella (German measles) is a viral disease that runs a mild and benign course in most people. Although rubella is not usually a serious illness in children or adults, it can cause birth defects or the loss of a fetus if a mother in the early stages of pregnancy becomes infected.

German physician Daniel Sennert first described the disease in 1619, calling it röteln, or rubella, for the red-coloured rash that accompanies the illness. Rubella was distinguished from a more serious infectious disease, measles, or rubeola, in the early 19th century. It came to be called German measles in the latter part of the 19th century when the disease was closely studied by German physicians. The rubella virus was first isolated in 1962, and a vaccine was made available in 1969. Rubella occurred worldwide before immunization programs were instituted, with minor epidemics arising every 6 to 9 years and major epidemics every 30 years. Because of its mildness it was not considered a dangerous illness until 1941, when Australian ophthalmologist N. McAlister Gregg discovered that prenatal infection with the virus was responsible for congenital malformations in children.

The rubella virus is spread through the respiratory route, being shed in droplets of respiratory secretions from an infected person. The incubation period is 12 to 19 days, with most cases occurring about 15 days after exposure. The first symptoms to appear are a sore throat and fever, followed by swollen glands and a rash that lasts about three days. Infected individuals tend to be most contagious when a rash is erupting. The duration and severity of the illness are variable and complications are rare, although encephalitis may follow. As many as 30 percent of infections are thought to occur without symptoms. Once infected, a person develops lifelong immunity to rubella.

Fetal infection occurs when the virus enters the placenta from the maternal bloodstream. Defects of the eye, heart, brain, and large arteries are most common and, together, are referred to as congenital rubella syndrome. The risk to the fetus is greatly reduced if the mother is infected after 20 weeks' gestation. If a woman of childbearing age has not had a natural infection with rubella virus, she should be immunized prior to pregnancy.

CHAPTER 7

VIRAL DISEASES: INFLUENZA

Influenza, which is also known simply as flu (or grippe), is an acute viral infection of the upper or lower respiratory tract that is marked by fever, chills, and a generalized feeling of weakness and pain in the muscles, together with varying degrees of soreness in the head and abdomen. Influenza, which has long been a major cause of infectious illness in humans, remains a widespread affliction today, despite the development of vaccines and drugs to prevent and treat the disease. Influenza viruses evolve at a very rapid rate. In fact, each "flu season" often brings with it a new strain of virus, against which the human body may possess only a limited degree of immunity. Thus, a new vaccine must be developed each year to ensure protection in susceptible populations, including very young children and the elderly. Because scientists are able to track influenza viruses as they circulate globally, they can accurately predict which strains are likely to give rise to seasonal influenza. This enables researchers to begin developing effective influenza vaccines ahead of time, and thus the vaccines often are made available to the public by the time flu season arrives.

Influenza viruses have caused some of the world's most devastating outbreaks of human disease in the modern era. These viruses, however, also infect animals, and it is the annual circulation through animal reservoirs, namely pigs and birds, that facilitates the emergence of new flu viruses that cause disease in humans. In addition, some strains that infect pigs and birds give rise to a flu-like illness in these animals. An outbreak of bird flu in the early 2000s spread to humans. The direct transmission of the virus to humans caused public alarm, and new concerns were raised in the scientific and medical communities about the seemingly unlimited disease potential of influenza viruses.

CLASSIFICATION OF INFLUENZA VIRUSES

Influenza is caused by any of several closely related viruses in the family Orthomyxoviridae (a group of RNA viruses). Influenza viruses are categorized as types A, B, and C. The three major types generally produce similar symptoms but are completely unrelated antigenically, so that infection with one type confers no immunity against the others. The A viruses cause the great influenza epidemics, and the B viruses cause smaller localized outbreaks. The C viruses are not important causes of disease in humans. Influenza A viruses are classified into subtypes, and both influenza B and subtypes of influenza A are further divided into strains. Subtypes of influenza A are differentiated mainly on the basis of two surface antigens (foreign proteins)—hemagglutinin (H) and neuraminidase (N). Examples of influenza A subtypes include H1N1, H5N1, and H3N2. Strains of influenza B and strains of influenza A subtypes are further distinguished by variations in genetic sequence.

EVOLUTION AND VIRULENCE OF INFLUENZA VIRUSES

Between worldwide outbreaks, known as pandemics, influenza viruses undergo constant, rapid evolution (a process called antigenic drift), which is driven by mutations in the genes' encoding antigen proteins. Periodically, the viruses undergo major evolutionary change by acquiring a new genome segment from another influenza virus (antigenic shift), effectively becoming a new subtype. Viral evolution is facilitated by animals such as pigs and birds, which serve as reservoirs of influenza viruses. When a pig is simultaneously infected with different influenza A viruses, such as human, swine, and avian strains, genetic reassortment can occur. This process gives rise to new strains of influenza A.

Newly emerged influenza viruses tend to be initially highly infectious and virulent in humans because they possess novel antigens to which the human body has no prepared immune defense (i.e., existing antibodies). Once a significant proportion of a population develops immunity through the production of antibodies capable of neutralizing the new virus, the infectiousness and virulence of the virus decreases. Although outbreaks of influenza viruses are generally most fatal to young children and the elderly, the fatality rate in people between ages 20 and 40 is sometimes unexpectedly high, even though the patients receive treatment. This phenomenon is believed to be

THOMAS FRANCIS, JR.

(b. July 15, 1900, Gas City, Ind., U.S.—d. Oct. 1, 1969, Ann Arbor, Mich.)

American microbiologist and epidemiologist Thomas Francis, Jr., isolated the viruses respon-
sible for influenza A (1934) and influenza B (1940) and developed a polyvalent vaccine effective
against both strains. He also conducted research that led to the development of antiserums for
the treatment of pneumonia.

Francis received his medical degree from Yale University (1925) and worked at the
Rockefeller Institute for Medical Research (1928–36), the Rockefeller Foundation (1936–38),
and the medical school of New York University (1938–41). He then joined the School of Public
Health at the University of Michigan. In 1954 he was appointed by the National Foundation for
Infantile Paralysis to direct the large-scale field tests that led to the widespread use of the Salk
vaccine against poliomyelitis.

due to hyper-reaction of the immune system to new strains of influenza virus. Such reaction results from the overproduction of inflammatory substances called cytokines. The release of excessive amounts of these molecules causes severe inflammation, particularly in the epithelial cells of the lungs. Individuals whose immune systems are not fully developed (such as infants) or are weakened (such as the elderly) cannot generate such a lethal immune response.

TRANSMISSION AND SYMPTOMS

The flu may affect individuals of all ages, though the highest incidence of the disease is among children and young adults. Influenza is generally more frequent during the colder months of the year. Infection is transmitted from person to person through the respiratory tract, by such means as inhalation of infected droplets resulting from coughing and sneezing. As the virus particles gain entrance to the body, they selectively attack and destroy the ciliated epithelial cells that line the upper respiratory tract, bronchial tubes, and trachea. The incubation period of the disease is one to two days, after which the onset of symptoms is abrupt, with sudden and distinct chills, fatigue, and muscle aches. The temperature rises rapidly to 38–40 °C (101–104 °F). A diffuse headache and severe muscular aches throughout the body are experienced, often accompanied by irritation or a sense of rawness in the throat. In three to four days the temperature begins to fall, and the person begins to recover. Symptoms associated with respiratory tract infection, such as coughing and nasal discharge, become more prominent and may be accompanied by lingering feelings of weakness. Death may occur, usually among older people already weakened by other debilitating disorders, and is caused in most of those cases by complications such as pneumonia or bronchitis.

TREATMENT AND PREVENTION

The antiviral drugs amantadine and rimantadine have beneficial effects on cases of influenza involving the type A virus. However, viral resistance to these agents has been observed, thereby reducing their effectiveness. A newer category of drugs, the neuraminidase inhibitors, which includes oseltamivir (Tamiflu) and zanamivir (Relenza), was introduced in the late 1990s. These drugs inhibit both the influenza A and B viruses. Other than this, the standard treatment remains bed rest, ingestion of fluids, and the use of analgesics to control fever. It is recommended that children and teenagers with the flu not be given aspirin, because treatment of viral infections with aspirin is associated with Reye syndrome, an extremely serious illness.

Individual protection against the flu may be bolstered by injection of a vaccine containing two or more circulating influenza viruses. These viruses are produced in chick embryos and rendered noninfective. Standard commercial preparations ordinarily include the type B influenza virus and several of the A subtypes. Protection from one vaccination seldom lasts more than a year, and yearly vaccination may be recommended, particularly for those individuals who are unusually susceptible to influenza or whose weak condition could lead to serious complications in case of infection. However, routine immunization in healthy people is also recommended. To prevent human-infecting bird flu viruses from mutating into more dangerous subtypes, public health authorities try to limit the viral "reservoir" where antigenic shift may take place by ordering the destruction of infected poultry flocks.

HISTORICAL AND MODERN INFLUENZA OUTBREAKS

Influenza pandemics are estimated to occur on average once every 50 years. Epidemics happen much more frequently, and seasonal influenza appears annually in most parts of the world, sometimes in epidemic proportions. Influenza type A virus is the most frequent cause of seasonal influenza. When an influenza A virus undergoes an antigenic shift, a pandemic affecting most of the world can occur within a matter of months. During the last century, four influenza pandemics have taken place, including the pandemic of 1918–19, the Asian flu of 1957, the Hong Kong flu of 1968, and the H1N1 flu of 2009. By far, the most destructive of these was the pandemic of 1918–19.

INFLUENZA PANDEMIC OF 1918–19

The influenza pandemic of 1918–19 (also known as the Spanish influenza pandemic, or Spanish flu) was the most severe influenza outbreak of the 20th century. In terms of total numbers of deaths, it was among the most devastating pandemics in human history. Influenza type A subtype H1N1 is now known to have been the cause of the extreme mortality of this pandemic, which resulted in an estimated 25 million deaths. However, some researchers have projected that it caused as many as 40–50 million deaths.

The pandemic occurred in three waves. The first apparently originated during World War I in Camp Funston, Kansas, U.S., in early March 1918. American troops that arrived in western Europe in April are thought to have brought the virus with them, and by July it had spread to Poland. The first wave of influenza was comparatively mild.

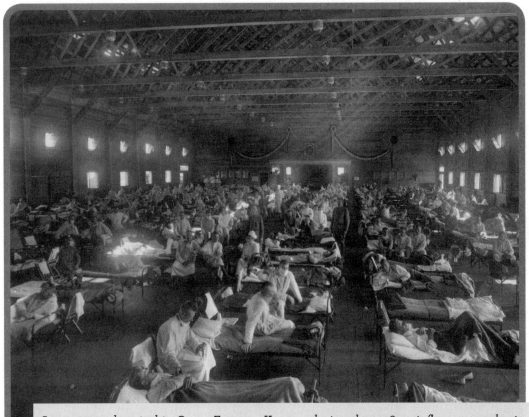

A temporary hospital in Camp Funston, Kansas, during the 1918–19 influenza pandemic. Courtesy of the National Museum of Health and Medicine, Armed Forces Institute of Pathology, Washington, D.C.

However, during the summer a more lethal type of disease was recognized, and this form fully emerged in August 1918. Pneumonia often developed quickly, with death usually coming two days after the first indications of the flu. For example, at Camp Devens, Massachusetts, U.S., six days after the first case of influenza was reported, there were 6,674 cases. The third wave of the pandemic occurred in the following winter, and by the spring the virus had run its course. In the two later waves about half the deaths were among 20- to 40-year-olds, an unusual mortality age pattern for influenza.

Outbreaks of the flu occurred in nearly every inhabited part of the world, first in ports, then spreading from city to city along the main transportation routes. India is believed to have suffered at least 12,500,000 deaths during the pandemic, and the disease reached distant islands in the South Pacific, including New Zealand and Samoa. In the United States about 550,000 people died. Altogether an estimated 25,000,000 persons throughout the world perished, most during the brutal second and third waves. Other outbreaks of Spanish influenza occurred in the 1920s, but with declining virulence.

ASIAN FLU OF 1957

The outbreak of Asian flu in 1957 was first identified in February of that year in East Asia, and it subsequently spread to countries worldwide. The 1957 Asian flu was the second major influenza pandemic to occur in the 20th century. It caused an estimated one million to two million deaths worldwide and is generally considered to have been the least severe of the three influenza pandemics of the 20th century.

The 1957 outbreak was caused by a virus known as influenza A subtype H2N2, or Asian flu virus. Research has indicated that this virus was a reassortant (mixed species) strain, originating from strains of avian influenza and human influenza viruses. In the 1960s the human H2N2 strain underwent a series of minor genetic modifications, a process known as antigenic drift. These slight modifications produced periodic epidemics. After 10 years of evolution, the Asian flu virus disappeared, having been replaced through antigenic shift by a new influenza A subtype, H3N2, which gave rise to the Hong Kong flu pandemic.

In the first months of the 1957 Asian flu pandemic, the virus spread throughout China and surrounding regions. By midsummer it had reached the United States, where it appears to have initially infected relatively few people. Several months later, however, numerous cases of infection were reported, especially in young children, the elderly, and pregnant women. This upsurge in cases was the result of a second pandemic wave of illness that struck the Northern Hemisphere in November 1957. At that time the pandemic was also already widespread in the United Kingdom. By December a total of some 3,550 deaths had been reported in England and Wales. The second wave was particularly devastating, and by

March 1958 an estimated 69,800 deaths had occurred in the United States.

Similar to the 1968 Hong Kong flu, the Asian flu was associated with variation in susceptibility and course of illness. Whereas some infected individuals experienced only minor symptoms, such as cough and mild fever, others experienced life-threatening complications such as pneumonia. Those persons who were unaffected by the virus were believed to have possessed protective antibodies to other, closely related strains of influenza. The rapid development of a vaccine against the H2N2 virus and the availability of antibiotics to treat secondary infections limited the spread and mortality of the pandemic.

Hong Kong Flu of 1968

The Hong Kong flu of 1968 was a global outbreak of influenza that originated in China in July 1968 and lasted until 1969–70. The outbreak was the third influenza pandemic to occur in the 20th century and resulted in an estimated one million to four million deaths.

The 1968 pandemic was initiated by the emergence of a virus known as influenza A subtype H3N2 (also called Hong Kong flu virus). It is suspected that this virus evolved from the strain of influenza that caused the 1957 pandemic. The 1957 Asian flu virus, or influenza A subtype H2N2, is believed to have given rise to H3N2 through antigenic shift, in which the hemagglutinin (H) antigen (a substance that stimulates an immune response) on the outer surface of the virus underwent genetic mutation to produce the new H3 antigen. Because the new virus retained the neuraminidase (N) antigen N2, persons who had been exposed to the 1957 virus apparently retained immune protection against the 1968 virus. This would explain the mildness of the 1968 outbreak relative to the pandemic of 1918–19.

Although the Hong Kong flu outbreak was associated with comparatively few deaths worldwide, the virus was highly contagious, a factor that facilitated its rapid global dissemination. Indeed, within two weeks of its emergence in July in Hong Kong, some 500,000 cases of illness had been reported, and the virus proceeded to spread swiftly throughout Southeast Asia. Within several months it had reached the Panama Canal Zone and the United States, where it had been taken overseas by soldiers returning to California from Vietnam. By the end of December the virus had spread throughout the United States and had reached the United Kingdom and countries in western Europe. Australia, Japan, and multiple countries in Africa, eastern Europe, and Central and South America were also affected. The pandemic occurred in two waves, and in most places the second wave caused a greater number of deaths than the first wave.

The 1968 Hong Kong flu caused illness of varying degrees of severity in different populations. For example, whereas illness was diffuse and affected only small numbers of people in Japan, it was widespread and deadly in the United States. Infection caused upper respiratory symptoms typical of influenza and produced symptoms of chills, fever, and muscle pain and weakness. These symptoms usually persisted for between four and six days. The highest levels of mortality were associated with the most susceptible groups, namely infants and the elderly. Although a vaccine was developed against the virus, it became available only after the pandemic had peaked in many countries.

The H3N2 virus that caused the 1968 pandemic is still in circulation today and is considered to be a strain of seasonal influenza. In the 1990s a closely related H3N2 virus was isolated from pigs. Scientists suspect that the human H3N2 virus jumped to pigs. Infected animals may show symptoms of swine flu.

INFLUENZA PANDEMIC (H1N1) OF 2009

The influenza pandemic of 2009 (also called H1N1 flu, or swine flu) was the first major influenza outbreak in the 21st century, noted for its rapid global spread, which was facilitated by an unusually high degree of viral contagiousness. Global dissemination of the virus was further expedited by the unprecedented rates of passenger travel that characterize the modern era.

The pandemic virus caused a respiratory disease typical of that resulting from infection with seasonal influenza.

However, despite local, national, and international efforts to contain the virus, its more contagious nature led to the infection of a substantial number of people. By mid-February 2010, 11 months after the outbreak was first detected in Mexico, more than 15,290 laboratory-confirmed deaths were reported by the World Health Organization (WHO). Because many countries stopped tracking individual cases in September and October 2009, WHO was unable to provide accurate global figures of laboratory-confirmed cases. Their final laboratory-confirmed case count, more than 622,482, was reported in late November 2009.

SYMPTOMS AND TRANSMISSION

Persons infected with H1N1 may experience fever and mild respiratory symptoms, such as coughing, runny nose, and congestion. In some cases symptoms may be severe and include diarrhea, chills, and vomiting, and in rare cases respiratory failure may occur. Although the H1N1 virus caused relatively few deaths in humans, it was most lethal in individuals affected by chronic disease.

The virus was passed from human to human primarily through inhalation of infectious particles or contact with an infected individual or a contaminated surface. These modes of transmission proved rapid and increased the potential for the virus's global spread. The H1N1 virus of 2009 was highly contagious. Between 22 and 33 percent of people who came into contact with an infected individual became infected themselves. This measure of the frequency of new cases of disease arising through contact with infected persons, which is known as the secondary attack rate, was higher for H1N1 flu than for seasonal influenza. (The typical secondary attack rate of seasonal influenza is between 5 and 15 percent.)

EARLY STAGES OF THE OUTBREAK

Evidence of an influenza-like illness first appeared in February 2009 in a small town called La Gloria in Veracruz, Mex. The following month the illness emerged in Mexico City. Officials investigating the outbreak quickly traced the illness to La Gloria, where a young boy, who later became known as "patient zero," was discovered to be infected with a previously unknown strain of influenza virus. The virus was a strain of swine influenza, and thus the outbreak adopted the name "swine flu." Although the boy represented the first known case, researchers who continue to investigate the virus suspect that it emerged sometime in 2008. Despite substantial progress made in the characterization of the virus, its origins remain unknown.

By the end of April more than 2,000 cases of the influenza-like illness had been reported in Mexico City and elsewhere in Mexico. Laboratory testing of a small subset of patients confirmed that a swine influenza virus was the cause of their illness. The virus that was detected was a subtype known as influenza A H1N1, though it was initially identified as a new strain of swine influenza virus because it consisted of genetic material from two different swine influenza viruses as well as genetic material from human and avian strains of influenza virus. The new H1N1 virus emerged in the United States in April 2009, in Texas, New York, California, and several other places. The virus was suspected of having been carried to those states by individuals who had been in affected areas in Mexico and then traveled from there.

On April 25, 2009, the director general of WHO, Margaret Chan, declared the outbreak a public health emergency of international concern. Within days of Chan's announcement, the H1N1 virus reached Spain, having been carried to that country by individuals traveling by airplane from Mexico. Confirmed cases of H1N1 infection also occurred in Germany, Austria, the United Kingdom, Israel, and New Zealand. Several provinces in Canada, including Nova Scotia, Alberta, Ontario, and British Columbia, also were affected. Although most persons who fell ill recovered, there were H1N1-related deaths in Mexico and the United States. In addition, many more cases of the disease were suspected in other countries, including Australia, Chile, Colombia, and France.

Although it was not clear whether all the cases in these other countries were caused by the H1N1 virus, several of the already confirmed cases in multiple countries demonstrated evidence of human-to-human transmission. This evidence prompted Chan and WHO on April 29 to declare a level 5 pandemic alert for the H1N1 outbreak. A level 5 pandemic alert indicated that WHO believed a swine flu pandemic was imminent and called for accelerated distribution of drugs to treatment facilities and rapid implementation of measures to control viral spread as much as possible.

At the end of April, there arose significant confusion concerning the name given to the outbreak. In some countries, "swine flu" was incorrectly believed to be caused by pigs, leading to the unnecessary slaughter of otherwise healthy pigs. This was most evident in Egypt, where a mandate for the slaughter of 400,000 pigs was issued by Minister of Health Hatem al-Gabali, though the animals showed no signs of viral infection. Egyptian pig farmers protested against the order, fueling riots that caused a great deal of concern among the country's citizens. To relieve tensions and to avoid further confusion, WHO officially renamed the outbreak influenza A (H1N1). It later assumed the name pandemic (H1N1) 2009, or some variation thereof, being known generally as H1N1 flu. The virus itself also was given various names, including novel influenza A (H1N1) virus.

Pandemic Status and Response

By early June 2009 more than 25,000 cases and nearly 140 deaths from H1N1 flu had been reported worldwide, the majority of deaths having occurred in Mexico and the greatest number of cases—more than 13,000—having appeared in the United States. The continued spread of the virus across multiple regions of the world prompted WHO to announce to its member countries on June 11, 2009, that it was raising the H1N1 flu pandemic alert from level 5 to level 6. This meant that the ongoing outbreak was officially declared a pandemic.

Prior to the announcement, an upsurge in cases had occurred in Chile, Japan, Australia, and the United Kingdom. The H1N1 flu pandemic was the first influenza pandemic to be declared since the 1968 outbreak of Hong Kong flu, which caused more than 750,000 deaths. However, despite the actuation of disease-control strategies determined to prevent the further spread of H1N1 flu, by late August 2009, six months into the outbreak, a total of 209,450 cases and nearly 2,200 deaths had been reported globally.

In mid-September in the United States, H1N1 flu activity increased dramatically, and 48 states reported widespread influenza-like illness by late October. This increase in disease activity was expected, however, since autumn traditionally marks the onset of the seasonal influenza season in the Northern Hemisphere. During the summer, in preparation for an increase in H1N1 activity, the U.S. Department of Health and Human Services had secured resources for the production of 120 million doses of vaccine, expecting that the full stock would be available by mid-October.

However, only about 11 million doses had been delivered by that time, and delays in vaccine production left a large percentage of the population susceptible to infection.

On October 24 U.S. Pres. Barack Obama declared the H1N1 flu outbreak a national emergency. The move was intended to ensure that, though faced with inadequate vaccine supplies, other federal resources would be available to support emergency measures, including the reimbursement of medical centres that set up treatment tents to facilitate H1N1 response efforts. At the time of Obama's announcement, the number of laboratory-confirmed H1N1 cases and deaths worldwide had increased to some 415,000 and 5,000, respectively.

In the United States the Centers for Disease Control and Prevention (CDC) periodically published updates on the number of H1N1 cases and deaths in that country. In late 2009 the CDC adjusted their methodology in assessing H1N1 data to account for affected individuals who had not sought medical care and who therefore had not undergone laboratory testing, which had formed the basis for earlier pandemic tracking in the country. The adjusted approach was believed to more accurately portray the actual impact of the outbreak in the United States. Based on this method, the CDC estimated that from April 2009 through mid-January 2010 between 8,330 and 17,160 deaths, between 41 million and 84 million cases, and between 183,000 and 378,000 H1N1-related hospitalizations had occurred in the United States.

THE H1N1 VIRUS

The influenza A H1N1 virus that caused the 2009 pandemic was suspected to have originated in pigs, although this remains a point of speculation. Because the virus was made up of genes from two strains of swine influenza virus as well as genes from human and avian influenza viruses, researchers concluded that it evolved through a process known as genetic reassortment. During reassortment, the three different types of influenza viruses—swine, human, and avian—presumably infected the same host and underwent an exchange of genetic material, thereby giving rise to the pandemic H1N1 strain. The details of how and when this occurred, however, are not clear.

Similar to all other influenza viruses, the 2009 H1N1 pandemic subtype was named for the composition of the proteins hemagglutinin (H) and neuraminidase (N) that form its viral coat. Although the pandemic virus was similar to the influenza viruses that circulate among humans seasonally, the pandemic subtype possessed unique antigens (molecules that stimulate an immune response, primarily through the production of antibodies).

H1N1 TREATMENT AND PREVENTION

Treatment for H1N1 infection consists of administration of the antiviral drugs oseltamivir (Tamiflu) or zanamivir (Relenza). However, there is some evidence that H1N1 viruses can develop resistance to oseltamivir, which commonly is used as first-line treatment for infection. In October 2009 an intravenously administered antiviral known as peramivir, though not formally approved by the U.S. Food and Drug Administration (FDA), was given emergency-use authorization for the treatment of hospitalized H1N1 patients who had not responded to oral or inhaled antivirals or who had life-threatening illness.

The spread of the virus can be controlled through basic sanitary practices, including washing hands, wearing face masks, and disinfecting potentially contaminated surfaces. However, the most effective method of prevention for high-risk persons, including young children, women who are pregnant, and individuals with compromised immune systems, is vaccination. When the H1N1 virus emerged, there were no vaccines available that could provide immunity against infection. However, the severity of the outbreak prompted the rapid development of a novel vaccine, which was tested in clinical trials beginning in early August 2009. Because the first vaccine tested required two doses, there was immediate concern that not enough vaccine could be manufactured before a potential second wave of illness arrived in the fall in the Northern Hemisphere. The vaccine also required a three-week wait between doses, introducing the possibility that it would not have time to take effect prior to the emergence of another period of high disease activity.

By September, pilot tests of novel single-dose vaccines—developed independently by Chinese biotechnology company Sinovac and Swiss pharmaceutical manufacturer Novartis AG—indicated that sufficient protection could be provided by one injection. Sinovac received approval from the Chinese government in early September to begin mass production of the vaccine, with the goal of generating enough of the agent to vaccinate 5 percent of the Chinese population by 2010. Efforts to increase the global supply of single-dose vaccines being developed by pharmaceutical companies around the world, as well as efforts to distribute these vaccines to countries affected by the pandemic, were considered vitally important to successfully stemming the spread of illness. To aid these efforts, WHO set a goal of obtaining some 200 million donated doses for allocation to 95 low- and middle-income countries. The first stocks of donated vaccine were scheduled for delivery to those countries between November 2009 and February 2010.

In late 2009 two types of H1N1 vaccines were made available: one that could be injected and one that could be inhaled. Whereas a single dose of vaccine was presumed to be sufficient for adolescents and adults, two doses were recommended for children between the ages of 6 months and 9 years.

INFLUENZA PANDEMIC PREPAREDNESS

Because influenza epidemics and pandemics can devastate large regions of the world very quickly, WHO constantly monitors influenza disease activity on a global scale. This monitoring is useful for gathering information that can be used to prepare vaccines and that can be disseminated to health centres in countries where seasonal influenza outbreaks are likely to occur. Monitoring by WHO also plays an important role in preventing and preparing for potential epidemics and pandemics.

In the event that a potentially pandemic influenza virus emerges, WHO adheres to its influenza pandemic preparedness plan. This plan consists of six phases of pandemic alert. Phases 1–3, which are the early stages in pandemic preparedness, are designed to prevent or contain small outbreaks. In these early phases, isolated incidences of animal-to-human transmission of an influenza virus are observed and provide warning that a virus has pandemic potential. Later, small outbreaks of disease may occur, generally resulting from multiple cases of animal-to-human transmission. Phase 3 signals to affected countries that the implementation of efforts to control the outbreak is needed to prevent a pandemic. Phases 4 and 5 are characterized by increasing urgency in mitigating the outbreak. Confirmed human-to-human viral transmission, with sustained disease in human communities which subsequently spread so that disease transmission between humans occurred in two countries, indicates that a pandemic is imminent. Phase 6, the highest level of pandemic alert, is characterized by widespread disease and sustained transmission of the virus between humans. Influenza pandemics sometimes occur in waves. Thus, a post-pandemic phase, when disease activity decreases, may be followed by another period of high prevalence of disease. As a result, influenza pandemics may last for a period of months.

BIRD FLU

Bird flu, or avian influenza, is a viral respiratory disease mainly of poultry and certain other bird species, including migratory waterbirds, some imported pet birds, and ostriches, that can be transmitted directly to humans. The first known cases in humans were reported in 1997, when an outbreak in poultry in Hong Kong led to severe illness in 18 people, a third of whom died. Symptoms of bird flu in humans resemble those of the human variety of influenza and include fever, sore throat, cough, headache, and muscle aches, which appear following an incubation period of several days. Severe infection can result in conjunctivitis or life-threatening complications such as bacterial or viral pneumonia and acute respiratory illness.

Between 2003 and late 2005, outbreaks of the most deadly variety of bird flu occurred among poultry in Cambodia, China, Indonesia, Japan, Kazakhstan, Laos, Malaysia, Romania, Russia, South Korea, Thailand, Turkey, and Vietnam. Hundreds of millions of birds in those countries died from the disease or were killed in attempts to control the epidemics. From 2003 through June 2010, some 499 people were reported to have been infected with bird flu, and about 60 percent of them died. The majority of human infections and deaths occurred in China, Egypt, Indonesia, Thailand, and Vietnam. Poultry-associated human infection with a less severe form of the disease was reported in the Netherlands.

Bird flu in avian species occurs in two forms, one mild and the other highly virulent and contagious. The latter form is known as fowl plague. Mutation of the virus causing the mild form is believed to have given rise to the virus causing the severe form. The infectious agents of bird

flu are any of several subtypes of type A orthomyxovirus. Other subtypes of this virus are responsible for most cases of human influenza and for the great influenza pandemics of the past. Genetic analysis suggests that the influenza A subtypes that afflict mainly nonavian animals, including humans, pigs, whales, and horses, derive at least partially from bird flu subtypes. All the subtypes are distinguished on the basis of variations in the surface proteins hemagglutinin and neuraminidase. The 1997 bird flu outbreak in Hong Kong was found to be caused by H5N1. This subtype, first identified in terns in South Africa in

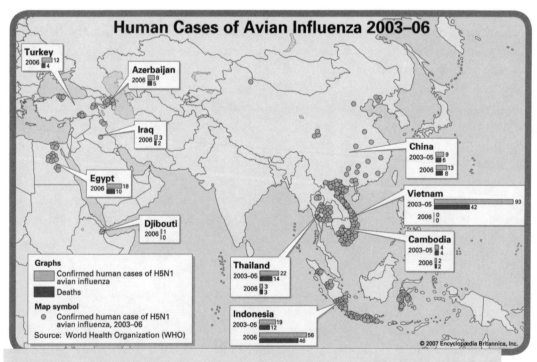

Map showing the locations and numbers of confirmed human bird flu (avian influenza) infections and related deaths from 2003 to 2006.

1961, has been responsible for nearly all laboratory-confirmed bird flu infections in humans and for the most devastating outbreaks in poultry. Other bird flu subtypes recognized to cause disease in birds and humans are H7N2, H7N3, H7N7, and H9N2.

Waterfowl such as wild ducks are thought to be primary hosts for all bird flu subtypes. Though normally resistant to the viruses, the birds carry them in their intestines and distribute them through feces into the environment, where they infect susceptible domestic birds. Sick birds pass the viruses to healthy birds through saliva, nasal secretions, and feces. Within a single region, bird flu is transmitted readily from farm to farm by airborne, feces-contaminated dust and soil, by contaminated clothing, feed, and equipment, or by wild animals carrying the virus on their bodies. The disease is spread from region to region by migratory birds and through international trade in live poultry. Humans who are in close contact with sick birds—for example, poultry farmers and slaughterhouse workers—are at the greatest risk of becoming infected. Virus-contaminated surfaces and intermediate hosts such as pigs can also be sources of infection for humans. Although isolated instances of person-to-person transmission appear to have occurred since 1997, sustained transmission has not been observed. However, through a rapid evolutionary process called antigenic shift, two viral subtypes (e.g., one a bird flu virus such as H5N1 and the other a human influenza virus) can combine parts of their genetic makeup to produce a previously unknown viral subtype. If the new subtype causes severe disease in humans, spreads easily between people, and has a combination of surface proteins to which few people have immunity, the stage will be set for a new influenza pandemic to occur.

Early detection of avian influenza is important in preventing and controlling outbreaks. One way the virus can be detected is by polymerase chain reaction (PCR), in which nucleic acids from blood or tissue samples are analyzed for the presence of molecules specific to bird flu. Other methods include viral antigen detection, which detects the reaction of antibodies to viral antigens in samples of skin cells or mucus, and viral culture, which is used to confirm the identity of specific subtypes of influenza based on the results of PCR or antigen detection and requires growth of the virus in cells in a laboratory. Tests based on lab-on-a-chip technology that take less than an hour to complete and can accurately identify specific subtypes of bird flu are being developed. This technology consists of a small device (the "chip") that contains on its surface a series of scaled-down laboratory analyses requiring only a tiny volume of sample (e.g., picolitres of saliva). These chip-based tests, which are portable and cost-effective, can be used to detect different subtypes of influenza in both poultry and humans.

Because of the many immunologically distinct viral subtypes that cause influenza in animals and the ability of the virus to rapidly evolve new strains, preparation of effective vaccines is complicated. The most effective control of outbreaks in poultry remains rapid culling of infected farm populations and decontamination of farms and equipment. This measure also serves to reduce the chances for human exposure to the virus. In 2007 the U.S. Food and Drug Administration approved a vaccine to protect humans against one subtype of the H5N1 virus. It was the first vaccine approved for use against bird flu in humans. Drug manufacturers and policy makers in developed and developing countries are working toward establishing a stockpile of the vaccine to provide some measure of protection against a future outbreak of bird flu. In addition, scientists are developing a vaccine that is effective against another subtype of H5N1, as well as a vaccine that might protect against all subtypes of H5N1. Studies suggest that antiviral drugs developed for human flu viruses would work against bird flu infection in humans. The H5N1 virus, however, appears resistant to at least two of the drugs, amantadine and rimantadine.

CHAPTER 8

VIRAL DISEASES: HEMORRHAGIC FEVERS AND ACUTE VIRAL INFECTIONS

Viral hemorrhagic fevers are highly fatal diseases that are characterized by massive external or internal bleeding or bleeding into the skin. Other symptoms vary by the type of viral hemorrhagic fever but often include fever, malaise, muscle aches, vomiting, and shock. Most viral hemorrhagic fevers are geographically restricted because they are transmitted by specific animal or insect hosts (reservoirs) that occupy narrow and sometimes localized ecological niches. Viral hemorrhagic fevers are caused by viruses of several different families, including Flaviviridae, Arenaviridae, Bunyaviridae, Togaviridae, and Filoviridae.

The most common viral hemorrhagic fevers are dengue and yellow fever, caused by related mosquitoborne flaviviruses. In the late 18th century, yellow fever epidemics in American coastal cities caused widespread panic, but the disease now occurs mainly in developing countries of Africa and South America. It is the only major viral hemorrhagic fever for which an effective preventive vaccine exists and is widely used. Most cases of dengue, seen in tropical areas, are mild and influenza-like, but all four dengue viruses may produce dengue hemorrhagic fever or its severe form, dengue shock syndrome. Dengue is unique among the fatal hemorrhagic fevers in that even severe cases can be effectively treated with simple fluid administration.

The arenaviruses cause the diseases Lassa fever (occurring in Africa), Argentine hemorrhagic fever, Bolivian hemorrhagic fever, Brazilian hemorrhagic fever, and Venezuelan hemorrhagic fever. Hantaviruses, Rift Valley fever virus (genus phlebovirus), and Crimean-Congo hemorrhagic fever virus (genus nairovirus) belong to the family Bunyaviridae. The hantaviruses, like the arenaviruses, are spread to humans by rodent contact. Hantaviruses cause Korean hemorrhagic fever and hantavirus pulmonary syndrome, which is highly fatal owing to accumulation of fluid in the lungs but features only minor hemorrhagic manifestations. Rift Valley fever, a mosquitoborne disease that is fatal in sheep and cattle, occurs in East and Southern Africa and the Middle East. Most people who contract Rift Valley fever survive, but a minority develop fatal hemorrhagic fevers, encephalitis, or severe eye disease. Crimean-Congo hemorrhagic fever, found in East and Southern Africa, the Middle East, and Russia, is a tickborne disease of cattle and other farm animals that is occasionally transmitted to humans.

The filoviruses, seen in Central and East Africa, include Ebola virus and Marburg virus. These are among the most highly fatal of the hemorrhagic fevers. Chikungunya virus, of the family Togaviridae, is the cause of chikungunya fever, a disease found primarily in eastern Africa, India, Southeast Asia, and several islands in the Indian Ocean. In the early 21st century, this disease spread to Europe, an event believed to have been tied to human travel and migration of the mosquito species that transmit the virus from person to person.

There are also several other acute viral infections that can occur in humans but that are distinct from the hemorrhagic fevers. Among the best known of these diseases are rabies, SARS (severe acute respiratory syndrome), and viral encephalitis.

CHIKUNGUNYA FEVER

Chikungunya fever is a viral disease transmitted to humans by infected mosquitoes. It is characterized by fever, headache, rash, and severe joint and muscle pain. The name *chikungunya*, which means "that which bends up," is derived from the Kimakonde language of the Makonde people. This African tribe lives on the eastern border between Mozambique and Tanzania, where chikungunya virus was first detected in an epidemic that occurred in 1952–53. The disease was given its name because severe musculoskeletal pain caused affected persons to walk in a stooped posture.

TRANSMISSION AND SYMPTOMS

The virus that causes chikungunya fever is carried by humans and is transmitted between humans by mosquitoes. Wild primates such as monkeys are suspected of serving as natural reservoirs for the virus in Africa. Outbreaks

CHIKUNGUNYA VIRUS

Chikungunya virus is an infectious agent of the genus *Alphavirus* in the family *Togaviridae*. The virus causes chikungunya fever, a disease that was first recorded in 1952–53 in an outbreak on the Makonde plateau, located on the border between Mozambique and Tanzania in Africa. The virus was initially isolated from a Tanzanian patient in 1953.

Similar to other alphaviruses, chikungunya virus is made up of a single strand of RNA that is about 12,000 nucleotides long. The RNA is contained within a protein shell, or capsid, which in turn is covered by a phospholipid layer, or envelope. A single chikungunya virion particle, which includes the capsid and envelope, is 60–70 nanometres in diameter. There are multiple strains of chikungunya virus, which differ from one another in their RNA sequences. These different strains are grouped within several distinct lineages of chikungunya virus, which are known as South/East African, West African, Central African, and Asian. Chikungunya viruses also have antigenic profiles that make them unique among viruses, including other alphaviruses. Antigens are proteins on the surfaces of virion particles that serve to promote viral infectiousness and to stimulate antibody production by the host's immune system. The antibodies generated and released into blood serum in response to chikungunya viral antigens enable these viruses to be detected by serological tests.

Nonhuman primates in Africa are believed to be the principal reservoir of chikungunya virus. The virus is considered enzootic in these animals—it circulates constantly in the African primate community but affects only a few animals at any given time. The virus is transmitted from its reservoir hosts to humans by arthropod vectors, the two known species of which are the mosquitoes *Aedes aegypti* and *A. albopictus*. The original vector of the virus was *A. aegypti*, which is native to Africa and India. However, genetic mutations enabled viral adaptation to *A. albopictus*, which is native to Asia. This mosquito is considered an invasive species, and factors involving changes in climate and increases in human travel have contributed to the subsequent spread of the mosquito and the virus, respectively, to multiple parts of the world. Where *A. albopictus* and the virus are coincident, outbreaks of chikungunya fever are likely to occur. Thus, chikungunya virus has appeared in areas of Europe and the southeastern United States and on multiple islands in the Indian Ocean largely because infected humans traveled from areas where the virus was endemic to areas where *A. albopictus* was invasive. The ability of the virus to carry out its life cycle between vector organisms and humans has facilitated its sustained spread in these geographical regions, which are distant from its nonhuman primate reservoirs in Africa.

Chikungunya virus, similar to several other alphaviruses, is known for causing severe joint and musculoskeletal pain. Symptoms of illness appear 3–7 days after viral transmission by an infected mosquito. Although the disease is typically self-limiting—most symptoms disappear within 10 days—chronic arthritis, lasting months or sometimes years, occurs in roughly 10–12 percent of cases.

of the illness historically were limited to Africa and India, where *Aedes aegypti*, the original mosquito vector described for chikungunya virus, thrived. However, viral mutation, climate change, and human travel and migration have caused shifts in the geographic occurrence of chikungunya fever. Mutations in the virus have enabled it to infect a second vector, *Aedes albopictus*, which is native to Asia but today is considered an invasive species in places with warm, marshlike environments, including certain areas in Australia, on islands in the Indian Ocean, in the southeastern United States, and in Europe. Infected humans traveling from regions where the virus is endemic to regions where *A. albopictus* is invasive have played a significant role in distributing the disease to previously unaffected parts of the world. Outbreaks of chikungunya fever typically occur following a period of heavy rain, since the resulting pools of water that form provide rich breeding sites for *Aedes* mosquitoes.

Chikungunya fever is debilitating, though it is rarely life-threatening. Onset of symptoms typically occurs within 3–7 days of being bitten by an infected mosquito, although some persons may not show signs of illness for up to 12 days. The symptoms of the disease resemble those of dengue, with acute illness characterized by sudden fever, headache, chills, nausea, vomiting, severe joint pain (arthralgia), and muscle pain. While many of these symptoms dissipate after a period of 10 days, joint pain may persist for weeks or months. Such chronic arthritis occurs in roughly 10–12 percent of patients.

DIAGNOSIS, TREATMENT, AND PREVENTION

Infection with chikungunya virus is diagnosed through serological tests for antibodies to the virus and is confirmed through reverse transcription-polymerase chain reaction (RT-PCR) detection of viral RNA. There are no vaccines or antiviral agents available for chikungunya fever. Thus, treatment is based on controlling symptoms of pain and fever. This is accomplished primarily through the administration of anti-inflammatory agents such as acetaminophen or ibuprofen.

Chikungunya fever can be prevented by managing *Aedes* mosquito populations. Using insect repellents and wearing long-sleeved shirts and pants are effective methods of preventing mosquito bites while outdoors. Secure screens in windows and doors and mosquito nets can be used to keep mosquitoes from entering houses or other buildings. In addition, emptying containers and other vessels that fill with rainwater eliminates potential mosquito breeding sites.

HISTORICAL AND MODERN OUTBREAKS

A disease similar to chikungunya fever that involved symptoms of fever and

Wearing long-sleeved shirts and pants and applying insect repellent can help prevent mosquito bites and, in turn, the infectious diseases they transmit. Yellow Dog Productions/The Image Bank/Getty Images

joint pain was described in India in 1824. The first epidemic in which the disease and the causative agent were characterized occurred in 1952–53 in an outbreak on the Makonde plateau in Africa. An outbreak in Bangkok in 1958 represented the first known incidence of the disease in Southeast Asia. Outbreaks in India, Sri Lanka, Cambodia, Vietnam, Myanmar, Laos, the Philippines, and Indonesia occurred in subsequent decades until about the mid-1980s, when the incidence of the disease in these areas decreased.

In 1998–99 chikungunya fever emerged in Malaysia, and in the early 2000s it reemerged in places such as India, Thailand, and Indonesia. The virus also appeared on Réunion, Mauritius, Comoros, and Seychelles—islands located in the western Indian Ocean. Beginning in 2005, a large outbreak occurred on Réunion that affected some 255,000 people by 2006. That same year an epidemic of the disease swept across multiple Indian states, including Tamil Nadu, Maharashtra, Gujarat, and Delhi, with some 1.25 million suspected cases reported. In 2007 chikungunya fever appeared for the first time in Europe, causing illness in more than 200 people in Ravenna, a city in northeastern Italy. The virus was believed to have been carried to Ravenna by a person traveling from an affected region of India. The unexpected outbreak of a tropical disease in this region of the world prompted concern about the invasiveness and adaptive abilities of *Aedes* mosquitoes in cool climates.

In 2009 a large outbreak of chikungunya fever occurred in Thailand. Between January and June of that year, some 24,000 cases of disease were reported. The outbreak initially affected only southern provinces—those near the border with West Malaysia, which also was experiencing an outbreak of the disease. However, by June cases had begun to appear in the northern provinces of Thailand as well. The disease also spread to Singapore, located on the southern edge of West Malaysia, and to many areas of East Malaysia, located on the northwestern edge of the island of Borneo.

DENGUE

Dengue (also known as breakbone, or dandy, fever) is an acute, infectious, mosquito-borne fever that is temporarily incapacitating but rarely fatal. Besides fever, the disease is characterized by an extreme pain in and stiffness of the joints (hence the name "breakbone fever"). Complication of dengue fever can give rise to a more severe form, called dengue hemorrhagic fever (DHF), which is characterized by hemorrhaging blood vessels and thus bleeding from the nose, mouth, and internal tissues. Untreated DHF may result in blood vessel collapse, causing a usually fatal condition known as dengue shock syndrome. Dengue is caused by one of four viral serotypes (closely related viruses), designated DEN-1, DEN-2, DEN-3, and DEN-4. These serotypes are members of the *Flavivirus* genus, which also contains the viruses that cause yellow fever, and can occur in any country where the carrier mosquitoes breed.

VIRAL TRANSMISSION

The carrier incriminated throughout most endemic areas is the yellow-fever mosquito, *Aedes aegypti*. The Asian tiger mosquito, *A. albopictus*, is another prominent carrier of the virus. A mosquito becomes infected only if it bites an infected individual (humans and perhaps also certain species of monkey) during the first three days of the victim's illness. It then requires 8 to 11 days to incubate the virus before the disease can be transmitted to another individual. Thereafter, the mosquito remains infected for life. The virus is injected into the skin of the victim in minute droplets of saliva. The spread of dengue is especially unpredictable because there are four serotypes of the virus. Infection with one type—though it confers lifetime immunity from reinfection with that type of dengue—does not prevent an individual from being infected by the other three types.

DIAGNOSIS AND TREATMENT

Diagnosis is made on clinical findings, namely, sudden onset, moderately high fever, excruciating joint pains, intense pain behind the eyes, a second rise in temperature after a brief remission, and particularly the type of rash and decided reduction in neutrophilic white blood cells. There is no specific therapy.

Therefore attention is focused on relieving the symptoms. In DHF prompt medical attention on maintaining circulating fluid volume can improve chances for survival.

Temporary preventive measures must be taken to segregate suspected as well as diagnosed cases during their first three days of illness and, by screens and repellents, to keep mosquitoes from biting more people. Fundamental in the control of the disease is the destruction of mosquitoes and their breeding places.

DENGUE THROUGH HISTORY

The earliest account of a denguelike disease comes from the Jin dynasty (265–420 CE) in China. There is also evidence that epidemics of illnesses resembling dengue occurred in the 17th century. However, three epidemics that took place in the late 18th century mark the arrival of the disease that is today recognized as dengue fever. Two of these outbreaks involved an illness decidedly similar in symptoms and progression to dengue, and both occurred in 1779—one in Cairo and the other in Batavia (now Jakarta) in the Dutch East Indies (now Indonesia), which was reported by Dutch physician David Bylon. The third epidemic happened in 1780 in Philadelphia, Pa. American statesman and physician Benjamin Rush, who treated afflicted patients during the Philadelphia epidemic, provided the first clinical description of dengue in his *Account of the Bilious, Remitting Fever*, which was published in

1789. Because all three 18th-century epidemics involved very similar diseases and occurred in port cities, it is believed that dengue virus was spread from one continent to another via ships. Thus, the spread of dengue depended on overseas survival of mosquito vectors, as well as on arrival in areas with both the necessary environmental conditions to support vector survival and a susceptible population into which the virus could be introduced. This pattern of transport probably also facilitated the emergence of new viral serotypes.

In the early 1900s Australian naturalist Thomas Lane Bancroft identified *Aedes aegypti* as a carrier of dengue fever and deduced that dengue was caused by an organism other than a bacterium or parasite. During World War II, dengue emerged in Southeast Asia and rapidly spread to other parts of the world, inciting a pandemic. Around this time the causative flavivirus was isolated and cultured independently by Japanese physicians Susumu Hotta and Ren Kimura and by American microbiologist Albert Bruce Sabin. In the 1950s hemorrhagic dengue appeared in Southeast Asia, where it became a common cause of death among children in the 1970s. The serotypes continued to spread on a pandemic level, eventually reaching areas of South and Central America, Cuba, and Puerto Rico, where in 1977 an epidemic lasting from July to December affected some 355,000 people. In the following decades the increasing incidence of dengue, particularly DHF, persisted.

In 2008 the World Health Organization reported that approximately 2.5 billion people worldwide were at risk of dengue and that the disease was endemic in more than 100 countries.

EBOLA

Ebola is a virus of the family Filoviridae that is responsible for a severe and often fatal viral hemorrhagic fever. Ebola outbreaks in primates—including gorillas, chimpanzees, and humans—and domestic pigs have been recorded. The disease is characterized by extreme fever, rash, and profuse hemorrhaging. In humans, certain strains of the virus can cause fatality in 50 to 90 percent of cases.

STRAINS OF EBOLA

The virus takes its name from the Ebola River in the northern Congo basin of central Africa, where it first emerged in 1976. Ebola is closely related to the Marburg virus, which was discovered in 1967, and the two are the only members of the Filoviridae that cause epidemic human disease. Five strains of Ebola virus, known as Ebola-Zaire, Ebola-Sudan, Ebola-Côte d'Ivoire, Ebola-Reston, and Ebola-Bundibugyo, named for their outbreak locations, have been described.

Ebola-Zaire causes death in 80 to 90 percent of cases, and Ebola-Sudan causes death in 50 percent of cases. Ebola-Côte d'Ivoire, found in dead chimpanzees in the Taï National Park in southwestern Côte d'Ivoire, can infect humans, although only two human cases have been documented, and both individuals survived. Ebola-Reston, which was originally discovered in laboratory monkeys in Reston, Va., in 1989, was also detected in laboratory monkeys in other locations in the United States in 1990 and 1996, as well as in Siena, Italy, in 1992. All the monkeys infected with Ebola-Reston have been traced to one export facility located in the Philippines, although the origin of the strain has not been identified. Similar to Ebola-Côte d'Ivoire, Ebola-Reston does not appear to cause death in humans. The fifth strain, Ebola-Bundibugyo, was discovered in November 2007 in an outbreak in Bundibugyo district, near the border of Uganda and Congo (Kinshasa). This strain causes death in about 25 percent of cases.

COURSE OF INFECTION AND TREATMENT

Viewed through an electron microscope, the Ebola virus appears as long filaments, sometimes branched or intertwined. The virion (virus particle) contains one molecule of noninfectious, single-stranded RNA (ribonucleic acid). It is not known how the Ebola virus attacks cells. However, it has been postulated that the virus produces proteins that suppress the immune system, allowing reproduction of the virus to continue unhindered. Viral hemorrhagic fevers similar to Ebola typically are carried by arthropods and rodents. The natural reservoir for the Ebola virus, however, has yet to

be discovered. Among the suspected reservoirs for Ebola are bats, primates, rodents, and insects that inhabit tropical forests in Africa and Asia. Ebola can be transmitted through contact with infected blood, bodily fluids, and possibly respiratory secretions. The virus has also been detected in the organs of patients after recovery from the fever. Unsanitary conditions and lack of adequate medical supplies may be factors in the spread of the disease.

The Ebola virus has an incubation period of 4 to 16 days. The onset is sudden and harsh. Infected persons develop fever, severe headaches and muscle aches, and loss of appetite. Within a few days the virus causes a condition known as disseminated intravascular coagulation, which is marked by both blood clots and hemorrhaging. In the case of Ebola fever, clots are concentrated in the liver, spleen, brain, and other internal organs, forcing capillaries to bleed into surrounding tissue. Nausea, vomiting and diarrhea with blood and mucus, conjunctivitis, and sore throat soon follow. A maculopapular rash (discoloured elevations of the skin) appears on the trunk and quickly spreads to the limbs and head. The patient is then beset by spontaneous bleeding from body orifices and any breaks in the skin, such as injection sites, and within the gastrointestinal tract, skin, and internal organs. Death is usually brought on by hemorrhaging, shock, or renal failure and occurs within 8 to 17 days.

There is no known treatment for Ebola fever, although immune plasma may be beneficial. Current therapy consists of maintenance of fluid and electrolyte balance and administration of blood and plasma to control bleeding. The spread of the virus can be contained by barrier nursing, handling of infected blood and tissue in isolated laboratory units, and proper decontamination of reusable equipment.

OUTBREAKS

The first outbreaks in 1976 in Zaire (now Congo [Kinshasa]) and The Sudan resulted in more than 400 deaths. A subsequent outbreak in Congo (Kinshasa) in May 1995 prompted temporary quarantine of the Kikwit region, and more than 250 people died. Later outbreaks in Uganda in 2000 and in Congo (Kinshasa) in 2002 also resulted in several hundred deaths. In September 2007 an outbreak was confirmed in Congo (Kinshasa) in the Kasai-Occidental (West Kasai) province, located in the south-central region of the country. However, while Ebola was detected in blood samples from some people that fell ill, other people were found to be infected with *Shigella*, the bacterium that causes dysentery—a disease whose symptoms are similar to the early symptoms of Ebola. As a result, although several hundred people became ill and more than 160 people died during the Ebola outbreak, it was unclear how many of the deaths were actually caused by Ebola. Less than two years later, in December 2008, a second outbreak of the disease was confirmed in

the Kasai-Occidental province. Ebola had been detected in just four people by early 2009. However, another 42 cases were suspected, and some 200 people were under close observation for infection. Although 13 deaths had been reported in association with the outbreak, samples collected from the victims did not test positive for Ebola.

In 2008, tissue samples from pigs that died of unknown causes in the Philippines were analyzed and found to contain Ebola-Reston virus. This was the first time that the virus was found in a mammalian species other than primates. Infections in pigs were unexpected and raised concerns about transmission of the virus from pigs to humans. In January 2009, antibodies to Ebola-Reston were found in five Filipinos, four of whom worked on pig farms and one of whom worked in a slaughterhouse. All five individuals were believed to have been infected with the virus through direct contact with infected pigs. The infected people were healthy and did not show signs of infection at the time antibodies to the virus were detected. To stop the spread of Ebola-Reston among pigs, Philippines officials authorized the slaughter of thousands of potentially infected swine.

PAPPATACI FEVER

Pappataci fever (also known as phlebotomus fever, three-day fever, or sandfly fever) is an acute, infectious, febrile disease caused by a phlebovirus (family

Bunyaviridae) and producing temporary incapacitation. It is transmitted to humans by the bloodsucking female sand fly (notably *Phlebotomus papatasii*, *P. perniciosus*, and *P. perfiliewsi*) and is prevalent in the moist subtropical countries of the Eastern Hemisphere lying between latitude 20° and 45° N, particularly around the Mediterranean Sea, in the Middle East, and in parts of India. It breaks out in epidemic form during the summer season following sand fly breeding. Hosts may include warm- and cold-blooded vertebrates and possibly plants and thrips (tiny winged insects of the order Thysanoptera). The sand fly can become infected as a result of biting an infected person any time from 48 hours before until 24 hours after the onset of fever. Once it has been transmitted, the virus requires 7 to 10 days to incubate, after which the sand fly remains infected for life.

In human hosts, the virus multiplies and becomes widely disseminated throughout the body. Within two and one-half to five days after exposure, there is suddenly a feeling of lassitude, abdominal distress, and dizziness, followed within one day by a chilly sensation and a rapid rise in temperature during the next day or two to 38.8–40.3 °C (102–104.5 °F). As in dengue, symptoms include severe frontal headache and postorbital pain, intense muscular and joint pains, and a flushed appearance of the face but, unlike dengue, no true rash or subsequent scaling occurs. During the first day of fever the pulse is accelerated. Usually after two days the temperature slowly returns to normal. Only rarely is there a second episode of fever. Following the febrile period, there is great fatigue and weakness, accompanied by slow pulse and frequently subnormal blood pressure. Convalescence may require a few days or several weeks, but the prognosis is always favourable. Treatment is entirely symptomatic.

Sand flies breed in vegetation within a few hundred feet of human habitations. However, these breeding places are difficult to discover, rendering larvicidal control impractical. The bloodsucking females feed only from sunset to sunrise and only at ground level, so that sleeping above the ground floor provides moderately good protection. Ordinary mosquito netting and screening are useless, because unfed female flies can pass through their 18-mesh squares. Insect repellents, such as dimethyl phthalate, when applied to exposed skin, will keep sand flies away for a few hours, but the use of insecticide sprays on verandas, on screens, around doors and windows, and within habitations will readily kill all adult sand flies that alight on the sprayed surfaces.

WEST NILE VIRUS

West Nile virus is an infectious agent belonging to the family Flaviviridae, and thus it is related to viruses that can cause yellow fever and dengue. It is, however, more closely related to viruses that can cause encephalitis (inflammation of the brain). Predominantly an infection of birds, West Nile virus is highly fatal for many avian species (e.g., crows and other corvids). A threat to human health occurs when infected birds are bitten by mosquitoes, which then transmit the virus to humans. Most human infections are inapparent or mild, causing a flulike illness that usually lasts only a few days. However, in a minority of infected persons, particularly in those older than age 50, the virus multiplies in the lymphoid tissue and circulates in the bloodstream (possibly also multiplying in leukocytes, or white blood cells) before reaching the brain, resulting in encephalitis. Symptoms of West Nile encephalitis include headache, fever, neck stiffness, disorientation, and muscle weakness. Death may result.

West Nile virus has been known and studied for decades, but historically it has been largely confined to Africa, the Middle East, and parts of Russia, India, and Indonesia, where it has caused occasional, usually minor, epidemics of denguelike illness or sporadic encephalitis. However, in recent years the virus has been imported more broadly into Europe by migratory birds. In 1999 West Nile virus was imported into the United States, spreading also into Canada and the Caribbean.

There is no specific treatment for infection with West Nile virus. In severe cases, intensive medical care is necessary, with continuous monitoring of respiratory function, management of fluid and electrolyte balance, and prevention of secondary infections.

YELLOW FEVER

Yellow fever is an acute infectious disease. It is one of the great epidemic diseases of the tropical world, though it sometimes has occurred in temperate zones as well. The disease, caused by a flavivirus, infects humans, all species of monkeys, and certain other small mammals. The virus is transmitted from animals to humans and among humans by several species of mosquitoes. Yellow fever appears with a sudden onset of fever, chills, headache, backache, nausea, and vomiting. The skin and eyes may appear yellow—a condition known as jaundice and a sign that gives rise to the disease's popular name. There is no specific treatment for those with yellow fever beyond good nursing and supportive care. However, yellow fever is an outstanding example of a completely preventable disease. People can be rendered immune to the virus through vaccination, and outbreaks can be contained by eliminating or controlling mosquito populations. Thanks to such measures, the great yellow fever epidemics of the late 19th and early 20th centuries are no more, though the disease is still present in tropical Africa and South America, where access to vaccine is sometimes lacking and the virus is held in vast natural reservoir by forest monkeys.

COURSE OF DISEASE

There are three substantially different patterns of transmission of the yellow fever virus: (1) urban, or classical, yellow fever, in which transmission is from person to person via the "domestic" (i.e., urban-dwelling) *Aedes aegypti* mosquito; (2) jungle, or sylvatic, yellow fever, in which transmission is from a mammalian host (usually a monkey) to humans via any one of a number of forest-living mosquitoes (e.g., *Haemagogus* in South America, *A. africanus* in Africa); and (3) intermediate, or savannah, yellow fever, in which transmission is from animal to person and from person to person via a number of "semidomestic" mosquitoes (e.g., *A. furcifer, A. taylori*).

The course of yellow fever is rapid. After the bite of the infecting mosquito, there is an incubation period of several days while the virus multiplies within the body. The onset of symptoms is then abrupt, with headache, backache, rapidly rising fever, nausea, and vomiting. This acute stage lasts two or three days, after which the patient either begins to recover or proceeds to a deeper toxic state marked by high fever, slow pulse rate, and the vomiting of dark blood. Death may occur six or seven days after the onset of symptoms. Because the virus destroys liver cells, jaundice (yellowing of the skin and eyes by deposition of bile pigment) is a common sign in persons with yellow fever.

The yellow fever patient's convalescence is prolonged, but, when recovery does occur, it is complete and is accompanied by a lifelong immunity. For reasons not yet understood, the mortality rate of yellow fever varies greatly. Many persons may experience only a mild infection that lasts a few days.

DIAGNOSIS, TREATMENT, AND CONTROL

In the early stages of yellow fever, its symptoms are similar to those of other tropical fevers such as malaria, leptospirosis, or dengue. Diagnosis is usually established by blood tests showing the presence of antibodies to the virus and by the patient's history of having been in an area where the disease is endemic. Treatment is supportive and is designed to correct the acid–base imbalance and electrolyte abnormalities caused by vomiting, heart failure, and kidney derangements. Good nursing and supportive care, particularly in reducing fever, are important both in maintaining comfort and in reducing mortality.

Before the introduction of yellow fever vaccine, the control of *Aedes aegypti* mosquitoes was the only procedure for preventing occurrence of the disease. Immunization is now the most practical and reliable way to prevent yellow fever in people who live in and travel to areas where it is endemic. Still, control of mosquito populations is an essential component of any program designed to prevent the spread of yellow fever, particularly in urban areas. When people must travel or live in regions where the jungle transmission cycle is maintained, individual immunization is necessary. In these regions, human cases will continue as long as there remain unimmunized persons, for there is no known practical way of eliminating the virus of yellow fever from the animal and mosquito populations of the vast tropical forests in South America and Africa.

YELLOW FEVER THROUGH HISTORY

Western Africa has long been regarded as the home of yellow fever, although the first recorded outbreaks of the disease were in central and coastal South America after the Spanish conquest in the 16th century. For the next 300 years, yellow fever, given various names such as Yellow Jack and "the saffron scourge," was one of the great plagues of the New World. The tropical and subtropical regions of the Americas were subjected to devastating epidemics, and serious outbreaks occurred as far north as Philadelphia, New York, and Boston but also as far away from the endemic centres as Spain, France, England, and Italy.

By the late 19th century there were several theories about the cause and transmission of yellow fever. The Scottish medical historian Charles Creighton, writing in the ninth edition of *Encyclopædia Britannica* (1885), pointed out that "yellow fever, in time and place,

has dogged the steps of the African slave trade." Dismissing as "altogether wide of the mark" recent suggestions that the disease might be passed by a microorganism, Dr. Creighton summarized the standard view that yellow fever was "a virulent filth-disease" brought to the New World in ships fouled by the excrement of African slaves:

> *To establish an epidemic in a distant port, it has been necessary that there should be carried thither a material quantity of the specifically poisonous harbour-filth in a ship's bilges, and that the conditions favourable to its increase and diffusion by fermentation should exist in the new soil.*

Treatment consisted of "vigorous measures" to purge the infection: doses of ipecacuanha to induce vomiting, castor oil to loosen the bowels, and enemas of cold water with turpentine to expel gas.

By the 1880s, however, new theories were already gaining acceptance. In 1881 Cuban epidemiologist Carlos Juan Finlay suggested that yellow fever was caused by an infectious agent transmitted by a mosquito now known as *Aedes aegypti*. In his investigation of Finlay's theory, U.S. Army pathologist and bacteriologist Major Walter Reed demonstrated in 1900 the transmission of yellow fever from one human to another through the bite of *A. aegypti*. Reed was further able to show that mosquitoes were the only vector of the disease. Reed's discoveries were

U.S. Army surgeon William Crawford Gorgas conducted experiments on the transmission of yellow fever by mosquitoes. His introduction of mosquito-control efforts enabled workers to complete the Panama Canal. Encyclopædia Britannica, Inc.

In 1927 researchers from the Rockefeller Institute for Medical Research, working in West Africa and the United States, demonstrated that yellow fever was transmitted by a specific virus, and over the next decade a vaccine was developed from attenuated strains of the virus (an achievement for which Rockefeller researcher Max Theiler eventually won a Nobel Prize). A distinct jungle transmission cycle, involving transmission of the virus from animal to animal and from animal to human, was first recognized in 1933, after which it became clear that the yellow fever virus was endemic in huge areas of the Amazon and Orinoco river basins in South America and in the forests of tropical central and western Africa. Outbreaks occurred periodically in these regions until major immunization programs were instituted after World War II. Since then, ravaging epidemics have not broken out as in the past. Nevertheless, the World Health Organization estimates that some 30,000 people die each year in areas where yellow fever is endemic. The disease has never crossed to tropical Asia, despite heavy travel to the region and the presence of large monkey populations that would serve as a viral reservoir. Researchers speculate that other flaviviruses endemic in Asia may stimulate some level of immunity to the yellow fever virus, that the ecology of tropical Asia does not favour the transmission cycles of the disease, and that Asian varieties of the *Aedes* mosquito may not be efficient carriers of the virus.

quickly taken up by American surgeon William Crawford Gorgas, who was able practically to eliminate yellow fever from Havana, Cuba, through the control of the *Aedes* mosquito. Gorgas's success was repeated in Rio de Janeiro, Brazil, and then in Panama during the building of the Panama Canal. The last outbreak of yellow fever in the United States occurred in 1905, when New Orleans, Louisiana, and other ports of the South were invaded.

RABIES

Rabies (also called hydrophobia, or lyssaacute) is a viral disease of the central nervous system that is usually spread among domestic dogs and wild carnivorous animals by a bite. All warm-blooded animals, including humans, are susceptible to rabies infection. The virus, a rhabdovirus, is often present in the salivary glands of rabid animals and is excreted in the saliva. Thus, the bite of the infected animal introduces the virus into a fresh wound. Under favourable conditions, the virus propagates along nerve tissue from the wound to the brain and becomes established in the central nervous system. After a time it spreads via nerves to the salivary glands, where it frequently produces a foaming at the mouth. The disease develops most often between four and six weeks after infection, but the incubation period may vary from 10 days to eight months.

Rabies virus travels quickly in a bitten animal (e.g., raccoons, skunks, bats, foxes, dogs, and cats, among other smaller animals) from the bite to the central nervous system. The disease often begins with excitation of the central nervous system expressed as irritability and viciousness. A rabid animal is most dangerous during the early stages of the disease because it appears to be healthy and may seem friendly but will bite at the slightest provocation. Wild animals that appear to be tame and that approach people or human habitations in the daytime should be suspected of having rabies.

Infected dogs usually show a short excitation phase that is characterized by restlessness, nervousness, irritability, and viciousness and is followed by depression and paralysis. After a few days they are unable to bite any more because the muscles of the throat are paralyzed. They seek only a quiet place to hide and die from the rapid spread of paralysis. Sudden death without recognizable signs of illness is also not uncommon. Dogs that develop the predominantly excited type of rabies invariably die of the infection, usually within three to five days after the onset of symptoms. Those that develop the paralytic type of rabies without any evidence of excitation or viciousness may recover on rare occasions. Paralysis of the "voice" muscles in rabid dogs may produce a characteristic change in the sound of the bark.

Rabies in humans is similar to that in animals. Symptoms include depression, headache, nausea, seizures, anorexia, muscle stiffness, and increased production of saliva. Abnormal sensations, such as itching, around the site of exposure are a common early symptom. The muscles of the throat become paralyzed so that the person cannot swallow or drink, and this leads to a dread of water (hydrophobia). The mental state of a person infected with rabies varies from maniacal excitement to dull apathy—the term *rabies* means "madness"—but soon the person falls into a coma and usually dies in less than one week owing to cardiac or respiratory failure. Sometimes rabies is characterized by paralysis without any evidence of excitation of the nervous system. In such cases the course of the disease may be prolonged to a week or more.

There is no cure for rabies. The incubation period (the time that elapses between the bite and the first symptom) is usually one to three months but in rare cases has been as long as several years. This provides a chance to interrupt the otherwise inevitable progress of the infection. The bite should be washed immediately because much, if not all, of the virus can be thus removed. The bitten patient should then receive a dose of antirabies serum. Serum is derived from horses or humans that have been immunized with attenuated rabies virus. It provides the patient with already prepared antibodies against the rabies antigen. The treatment is effective if given within 24 hours after exposure but has little, if any, value if given three or more days after infection by rabies.

Active immunization with rabies vaccine should also be initiated to allow the patient's body to make its own antibody. The safest and most effective vaccines are human diploid cell vaccine (HDCV), purified chick embryo cell culture (PCEC), and rabies vaccine adsorbed (RVA). With older vaccines, at least 16 injections were required, whereas with HDCV, PCEC, or RVA, 5 are usually sufficient. Persons at risk of rabies by virtue of occupation (e.g., veterinarians) or travel to endemic areas should receive rabies vaccine as a form of preexposure prophylaxis.

SARS

SARS (severe acute respiratory syndrome) is a highly contagious respiratory illness characterized by a persistent fever, headache, and bodily discomfort, followed by a dry cough that may progress to great difficulty in breathing. SARS appeared in November 2002 in Guangdong province, China, where it was first diagnosed as an atypical pneumonia. From Guangdong it was brought by an infected doctor to the important business centre of Hong Kong, and from Hong Kong it was quickly spread by global travelers throughout East Asia, to North America, and to Europe and the rest of the world. The most notable affected group was health care workers infected before SARS was officially identified as a distinct disease threat by the World Health Organization in March 2003. By the end of May more than 8,000 cases, most of them in mainland China and Hong Kong, had been reported, and some 800 people had died from the disease. Near-panic conditions gripped major Asian cities from Singapore to Beijing, with many schools and public buildings closing and citizens avoiding places where infection might spread. Health authorities around the world instituted strict control measures, including prohibitions on travel to and from affected countries as well as quarantines of hospitals and other places where persons were found to be infected. By June 2003 the contagion had been controlled to the point where restrictions were eased.

SARS is caused by a coronavirus, a type of virus usually associated with pneumonia and the common cold. The virus is named for the appearance in electron-microscope images of a halo-like corona, or crown, around its surface. SARS coronavirus jumped to humans from an animal reservoir, believed to be horseshoe bats. The ability of the SARS coronavirus to jump to humans undoubtedly required genetic changes in the virus. These changes are suspected to have occurred in the palm civet since the SARS virus present in horseshoe bats is unable to infect humans directly.

Among humans the virus is transmitted from an infected person through bodily secretions, usually droplets expelled by sneezing or coughing. After the virus incubates for approximately one week, the illness appears with a fever that remains above 38 °C (100.4 °F). Aches and discomfort frequently accompany the fever, and soon a dry cough appears. In a minority of patients, respiratory distress progresses to the point where mechanical ventilation is necessary. Diagnosis of SARS is made after other illnesses such as pneumonia or influenza are ruled out and a history of the patient's movements has established the likelihood of exposure to an infected person. Since no specific medication is available against the SARS coronavirus, treatment is usually restricted to easing the patient's symptoms until the illness has run its course. A SARS patient is either quarantined or advised to remain isolated, and all persons such as hospital workers or family members who come into close contact with a patient must follow strict routines of cleanliness. The patient is considered to be noninfectious 10 days after the fever subsides. Researchers have yet to establish the long-term prospects of recovered patients or the potential for recurrent epidemics, and a specific vaccine has not been developed.

VIRAL ENCEPHALITIS

Viral encephalitis is an inflammation of the brain. (The word *encephalitis* is from Greek *enkephalos*, meaning "brain," and *itis*, meaning "inflammation.") Inflammation affecting the brain may also involve adjoining structures. Encephalomyelitis is inflammation of the brain and spinal cord, and meningoencephalitis is inflammation of the brain and meninges (the membranes covering the brain). Encephalitis is most often caused by an infectious organism and sometimes by such noninfective agents as chemicals, including lead, arsenic, and mercury. Although encephalitis can be produced by many different types of organisms, such as bacteria, protozoans, and helminths (worms), the most frequent causal agents are viruses. The encephalitis-producing viruses are divided into two groups: (1) those that invade the body and produce no damage until they are carried by the bloodstream to the nerve cells of the brain (e.g., the rabies and arthropod-borne viruses) and (2) those that invade the body and first injure nonnervous tissues and then second-arily invade brain cells (e.g., the viruses causing herpes simplex, herpes zoster, dengue, acquired immune deficiency syndrome [AIDS], and yellow fever).

Symptoms common to most types of encephalitis are fever, headache, drowsi-ness, lethargy, coma, tremors, and a stiff neck and back. Convulsions may occur in patients of any age but are most common in infants. Characteristic neurological signs include uncoordinated and invol-untary movements, weakness of the arms, legs, or other parts of the body, or unusual sensitivity of the skin to various types of stimuli. These symptoms and signs and an examination of the cerebro-spinal fluid by a lumbar puncture (spinal tap) can usually establish the presence of encephalitis, but they do not necessarily establish the cause, which often remains unknown. This makes specific treatment difficult, and, even when the causative virus is known, there may be no effec-tive treatment. Treatment of encephalitis is therefore largely supportive. Patients require intensive medical care, with con-tinuous monitoring of their heart and respiratory functions and management of their fluid and electrolyte balances. Symptoms remaining after recovery from the acute phase of brain inflammation

vary considerably, depending on the type of encephalitis and on the age and general health of the patient. Many indi-viduals are weak and debilitated after an attack but recover with no serious effects. Some encephalitides may cause irrepa-rable brain damage. Prognosis depends upon the specific viral agent that caused the encephalitis. Mortality can be as high as 70 percent.

A large number of acute enceph-alitides are of the type known as demyelinating encephalitis, which may develop in children as a complication of such viral diseases as measles or chicken-pox or as a result of vaccination against such viral diseases as smallpox. Damage to the nerve cell body does not occur, but the insulation (myelin sheath) surround-ing the nerve fibres is gradually destroyed.

Encephalitis lethargica, or sleeping sickness (to be distinguished from African sleeping sickness, or African trypanoso-miasis), occurred in epidemics in Europe and in the United States about the time of World War I but has not been reported since 1930, although certain individuals may rarely exhibit residual symptoms (postencephalitic Parkinsonism). The causative agent of sleeping sickness was never established, although the influenza virus was suspected.

CHAPTER 9

VIRAL DISEASES: AIDS

AIDS (acquired immunodeficiency syndrome) is a transmissible disease of the immune system caused by the human immunodeficiency virus (HIV). HIV is a lentivirus (literally meaning "slow virus"; a member of the retrovirus family) that slowly attacks and destroys the immune system, the body's defense against infection, leaving an individual vulnerable to a variety of other infections and certain malignancies that eventually cause death. AIDS is the final stage of HIV infection, during which time fatal infections and cancers frequently arise.

THE EMERGENCE OF HIV/AIDS

Details of the origin of HIV remain unclear. However, a lentivirus that is genetically similar to HIV has been found in chimpanzees and gorillas in western equatorial Africa. This virus is known as simian immunodeficiency virus (SIV), and it was once widely thought to be harmless in chimpanzees. However, in 2009 a team of researchers investigating chimpanzee populations in Africa found that SIV in fact causes AIDS-like illness in the animals. SIV-infected chimpanzees have a death rate that is 10 to 16 times higher than their uninfected counterparts. The practice of hunting, butchering, and eating the meat of chimpanzees may have allowed transmission of the virus to humans, probably in the late 19th or early 20th century. The strain of SIV found in gorillas is known as

LUC MONTAGNIER

(b. Aug. 18, 1932, Chabris, France)

French research scientist Luc Montagnier received, with Harald zur Hausen and Françoise Barré-Sinoussi, the 2008 Nobel Prize for Physiology or Medicine. Montagnier and Barré-Sinoussi shared half the prize for their work in identifying the human immunodeficiency virus (HIV), the cause of acquired immunodeficiency syndrome (AIDS).

Montagnier was educated at the Universities of Poitiers and Paris, earning degrees in science and medicine. He began his career as a research scientist in 1955 and joined the Pasteur Institute in Paris in 1972. Montagnier served as president of the Administrative Council of the European Federation for AIDS Research.

In the early 1980s Montagnier, working at the Pasteur Institute with a team that included Barré-Sinoussi, identified the retrovirus that eventually became known as HIV. In the ensuing years there was much controversy over who first isolated the virus, Montagnier or American scientist Robert Gallo, and in 1987 the U.S. and French governments agreed to share credit for the discovery. Subsequently, however, Montagnier's team was generally acknowledged as having first identified the virus.

SIVgor, and it is distinct from the strain found in chimpanzees. Because primates are suspected to be the source of HIV, AIDS is considered a zoonosis, an infection that is shared by humans and other vertebrate animals.

Genetic studies of a pandemic strain of HIV, known as HIV-1 group M, have indicated that the virus emerged between 1884 and 1924 in central and western Africa. Researchers estimate that this strain of the virus began spreading throughout these areas in the late 1950s. Later, in the mid-1960s, an evolved strain called HIV-1 group M subtype B spread from Africa to Haiti. In Haiti this subtype acquired unique characteristics, presumably through the process of genetic recombination. Sometime between 1969 and 1972, the virus migrated from Haiti to the United States. The virus spread within the United States for about a decade before it was discovered in the early 1980s. The worldwide spread of HIV-1 was likely facilitated by several factors, including increasing urbanization and long-distance travel in Africa, international travel, changing sexual mores, and intravenous drug use.

In 1981 investigators in New York and California reported the first official case of AIDS. Initially, most cases of AIDS in the United States were diagnosed in homosexual men, who contracted the virus primarily through sexual contact, and in intravenous drug users,

FRANÇOISE BARRÉ-SINOUSSI

(b. July 30, 1947, Paris, France)

French virologist Françoise Barré-Sinoussi was a corecipient, with Luc Montagnier and Harald zur Hausen, of the 2008 Nobel Prize for Physiology or Medicine. She and Montagnier shared half the prize for their work in identifying HIV, the cause of AIDS.

Barré-Sinoussi earned a Ph.D. (1975) at the Pasteur Institute in Garches, France, and did postdoctoral work in the United States at the National Cancer Institute in Bethesda, Md. In 1975 she joined the Pasteur Institute in Paris, and in 1996 she became head of the Retrovirus Biology Unit (later called Regulation of Retroviral Infections Unit) there.

When Montagnier led efforts at the Pasteur Institute in 1982 to determine a cause for AIDS, Barré-Sinoussi was a member of his team. Through dissection of an infected patient's lymph node, they determined that AIDS was caused by a retrovirus, which came to be known as HIV. Their work led to the development of new antiviral drugs and diagnostic methods.

who became infected mainly by sharing contaminated hypodermic needles. In 1983 French and American researchers isolated the causative agent, HIV. (In 2008 French virologists Françoise Barré-Sinoussi and Luc Montagnier were awarded the Nobel Prize for Physiology or Medicine for their discovery of HIV.) By 1985 serological tests to detect the virus had been developed. According to the 2007 United Nations report on AIDS, an estimated 33.2 million people were living with HIV, approximately 2.5 million people were newly infected with HIV, and about 2.1 million people died of AIDS. Relative to previous years, the statistics for 2007 reflect a decrease in the annual number of new infections and deaths from AIDS and an increase in the overall number of people living with AIDS. Some 25 million people have died of the disease since 1981.

People living in sub-Saharan Africa account for about 70 percent of all infections, and in some countries of the region the prevalence of HIV infection of inhabitants exceeded 10 percent of the population. Rates of infection are lower in other parts of the world, but different subtypes of the virus have spread to Europe, India, South and Southeast Asia, Latin America, and the Caribbean. Rates of infection have leveled off somewhat in the United States and Europe. In the United States nearly one million people are living with HIV/AIDS, and half of all new infections are among African Americans. In Asia the sharpest increases in HIV infections are found in China, Indonesia, and Vietnam. Access to retroviral treatment for AIDS remains limited in some areas of the world, although more people are receiving treatment today than in the past.

GROUPS AND SUBTYPES OF HIV

Genetic studies have led to a general classification system for HIV that is primarily based on the degree of similarity in viral gene sequence. The two major classes of HIV are HIV-1 and HIV-2. HIV-1 is divided into three groups, known as group M (main group), group O (outlier group), and group N (new group). Worldwide, HIV-1 group M causes the majority of HIV infections, and it is further subdivided into subtypes A through K, which differ in expression of viral genes, virulence, and mechanisms of transmission. In addition, some subtypes combine with one another to create recombinant subtypes. HIV-1 group M subtype B is the virus that spread from Africa to Haiti and eventually to the United States. Pandemic forms of subtype B are found in North and South America, Europe, Japan, and Australia. Subtypes A, C, and D are found in sub-Saharan Africa, although subtypes A and C are also found in Asia and some other parts of the world. Most other subtypes of group M are generally located in specific regions of Africa, South America, or Central America.

In 2009 a new strain of HIV-1 was discovered in a woman from Cameroon. The virus was closely related to a strain of SIV found in wild gorillas. Researchers placed the new virus into its own group, HIV-1 group P, because it was unique from all other types of HIV-1. It was unclear whether the newly identified virus causes disease in humans.

HIV-2 is divided into groups A through E, with subtypes A and B being the most relevant to human infection. HIV-2, which is found primarily in western Africa, can cause AIDS, but it does so more slowly than HIV-1. There is some evidence that HIV-2 may have arisen from a form of SIV that infects African green monkeys.

TRANSMISSION

HIV is transmitted by the direct transfer of bodily fluids, such as blood and blood products, semen and other genital secretions, or breast milk, from an infected person to an uninfected person. The primary means of transmission worldwide is sexual contact with an infected individual. HIV frequently is spread among intravenous drug users who share needles or syringes. Prior to the development of screening procedures and heat-treating techniques that destroy HIV in blood products, transmission also occurred through contaminated blood products. Many people with hemophilia contracted HIV in this way. Today the risk of contracting HIV from a blood transfusion is extremely small. In rare cases transmission to health care workers may occur by an accidental stick with a needle used to obtain blood from an infected person. The virus also can be transmitted across the placenta or through the breast milk from mother to infant. Administration of antiretroviral medications to both the mother and infant around the time of birth reduces the chance that the child will be infected with HIV. HIV is not spread by coughing, sneezing, or casual contact (e.g., shaking hands), because HIV is fragile and cannot survive long outside of the body. Therefore, direct transfer of bodily fluids is required for transmission. Other sexually transmitted diseases, such as syphilis, genital herpes, gonorrhea, and chlamydia, increase the risk of contracting HIV through sexual contact, probably through the genital lesions that they cause.

LIFE CYCLE OF HIV

The main cellular target of HIV is a special class of white blood cells critical to the immune system known as helper T lymphocytes, or helper T cells. Helper T cells are also called CD4+ T cells because they have on their surfaces a protein called CD4. Helper T cells play a central role in normal immune responses by producing factors that activate virtually all the other immune

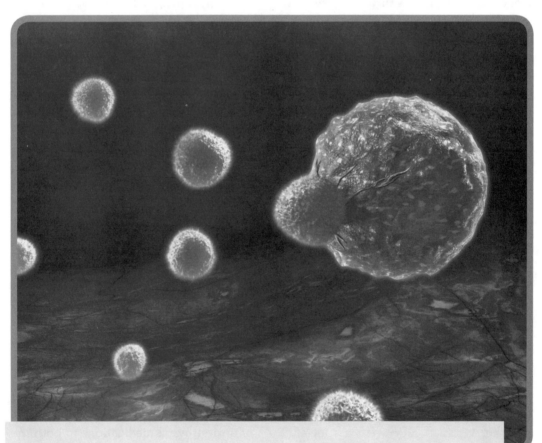

Helper T cells are instrumental in the immune response, so AIDS results after most helper T cells in the body are lost. Shutterstock.com

system cells. These include B lymphocytes, which produce antibodies needed to fight infection; cytotoxic T lymphocytes, which kill cells infected with a virus; and macrophages and other effector cells, which attack invading pathogens. AIDS results from the loss of most of the helper T cells in the body.

HIV is a retrovirus, one of a unique family of viruses that consist of genetic material in the form of RNA (instead of DNA) surrounded by a lipoprotein envelope. HIV cannot replicate on its own and instead relies on the mechanisms of the host cell to produce new viral particles. HIV infects helper T cells by means of a protein embedded in its envelope called gp120. The gp120 protein binds to a molecule called CD4 on the surface of the helper T cell, an event that initiates a complex set of reactions that allow the HIV genetic information into the cell. Entry of HIV into the host cell also requires the participation of a set of cell surface proteins that normally serve as receptors for chemokines (hormone-like mediators that attract immune system cells to particular sites in the body). It appears that the binding of gp120 to CD4 exposes a region of gp120 that interacts with the chemokine receptors. This interaction triggers a conformational change that exposes a region of the viral envelope protein gp41, which inserts itself into the membrane of the host cell so that it bridges the viral envelope and the cell membrane. An additional conformational change in gp41 pulls these two membranes together, allowing fusion to

occur. After fusion the viral genetic information can enter the host cell.

Once the virus has infected a T cell, HIV copies its RNA into a double-stranded DNA copy by means of the viral enzyme reverse transcriptase. This process is called reverse transcription because it violates the usual way in which genetic information is transcribed. Because reverse transcriptase lacks the "proofreading" function that most DNA synthesizing enzymes have, many mutations arise as the virus replicates, further hindering the ability of the immune system to combat the virus. These mutations allow the virus to evolve very rapidly, approximately one million times faster than the human genome evolves. This rapid evolution allows the virus to escape from antiviral immune responses and antiretroviral drugs. The next step in the virus life cycle is the integration of the viral genome into the host cell DNA. Integration occurs at essentially any accessible site in the host genome and results in the permanent acquisition of viral genes by the host cell. Under appropriate conditions these genes are transcribed into viral RNA molecules. Some viral RNA molecules are incorporated into new virus particles, while others are used as messenger RNA for the production of new viral proteins. Viral proteins assemble at the plasma membrane together with the genomic viral RNA to form a virus particle that buds from the surface of the infected cell, taking with it some of the host cell membrane that serves as the viral envelope. Embedded in this envelope are the gp120/gp41 complexes that allow attachment of the helper T cells in the next round of infection. Most infected cells die quickly (in about one day). The number of helper T cells that are lost through direct infection or other mechanisms exceeds the number of new cells produced by the immune system, eventually resulting in a decline in the number of helper T cells. Physicians follow the course of the disease by determining the number of helper T cells (CD4+ cells) in the blood. This measurement, called the CD4 count, provides a good indication of the status of the immune system. Physicians also measure the amount of virus in the bloodstream (i.e., the viral load), which provides an indication of how fast the virus is replicating and destroying helper T cells.

GENOME OF HIV

The genome of HIV mutates at a very high rate, and thus the virus in each infected individual is slightly different. The genetic mechanisms that underlie this individual variation have been investigated through approaches based on genome sequencing. The HIV-1 genome in 2009 was the first HIV genome to be sequenced in its entirety. Prior to this achievement, the ability of HIV RNA to fold into highly intricate structures had complicated attempts to elucidate the genomic sequence, and scientists could sequence only small segments of the genome. The HIV-1 genome is composed

of 9,173 nucleotides of RNA (nucleotides are the building blocks of nucleic acids).

Sequencing revealed that variation occurs throughout the HIV genome but is especially pronounced in the gene encoding the gp120 protein. By constantly changing the structure of its predominant surface protein, the virus can avoid recognition by antibodies produced by the immune system. Sequencing also has provided useful insight into genetic factors that influence viral activity. Knowledge of these factors is expected to contribute to the development of new drugs for the treatment of AIDS.

COURSE OF INFECTION

The course of HIV infection involves three stages: primary HIV infection, the asymptomatic phase, and AIDS. During the first stage the transmitted HIV replicates rapidly, and some persons may experience an acute flulike illness that usually persists for one to two weeks. During this time a variety of symptoms may occur, such as fever, enlarged lymph nodes, sore throat, muscle and joint pain, rash, and malaise. Standard HIV tests, which measure antibodies to the virus, are initially negative because HIV antibodies generally do not reach detectable levels in the blood until a few weeks after the onset of the acute illness. As the immune response to the virus develops, the level of HIV in the blood decreases.

The second phase of HIV infection, the asymptomatic period, lasts an average of 10 years. During this period the virus continues to replicate, and there is a slow decrease in the CD4 count (the number of helper T cells). When the CD4 count falls to about 200 cells per microlitre of blood (in an uninfected adult it is typically about 1,000 cells per microlitre), patients begin to experience opportunistic infections (i.e., infections that arise only in individuals with a defective immune system). This is AIDS, the final stage of HIV infection. The most common opportunistic infections are *Pneumocystis carinii* pneumonia, tuberculosis, *Mycobacterium avium* infection, herpes simplex infection, bacterial pneumonia, toxoplasmosis, and cytomegalovirus infection. In addition, patients can develop dementia and certain cancers, including Kaposi sarcoma and lymphomas. Death ultimately results from the relentless attack of opportunistic pathogens or from the body's inability to fight off malignancies.

A small proportion of individuals infected with HIV have survived longer than 10 years without developing AIDS. It was suspected for many years that such individuals mount a more vigorous immune response to the virus, but scientists could not explain why. Then, in 2006, a variation called a single nucleotide polymorphism, or SNP, in the *HLA-G* gene—human leukocyte antigen G, a gene that codes for a molecule that stimulates immune response—was identified in a subset of female prostitutes who had remained HIV-negative despite having had sexual contact with more than 500 HIV-positive men. In

2007 scientists identified three additional SNPs responsible for an estimated 15 percent of the variability in viral load and disease progression between HIV-infected individuals. Two of these SNPs are located in genes that code for HLA-B and HLA-C, molecules that are similar to HLA-G in that they specialize in pathogen recognition and immune system activation. The third SNP is located in a gene called *HCP5* (HLA complex P5), an inactive retrovirus first incorporated into the human genome millions of years ago that shares similarities in DNA sequence with HIV and is thought to interfere with viral replication.

In 2009 scientists discovered that HIV is capable of rapidly mutating to escape recognition by certain HLA immune molecules. In particular, researchers identified two forms of the *HLA-B* gene, known as *HLA-B*51* and *HLA-B*27*, that produced immune molecules particularly susceptible to escape by HIV. The mutation of HIV to avoid these molecules is directly correlated to the frequency at which the *HLA-B*51* and *HLA-B*27* genes occur within populations. For example, the percentage of HIV-infected individuals that carried mutant virus capable of escaping immune detection by HLA-B*51 and HLA-B*27 molecules was high in populations with the highest frequencies of the *HLA-B*51* and *HLA-B*27* genes. In contrast, in populations with the lowest frequencies of these genes, only a small percentage of HIV-infected individuals were infected with mutant virus. The ability of HIV to mutate and hence rapidly evolve to escape immune detection by the most prevalent HLA molecules is similar to the rapid adaptation and mutation of other infectious viruses such as influenza.

DIAGNOSIS, TREATMENT, AND PREVENTION

Tests for the disease check for antibodies to HIV, which appear from four weeks to six months after exposure. The most common test for HIV is the enzyme-linked immunosorbent assay (ELISA). If the result is positive, the test is repeated on the same blood sample. Another positive result is confirmed using a more specific test such as the Western blot. A problem with ELISA is that it produces false positive results in people who have been exposed to parasitic diseases such as malaria. This is particularly troublesome in Africa, where both AIDS and malaria are rampant. Polymerase chain reaction (PCR) tests, which screen for viral RNA and therefore allow detection of the virus after very recent exposure, and Single Use Diagnostic Screening (SUDS) are other options. Because these tests are very expensive, they are often out of reach for the majority of the population at risk for the disease. Pharmaceutical companies are developing new tests that are less expensive and that do not need refrigeration, allowing for a greater testing of the at-risk population around the world.

There is no cure for HIV infection. Efforts at prevention have focused primarily on changes in sexual behaviour such as the practice of abstinence and the use of condoms. Attempts to reduce intravenous drug use and to discourage the sharing of needles also led to a reduction in infection rates in some areas. The first vaccine to demonstrate some level of effectiveness in preventing HIV infection was RV144, which actually consisted of two different vaccines given in succession, a strategy known as "prime boost." Each vaccine was designed to work against strains of HIV circulating in Southeast Asia. In 2009, results from a clinical trial involving more than 16,000 volunteers in Thailand revealed that RV144 reduced the risk of HIV infection by 31.2 percent in healthy men and women between ages 18 and 30.

HIV infection is treated with three classes of antiretroviral medications. Protease inhibitors, which inhibit the action of an HIV enzyme called protease, include ritonavir, saquinivir, indinavir, amprenivir, nelfinavir, and lopinavir. Nucleoside reverse transcriptase (RT) inhibitors (e.g., abacavir [ABC], zidovudine [AZT], zalcitabine [ddC], didanosine [ddI], stavudine [d4T], and lamivudine [3TC]) and non-nucleoside RT inhibitors (e.g., efavirenz, delavirdine, and nevirapine) both inhibit the action of reverse transcriptase. Each drug has unique side effects, and, in addition, treatment with combinations of these drugs leads to additional side effects including a fat-redistribution condition called lipodystrophy.

Because HIV rapidly becomes resistant to any single antiretroviral drug, combination treatment is necessary for effective suppression of the virus. Highly active antiretroviral therapy (HAART), a combination of three or more RT and protease inhibitors, has resulted in a marked drop in the mortality rate from HIV infection in the United States and other industrialized states since its introduction in 1996. Because of its high cost, HAART is generally not available in regions of the world hit hardest by the AIDS epidemic. Although HAART does not appear to eradicate HIV, it largely halts viral replication, thereby allowing the immune system to reconstitute itself. Levels of free virus in the blood become undetectable. However, the virus is still present in reservoirs, the best-known of which is a latent reservoir in a subset of helper T cells called resting memory T cells. The virus can persist in a latent state in these cells, which have a long life span due to their role in allowing the immune system to respond readily to previously encountered infections. These latently infected cells represent a major barrier to curing the infection. Patients successfully treated with HAART no longer suffer from the AIDS-associated conditions mentioned above, although severe side effects may accompany the treatment. Patients must continue to take all of the drugs without missing doses in the prescribed combination or risk developing a drug-resistant virus. Viral replication resumes if HAART is discontinued.

Antiretroviral therapy is typically initiated once CD4 levels have fallen to 200 cells per microlitre of blood, which generally coincides with the establishment of symptomatic disease. In most patients, initiating treatment at this point provides maximal therapeutic effectiveness, in that it minimizes the severity of drug toxicities and thus the risk for discontinuance of treatment and development of drug resistance. However, studies have indicated that in patients with morbidity-increasing factors, such as coinfection with a hepatitis virus or unusually rapid CD4 decline or high viral load, initiating treatment earlier, when CD4 levels have declined to 350 cells per microlitre, can improve survival and delay the onset of AIDS-related diseases significantly. Other studies have indicated that beginning antiretroviral treatment in infants immediately following diagnosis, rather than waiting until symptoms appear, can reduce infant mortality and disease progression dramatically. Such studies have resulted in the consideration of treatment recommendations that are more dynamic today than in the past, thereby improving treatment outcomes for certain subsets of patients with HIV.

The identification of gene variations in *HLA-B*, *HLA-C*, *HLA-G*, and *HCP5* has opened avenues of drug and vaccine development that had not been previously explored for HIV infection. Scientists anticipate that therapies aimed at these genes will serve as ways to boost immune response.

WORLD AIDS DAY

The AIDS ribbon. © AbleStock.com/Jupiterimages

World AIDS Day is an annual observance aimed at raising awareness of the global epidemic of AIDS and the spread of HIV. World AIDS Day occurs on December 1 and was established by the World Health Organization (WHO) in 1988 to facilitate the exchange of information among national and local governments, international organizations, and individuals. When the first World AIDS Day was held in 1988, an estimated 90,000 to 150,000 people were infected with HIV, which causes AIDS. Within two decades more than 33 million people were living with HIV infection, and between 1981, when the first AIDS case was reported, and 2008, some 25 million people had died of the disease. As a result, AIDS awareness became increasingly concerned with educating societies about HIV/AIDS through the unification and monetary support of international organizations.

A primary goal of World AIDS Day activities is the distribution of information. Each country creates and organizes its own agenda for World AIDS Day, and some countries launch weeklong campaigns. In addition, many countries and cities hold ceremonies that serve to commence World AIDS Day activities on international, national, and local levels. For example, in the United States the president delivers an annual proclamation, and in other countries, such as South Africa, Bermuda, and Brunei, ministers of health make annual speeches drawing attention to AIDS concerns. Typical World AIDS Day activities include concerts, rallies, memorials to those who have died from AIDS, discussions, and debates. A major international symbol of World AIDS Day is the red ribbon, worn as a demonstration of commitment to the fight against AIDS. In the United States a symbol commemorating those who have died of AIDS is the AIDS Memorial Quilt, sections of which are displayed in various cities and towns throughout the country on World AIDS Day.

WHO organized World AIDS Day, developing the annual themes and activities, until 1996, when these responsibilities were assumed by UNAIDS, the Joint United Nations Programme on HIV/AIDS. In 1997 UNAIDS created the World AIDS Campaign (WAC) to increase AIDS awareness and to integrate AIDS information on a global level. In 2005 the WAC became an independent body, functioning as a global AIDS advocacy movement, based in Cape Town, S.Af., and Amsterdam, Neth. In addition to ensuring the support of leaders and AIDS organizations, the WAC prepares information that is distributed for World AIDS Day. World AIDS Day's first theme was "Communication." For 2005 to 2010 the WAC fostered the theme "Stop AIDS. Keep the Promise," which the organization used not only on World AIDS Day but also throughout the year to raise awareness of AIDS.

SOCIAL, LEGAL, AND CULTURAL ASPECTS

As with any epidemic for which there is no cure, tragedy shadows the disease's advance. From wreaking havoc on certain populations (such as the gay community in San Francisco in the 1980s) to infecting more than one-third of adults in sub-Saharan African countries such as Botswana, Swaziland, and Zimbabwe at the turn of the 21st century, AIDS has had a devastating social impact. Its collateral cultural effect has been no less far-reaching, sparking new research in medicine and complex legal debates, as well as intense competition among scientists, pharmaceutical companies, and research institutions. Since the mid-1980s, the International AIDS Society has held regular conferences at which new research and medical advances were discussed.

In order to raise public awareness, advocates promote the wearing of a loop of red ribbon to indicate their concern. Activist groups lobby governments for funding for education, research, and treatment, and support groups provide a wide range of services including medical, nursing, and hospice care, housing, psychological counseling, meals, and legal services. Those who have died of AIDS have been memorialized in the more than 44,000 panels of the AIDS Memorial Quilt, which has been displayed worldwide both to raise funds and to emphasize the human dimension of the tragedy. The United Nations designated December 1 as World AIDS Day.

Regarding access to the latest medical treatments for AIDS, the determining factors tend often to be geographic and economic. Simply put, developing nations often lack the means and funding to support the advanced treatments available in industrialized countries. On the other hand, in many developed countries specialized health care has caused the disease to be perceived as treatable or even manageable. This perception has fostered a lax attitude toward HIV prevention (such as safe sex practices or sterile needle distribution programs), which in turn has led to new increases in HIV infection rates.

Because of the magnitude of the disease in Africa, and in sub-Saharan Africa in particular, the governments of this region have tried to fight the disease in a variety of ways. Some countries have made arrangements with multinational pharmaceutical companies to make HIV drugs available in Africa at lower costs. Other countries, such as South Africa, have begun manufacturing these drugs themselves instead of importing them. Plants indigenous to Africa are also being scrutinized for their usefulness in developing various HIV treatments.

In the absence of financial resources to pay for new drug therapies, many African countries have found education to be the best defense against the disease. In Uganda, for example, songs about the disease, nationally distributed posters, and public awareness campaigns starting as early as kindergarten have all helped to stem the spread of AIDS. Prostitutes in Senegal are licensed and regularly tested for HIV, and the clergy, including Islamic religious leaders, work to inform the public about the disease. Other parts of Africa, however, have seen little progress. For example, the practice of sexually violating very young girls has developed among some HIV-positive African men because of the misguided belief that such acts will somehow cure them of the disease. In sub-Saharan Africa the stigma associated with homosexuality and the illegal nature of this sexual orientation in some countries there have discouraged gay men from seeking treatment for the disease and have severely hindered the extension of AIDS outreach programs to this population. In 2009 the incidence of AIDS among homosexual males in certain African countries was found to be alarmingly high—some 10 times higher than in the male population at large. Furthermore, many homosexual men in those areas were reportedly unaware that the disease could be transmitted from male to male. In the opinion of many, only better education can battle the damaging stereotypes, misinformation, and disturbing practices associated with AIDS.

Laws concerning HIV and AIDS typically fall into four broad categories: mandatory reporting, mandatory testing, laws against transmission, and immigration. The mandatory reporting of newly discovered HIV infections is meant to encourage early treatment. Many countries, including Canada, Switzerland, Denmark, and Germany, have enacted mandatory screening laws for HIV. Some countries, such as Estonia, require mandatory testing of prison populations (in response to explosive rates of infection among the incarcerated). Most of the United States requires some form of testing for convicted sex offenders. Other legal and international issues concern the criminalization of knowing or unknowing transmission (more prevalent in the United States and Canada) and the rights of HIV-positive individuals to immigrate to or even enter foreign countries. In 1987 the United States added AIDS to its list of communicable diseases that prevent an infected person's entry into the country. Eleven other countries—including Saudi Arabia, Libya, Qatar, Russia, and South Korea—also imposed immigration bans against persons infected with HIV.

On Jan. 4, 2010, U.S. Pres. Barack Obama lifted the U.S. ban, declaring that it contradicted the country's goal of serving as a leader in the global fight against AIDS.

In the United States some communities have fought the opening of AIDS clinics or the right of HIV-positive children to attend public schools. Several countries—notably Thailand, India, and Brazil—have challenged international drug patent laws, arguing that the societal need for up-to-date treatments supersedes the rights of pharmaceutical companies. At the start of the 21st century many Western countries were also battling the reluctance of some governments to direct public awareness campaigns at high-risk groups such as homosexuals, prostitutes, and drug users out of fear of appearing to condone their lifestyles.

For the world of art and popular culture, HIV/AIDS has been double-edged. On the one hand, AIDS removed from the artistic heritage many talented photographers, singers, actors, dancers, and writers in the world. On the other hand, as with the tragedy of war and even the horror of the Holocaust, AIDS has spurred moving works of art as well as inspiring stories of perseverance. From Paul Monette's *Love Alone*, to John Corigliano's Symphony No. 1, to the courage with which American tennis star Arthur Ashe publicly lived his final days after acquiring AIDS from a blood transfusion—these, as much as the staggering rates of infection, constitute the legacy of AIDS.

CHAPTER 10

PROTOZOAL DISEASES

Protozoal diseases are infections caused by single-celled organisms known as protozoans. These organisms may remain in the human host for their entire life cycle, but many carry out part of their reproductive cycle in insects or other hosts. For example, mosquitoes are vectors of *Plasmodium* organisms that cause malaria.

In addition to malaria, other important protozoal infections include those categorized as neglected protozoal diseases, which are part of the larger group of neglected tropical diseases. These diseases are so-named because they have received little attention from national health organizations. As a result, neglected protozoal diseases—such as Chagas' disease, leishmaniasis, and sleeping sickness, for which treatments exist—have been allowed to fester in their endemic regions, causing extreme suffering and death in many instances.

MALARIA

Malaria is a serious relapsing infection in humans that is characterized by periodic attacks of chills and fever, anemia, splenomegaly (enlargement of the spleen), and often fatal complications. It is caused by one-celled parasites of the genus *Plasmodium* that are transmitted to humans by the bite of *Anopheles* mosquitoes. Malaria can occur in temperate regions, but it is most common in the tropics and

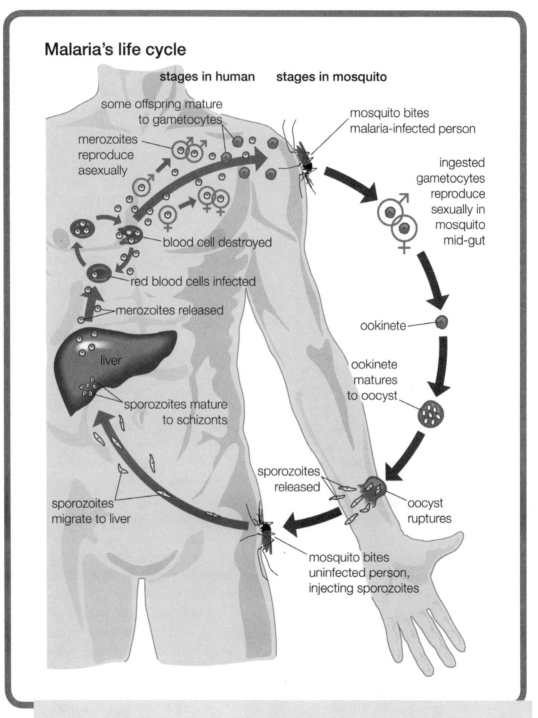

Malaria's life cycle

stages in human   **stages in mosquito**

some offspring mature to gametocytes

merozoites reproduce asexually

mosquito bites malaria-infected person

ingested gametocytes reproduce sexually in mosquito mid-gut

blood cell destroyed

red blood cells infected

merozoites released

ookinete

ookinete matures to oocyst

liver

sporozoites mature to schizonts

sporozoites released

oocyst ruptures

sporozoites migrate to liver

mosquito bites uninfected person, injecting sporozoites

Life cycle of a malaria parasite. Encyclopædia Britannica, Inc.

subtropics. In many parts of sub-Saharan Africa, entire populations are infected more or less constantly. Malaria is also common in Central America, the northern half of South America, and in South and Southeast Asia. The disease also occurs in countries bordering on the Mediterranean, in the Middle East, and in East Asia. In Europe, North America, and the developed countries of East Asia, malaria is still encountered in travelers arriving or returning from affected tropical zones. Annual cases of malaria worldwide are estimated at 250 million, with roughly 900,000 deaths resulting—most of them young children in Africa.

COURSE OF DISEASE

Malaria in humans is caused by five related protozoan (single-celled) parasites: *Plasmodium falciparum*, *P. vivax*, *P. ovale*, *P. malariae*, and *P. knowlesi*. The most common worldwide is *P. vivax*. The deadliest is *P. falciparum*. In 2008 *P. knowlesi*, which was thought to infect primarily Old World monkeys and to occur only rarely in humans, was identified as a major cause of malaria in humans in Southeast Asia, accounting for as many as 70 percent of cases in some areas. *P. knowlesi* was found to be easily confused with *P. malariae* during microscopic examination, resulting in many cases being attributed to *P. malariae* when in fact they may have been caused by *P. knowlesi*.

Plasmodium parasites are spread by the bite of infected female *Anopheles* mosquitoes, which feed on human blood to nourish their own eggs. While taking its meal (usually between dusk and dawn), an infected mosquito injects immature forms of the parasite, called sporozoites, into the person's bloodstream. The sporozoites are carried by the blood to the liver, where they mature into forms known as schizonts. Over the next one to two weeks, each schizont multiplies into thousands of other forms known as merozoites. The merozoites break out of the liver and reenter the bloodstream, where they invade red blood cells, grow and divide further, and destroy the blood cells in the process. The interval between invasion of a blood cell and rupture of that cell by the next generation of merozoites is about 48 hours for *P. falciparum*, *P. vivax*, and *P. ovale*. In *P. malariae* the cycle is 72 hours long. *P. knowlesi* has the shortest life cycle—24 hours—of the known human *Plasmodium* pathogens, and thus parasites rupture daily from infected blood cells.

Most merozoites reproduce asexually—that is, by making identical copies of themselves rather than by mixing the genetic material of their parents. A few, however, develop into a sexual stage known as a gametocyte. These will mate only when they enter the gut of another mosquito that bites the infected person. Mating between gametocytes produces embryonic forms called ookinetes. These embed themselves in the mosquito's gut, where they mature after 9 to 14 days into oocysts, which in turn break open and release thousands of

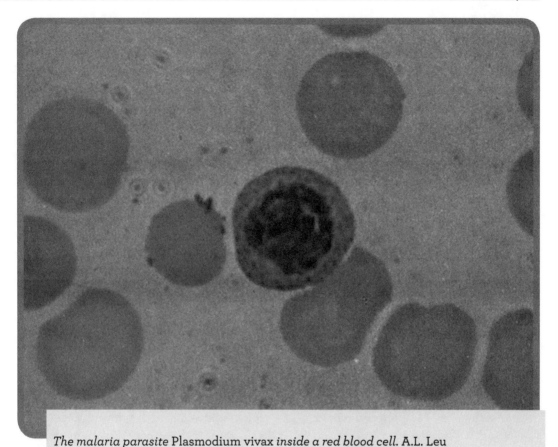

The malaria parasite Plasmodium vivax *inside a red blood cell.* A.L. Leu

sporozoites that migrate to the insect's salivary glands, ready to infect the next person in the cycle.

Typically, victims who are bitten by malaria-carrying mosquitoes experience no symptoms until 10 to 28 days after infection. The first clinical signs may be any combination of chills, fever, headache, muscle ache, nausea, vomiting, diarrhea, and abdominal cramps. Chills and fever occur in periodic attacks. These last 4 to 10 hours and consist first of a stage of shaking and chills, then a stage of fever and severe headache, and finally a stage of profuse sweating during which the temperature drops back to normal. Between attacks the temperature may be normal or below normal. The classic attack cycles, recurring at intervals of 48 hours (in so-called tertian malaria) or 72 hours (quartan malaria), coincide with the synchronized release of each new generation of merozoites into the bloodstream. Often, however, a victim may be infected with different species of parasites at the same time or may have different generations of the same species being released out of synchrony—in which case the classic two- or three-day pattern may be replaced by more frequent rigours of chills, fever, and sweating. The parasites continue to multiply—unless the victim is treated with appropriate drugs or dies in the interim.

Besides attacks, persons with malaria commonly have anemia (owing to the destruction of red blood cells by the parasites), enlargement of the spleen (the organ responsible for ridding the body of degenerate red blood cells), and general weakness and debility. Infections caused by *P. falciparum* are by far the most dangerous. Victims of this "malignant tertian" form of the disease may deteriorate rapidly from mild symptoms to coma and death unless they are diagnosed and treated promptly and properly. The greater virulence of *P. falciparum* is associated with its tendency to infect a large proportion of the red blood cells. Patients infected with that species will exhibit ten times the number of parasites per cubic millimetre of blood than patients infected with the other three malaria species. In addition, red blood cells infected with *P. falciparum* have a special tendency to adhere to the walls of the tiniest blood vessels, or capillaries. This results in obstruction of the blood flow in various organs, but the consequences are gravest when capillaries in the brain are affected, as they often are. It is this latter complication—known as cerebral malaria and manifested by confusion, convulsions, and coma—that frequently kills victims of *P. falciparum* malaria. Several strains of *P. falciparum* have developed that are resistant to some of the drugs used to treat or prevent malaria.

Infections of *P. vivax* and *P. ovale* differ from the other two types of malaria. Some of the sporozoites may remain dormant in the liver in a "hypnozoite" stage for months or even years before emerging to attack red blood cells and cause a relapse of the disease.

DIAGNOSIS AND TREATMENT

If diagnosis is based on clinical symptoms alone, malaria may easily be confused with any of several other diseases. For example, an enlarged spleen can also sometimes be caused by other less-prevalent tropical infections such as schistosomiasis, kala-azar (a type of leishmaniasis), and typhoid fever. For this reason the most reliable method of diagnosis is a laboratory test in which a trained technician is able to distinguish between the four species of parasites when a smear of blood from the infected person is examined under a microscope. The method has drawbacks, however. For example, the test is time-consuming, may fail to detect cases where there are very few parasites, and relies on a laboratory and skilled staff. Therefore, symptoms will continue to be an important clue in detecting malaria, especially for people who live in rural areas that lack sophisticated laboratory facilities but also for international travelers. Most travelers will not develop symptoms until they return home to countries where malaria may not be endemic. This makes it vital that they recognize the possible early signs of infection themselves and tell their doctors where they have been. Otherwise, their illness may be dismissed as flu, with potentially fatal consequences. In some cases, malaria can kill within hours.

An effective treatment for malaria was known long before the cause of the disease was understood: the bark of the cinchona tree, whose most active principle, quinine, was used to alleviate malarial fevers as early as the 17th century. Quinine has been extracted from cultivated cinchona trees since the early 19th century. Despite a range of side effects such as tinnitus (ringing in the ears), blurred vision, and, less commonly, blood disorders and various allergic reactions, it is still used, especially for severe malaria and in cases in which the parasites are resistant to other, newer drugs. Chief among these newer drugs are chloroquine, a combination of pyrimethamine and sulfadoxine, mefloquine, primaquine, and artemisinin—the latter a derivative of *Artemisia annua*, a type of wormwood whose dried leaves have been used against malarial fevers since ancient times in China. All these drugs destroy the malarial parasites while they are living inside red blood cells. For the treatment of malignant or cerebral malaria, the antimalarial drug must be given intravenously without delay, and measures are taken to restore the red blood cell level, correct the severe upset of the body's fluids and electrolytes, and

get rid of urea that accumulates in the blood when the kidneys fail.

In their initial decades of use, chloroquine and related drugs could relieve symptoms of an attack that had already started, prevent attacks altogether, and even wipe out the plasmodial infection entirely. By the late 20th century, however, some strains of *P. vivax* as well as most strains of *P. falciparum* had become resistant to the drugs, which were thus rendered ineffective. As a result, the incidence of malaria began to increase after having steadily declined for decades.

Unlike some infectious diseases, infection with malaria induces the human body to develop immunity very slowly. Unprotected children in tropical countries acquire sufficient immunity to suppress clinical attacks only after many months or a few years of constant exposure to *Plasmodium* parasites by hungry mosquitoes. Even then, the immunity is effective only against the specific parasite to which the child has been exposed, and the immunity wanes after several months if the child is removed from constant exposure. One interesting group that shows unusual resistance to malaria are carriers of a gene for the sickle-cell trait. Apparently, infection of the red blood cells induces the sickling effect, and the cells are destroyed along with the parasites.

International efforts have been under way for decades to produce a vaccine, so far without success. To immunize against *Plasmodium*, a different response must be elicited from the immune system at each of the parasites' different life-cycle stages. Moreover, the parasites' surface proteins change rapidly, so a vaccine based on a particular "cocktail" of proteins might not necessarily protect against all forms of the parasite that the immunized person might encounter. Still, work continues on vaccines that would aim to limit or completely prevent infection by parasites by stimulating the production of antibodies to specific surface proteins. Another strategy is to develop an "antidisease" vaccine, which would block not the infection itself but rather the immune system's responses to infection, which are responsible for many of the harmful symptoms. A third approach, known as the "altruistic" vaccine, would not stop either infection or symptoms but would prevent infection from spreading to others by blocking the ability of the parasites to reproduce in the gut of the mosquito.

While the world awaits a vaccine, the mainstay of prevention in much of Africa and Southeast Asia is the bednet treated with insecticide. For travelers to malarious regions, essential equipment in addition to a bednet would include a spray-on or roll-on insecticide such as diethyl toluamide. Travelers should also take antimalarial drugs prophylactically, though none is completely effective against the parasites. The most comprehensive method of prevention is to eliminate the breeding places of *Anopheles* mosquitoes by draining and filling marshes, swamps, stagnant pools, and other large or small bodies of standing freshwater. Insecticides have proved potent in controlling mosquito populations in affected areas.

In 2008 scientists reported the discovery of a group of proteins synthesized by *Plasmodium* that mediate the parasite's ability to make human red blood cells "sticky." Stickiness causes the infected human cells to adhere to the walls of blood vessels, allowing the parasite to evade transport to the spleen and hence destruction by the host's immune system. Scientists found that blocking the synthesis of one of the proteins involved in mediating this adherence process renders the parasite susceptible to elimination by the host's immune system. These adherence proteins represent possible targets for the development of novel antimalarial drugs.

Malaria Through History

The human species has suffered from malaria for thousands of years. In ancient Egypt malaria probably occurred in lowland areas. The enlarged spleens of some Egyptian mummies are surviving traces of its presence. Tutankhamen, who reigned as king of ancient Egypt from 1333 to 1323 BCE, may have been afflicted by the disease. In 2010 scientists recovered traces of malaria parasites from the mummified remains of his blood.

In ancient Greece, malaria appeared annually as an autumnal fever and was described by Hippocrates and others. Some scholars have surmised that malaria occurring in Greece in those times was probably caused by *P. vivax* and *P. malariae*. By the later classical period of the Roman Empire, however, malaria was a much more serious disease than it had previously been in the lands along the north shore of the Mediterranean Sea, and the association of malaria with the Pontine Marshes of the Roman Campagna was well established. Modern malariologists have attributed this increase in the severity of malaria to ecological changes associated with deforestation that had accompanied intensified agricultural activities—changes that allowed new species of mosquitoes from North Africa to be introduced and successfully established in southern Europe. Two of the introduced species were better transmitters of *P. falciparum* than any of the native European insects.

Alexander the Great, whose death on the banks of the Euphrates River in June 323 BCE was attributed to malaria, shared that fate with numerous illustrious victims. In the Italian peninsula, malaria killed Pope Innocent III as he was preparing to lead a Crusade to the Holy Land in 1216, the poet Dante Alighieri in 1321, and Pope Leo X in 1521. The artist Raphael, who painted a famous portrait of Leo X, also died of malaria (in 1520). Thirty-eight years later the former Holy Roman emperor Charles V reportedly succumbed to the disease in Spain.

Malarial fevers were associated with swamps and marshes as early as classical Greece, but the role of mosquitoes in transmitting the infection was completely unknown. Many of the early Greeks thought the disease was contracted by drinking swamp water. Later, because the Romans attributed it to breathing "miasmas," or vapours, arising from bodies of stagnant water, the disease came to be called *mal aria*, or "bad air." Since early Greek times, attempts were made to control malaria by draining swamps and stagnant marshes, but a specific treatment for the disease did not become available in Europe until the 1630s, when bark of the cinchona tree was introduced into Spain from Peru. The skillful use of "Peruvian bark" by the great English physician Thomas Sydenham helped to separate malaria from other fevers and served as one of the first practices of specific drug therapy. The lifesaving drug became much more widely available by the mid-19th century, after the active ingredient of cinchona, quinine, was successfully isolated and the Dutch began to cultivate the cinchona tree in plantations on the island of Java.

Following the introduction of cinchona bark, no comparably significant advance in the understanding of malaria or its control came until after the 1870s, when pioneering studies by Louis Pasteur in France and Robert Koch in Germany laid the foundations of modern microbiology. In November 1880 Alphonse Laveran, a French military physician working in Algeria, showed that the elements seen in red blood cells of certain patients were parasites responsible for their hosts' malaria. Laveran won a Nobel Prize in 1907 in part for this discovery. In August 1897, in India, British bacteriologist Ronald Ross discovered parasites of a malaria of birds in the stomach of a *Culex* mosquito, and in 1898, in Rome, Giovanni Grassi and his colleagues discovered a parasite of human malaria in an *Anopheles* mosquito. A bitter controversy that ensued between Ross and Grassi and their respective partisans over priority of discovery was one of the most vitriolic public quarrels in modern science. (Ross was awarded a Nobel Prize in 1902.)

Immediately following the discovery that mosquitoes were the vectors for transmitting malaria to humans, William C. Gorgas, an American army surgeon, led two campaigns of mosquito reduction using sanitary measures (drainage and larviciding) in Cuba and Panama. Gorgas's campaign made the U.S. construction of the Panama Canal possible. It also made the killing of mosquito larvae by spreading oil on their breeding sites another widely accepted means of controlling the disease. In 1939–40 Fred Soper of the Rockefeller Foundation led a vigorous effort in Brazil that eradicated the *Anopheles gambiae* mosquito, using a dust larvicide (Paris green) against the larvae and a newly discovered insecticide (pyrethrum) against the adult insects. The entire antimalarial effort was given an enormous boost in 1939 when the Swiss chemist Paul Müller discovered the insecticidal properties of DDT. (Müller received a Nobel Prize in 1948 for his work.) After a six-year campaign (1946–51) of spraying DDT in Sardinia,

malaria virtually disappeared from that Mediterranean island. Similar success was achieved in Greece, and with that, public health officials began to contemplate the possible eradication of malaria from the globe.

Even as these multiple methods of attacking the mosquito vector were being improved, direct means of attacking the parasite itself were also refined. Chloroquine, the mainstay of modern antimalarial drugs, was first synthesized in Germany in 1934, and pyrimethamine was synthesized in the United States during World War II (1939–45) by a team that included future Nobel laureates George H. Hitchings and Gertrude B. Elion. The value of the synthetic antimalarials was heightened for the wartime Allies after Japan seized Java, where the Dutch cinchona plantations were the main source of quinine. Because the synthetics were cheaper, more plentiful, and caused fewer side effects than the natural products from bark, they too raised hopes after the war of winning a global campaign against malaria.

In 1955 the World Health Organization (WHO) inaugurated its Global Malaria Eradication Campaign, to be based mainly on the spraying of insecticide in designated "malarious areas" of the world. The program resulted in the elimination of endemic malaria from Europe, Australia, and other developed areas and in a radical reduction of cases in less-developed countries such as India. However, by 1969 WHO was forced to abandon its dream of complete eradi-cation. Species of *Anopheles* mosquitoes had quickly developed resistance to DDT, and the insecticide itself fell out of favour owing to its cost and ecological effects. More disturbing was the appearance of drug-resistant strains of *Plasmodium*. The first chloroquine-resistant para-sites emerged in the late 1950s and early 1960s in Asia and Latin America, and soon almost no country with endemic malaria was without drug-resistant para-sites. In the late 1990s and early 2000s partnership-based aid programs, such as the Multilateral Initiative on Malaria and the Malaria Vaccine Initiative, were established to support the fight against malaria. Some of these programs aim to fund a broad range of malaria research, whereas others aim to fund ongoing malaria control efforts in endemic areas. These control efforts, which are the focus of antimalarial strategies established by WHO, include the dissemination of insecticide-treated netting, the provision of prophylactic drugs to pregnant women, and earlier and more effective treatment of clinical cases, preferably through the use of multidrug "combination therapy" to attack drug-resistant parasites.

EVOLUTION OF MALARIA PARASITES IN PRIMATES

The malaria parasites of humans are thought to have evolved in tropical Africa from 2.5 million to 30 million years ago (*P. vivax*, *P. ovale*, and *P. malariae* are among the oldest of the group). Scientists suspect that the human-specific parasites in existence today diverged from ancient lineages that infected early apes.

One of the first species of malaria par-asites to be discovered in primates (other than humans) was *P. reichenowi*, which occurs in both chimpanzees and gorillas. This organism, first described between 1917 and 1920, was found to be very simi-lar morphologically to *P. falciparum*, suggesting that the two must be closely related. However, subsequent studies conducted in the 1920s and '30s demon-strated that the two parasites appeared to be host-specific: *P. falciparum* could not infect chimpanzees, nor could *P. reichenowi* infect humans. This finding indicated that there existed important differences between the organisms. In 2002 the full genomic sequence of *P. falci-parum* was published, enabling scientists to more closely investigate its genetic history. According to what is known about the phylogenetic relationships of *Plasmodium* species, *P. falciparum* is the most recent of the human parasites, which may help to explain its greater virulence. Although it is widely accepted that *P. falciparum* and *P. reichenowi* share a common ancestor, research on the tim-ing of their evolutionary divergence has led to various and often inconsistent conclusions.

In 2009 and 2010 several new strains of *Plasmodium* were discovered in captive and wild African gorillas and chimpanzees. These new strains included

WORLD MALARIA DAY

World Malaria Day is an annual observance held on April 25 to raise awareness of the global effort to control and ultimately eradicate malaria. World Malaria Day, which was first held in 2008, developed from Africa Malaria Day, an event that had been observed since 2001 by African governments. The observance served as a time to assess progress toward goals aimed at controlling malaria and reducing its mortality in African countries. In 2007, at the 60th session of the World Health Assembly (a meeting sponsored by the World Health Organization), it was proposed that Africa Malaria Day be changed to World Malaria Day to recognize the existence of malaria in countries worldwide and to bring greater awareness to the global fight against the disease.

Malaria exists in more than 100 countries worldwide, and some 900,000 people die from the disease each year. However, malaria is preventable with the use of medicines and other precautionary measures, such as insecticide-treated bed nets and indoor insecticide spraying. On the first World Malaria Day the secretary-general of the United Nations, Ban Ki-moon, emphasized the need to increase the availability of bed nets, medicines, public health facilities, and trained health workers to people in areas of the world affected by malaria. Ban challenged global initiative programs, such as the Bill & Melinda Gates Foundation, the Roll Back Malaria Partnership, and the Global Fund for AIDS, Tuberculosis, and Malaria, by stating that he expected such universal access to be in place by the end of 2010. This call for action prompted the formation of the Global Malaria Action Plan (GMAP), an aggressive unified strategy designed to reduce the incidence of malaria worldwide. The three components of this strategy are control, elimination, and research. Research to develop new drugs and new approaches to prevention is fundamental to efforts aimed at first controlling and then eliminating malaria from areas severely affected by the disease. The long-term goal of the plan is global eradication of the disease by 2015.

In addition to bringing together international agencies and research institutions to discuss the progress of the GMAP, World Malaria Day also provides health organizations and scientists with an opportunity to communicate information about the disease and about current research efforts to the public. This is accomplished through public educational programs, charity events, and other community activities.

P. GorA and *P. GorB*, which were found in gorillas, and *P. gaboni*, which was found in chimpanzees. Gorillas in Africa were also found to be infected with *P. falciparum*, providing the first evidence that this organism is able to naturally infect a primate species other than humans.

This discovery raised concern over the close interactions between humans and nonhuman primates in Africa, which appear to increase the potential for interspecies parasite transmission. In contrast to human parasites, the parasites occurring in wild African apes generally do not cause severe illness. It is presumed that the long evolutionary history between apes and *Plasmodium* has dampened parasite virulency.

NEGLECTED PROTOZOAL DISEASES

Neglected protozoal diseases have a significant, negative impact not only on human health but also on the economies of the communities in which they exist. In many instances, these diseases occur in rural villages affected by poverty or urban regions affected by violence, thereby placing them beyond the resources and aid of national health departments. In other instances, however, protozoal infections simply have been designated as low-priority diseases within the context of larger national concerns, and therefore little effort has been made toward reducing their prevalence.

Awareness of neglected protozoal diseases increased dramatically in the early 21st century, largely because of programs such as the Neglected Tropical Diseases department of the World Health Organization. These efforts have led to increased funding for scientific investigation into protozoal diseases and to increased availability of resources necessary for their prevention and treatment. Millions of people worldwide are afflicted by neglected protozoal diseases, and infections such as amebic dysentery, leishmaniasis, and sleeping sickness are among the most devastating.

AMEBIC DYSENTERY

Dysentery is an infectious disease characterized by inflammation of the intestine, abdominal pain, and diarrhea with stools that often contain blood and mucus. There are two major classifications of dysentery: bacillary and amebic, caused respectively by bacteria and by amoebas.

Amebic dysentery, or intestinal amebiasis, is caused by the protozoan *Entamoeba histolytica*. This form of dysentery, which traditionally occurs in the tropics, is usually much more chronic and insidious than the bacillary disease and is more difficult to treat because the causative organism occurs in two forms, a motile one and a cyst, each of which produces a different disease course. The motile form causes an acute dysentery, the symptoms of which resemble those of bacillary dysentery. The cyst form produces a chronic illness marked by intermittent episodes of diarrhea and abdominal pain. Bloody stools occur in some patients. The chronic type is the more common of the two and is marked by frequent remissions and exacerbations of symptoms. The chronic form may also produce ulcerations of the large intestine and pockets of infection in the liver. Both forms of amebic dysentery are treated with drugs that specifically kill the amebic parasites that thrive in the intestines.

Dysentery is transmitted through the ingestion of food or water that has been

ENTAMOEBA

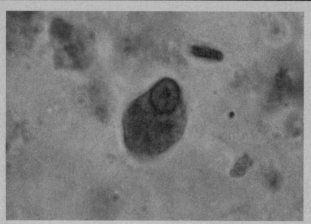

Entamoeba coli. A.L. Leu

Entamoeba is a protozoan genus of the rhizopodian order Amoebida. Most species are parasitic in the intestines of many vertebrates, including humans. E. histolytica is the cause of human amebic dysentery. The cell nucleus, which is distinctive for the genus, contains a central body, the endosome, and a ring of uniformly sized granules attached to the nuclear membrane.

Primary infection of the large intestine with E. histolytica (amebiasis) is often asymptomatic. However, diarrhea, abdominal pain, and fever may result from invasion and ulceration of intestinal walls. Secondary infection occurs in the liver, lungs, brain, and spleen after the amoebas enter the circulation by way of the portal vein and produce abscesses in these tissues. Encysted E. histolytica are transmitted through food and water, often by fly and cockroach droppings. Excystment (emergence from the cyst) occurs in the vertebrate intestine. The species sometimes is separated by size into the larger, pathogenic form and the smaller, nonpathogenic form, E. hartmanni.

Another species, E. gingivalis, is found around the gum margins, especially in unhealthy or pyorrheic mouths. It has not, however, been shown to cause disease.

contaminated by the feces of a human carrier of the infective organism. The transmission is often by infected individuals who handle food with unwashed hands. The spread of amebic dysentery is often accomplished by people who are carriers of the disease but who at the time show no symptoms. Dysentery is commonly found when people are crowded together and have access only to primitive sanitary facilities. Spread of the disease can be controlled by boiling drinking water and by adequately disposing of human waste to avoid the contamination of food.

CHAGAS' DISEASE

Chagas' disease (also called American trypanosomiasis) is caused by the flagellate protozoan *Trypanosoma cruzi*. It is transmitted to humans by bloodsucking reduviid bugs and is endemic in most rural areas of Central and South America. The disease is most often transmitted by contact with the feces of infected insects, commonly through scratching of the skin at the site of the insects' bites, or through the mucous membranes of the eye and mouth. About a week following inoculation, local signs appear, including edema (swelling) and lymph node enlargement. The patient may have fever and prostration for several weeks. The disease may then enter a chronic stage, characterized chiefly by heart symptoms, mainly disturbances of the rhythm. Heart failure sometimes occurs because of the development of the parasite in the muscle fibres of the heart and the accompanying inflammatory reaction. The infection may end in death, especially in children, or the course may be mild. Nifurtimox is the drug of choice for treating acute *T. cruzi* infections, though benznidazole is an alternative agent. There is no effective treatment for chronic infections. Prevention is centred on control of the insect carrier and screening of the blood supply to avoid transfusion of infected blood.

LEISHMANIASIS

Leishmaniasis is a human protozoal infection spread by the bite of a sand fly. Leishmaniasis occurs worldwide but is especially prevalent in tropical areas. Three major forms of the disease are recognized: visceral, cutaneous, and mucocutaneous.

Leishmaniasis is caused by various species of the flagellate protozoan *Leishmania*, of the order Kinetoplastida. These parasites infect a variety of vertebrate animals, such as rodents and canines. They are transmitted to humans by the bite of a bloodsucking sand fly, which belongs to the genus *Lutzomyia* in the Americas and to *Phlebotomus* in the Old World. Leishmanial parasites have two morphologic stages in their life cycle. One form, which inhabits the digestive tract of the sand fly, is an elongated, motile, flagellated form called a promastigote or leptimonad. The other, a round or oval, nonmotile form, called an amastigote, is found in certain cells (i.e., macrophages) of vertebrates. If a sand fly dines on an infected vertebrate, it will ingest cells containing amastigotes, which develop into promastigotes in its gut. There the promastigotes multiply, eventually entering the fly's saliva. From here they can enter another vertebrate through the wound made during the sand fly's next blood meal, thus initiating a new infection.

Depending on the species of *Leishmania* that invades a host and on the host's immunologic response to the infection, one of three principal types of leishmaniasis can arise. Visceral leishmaniasis, also called kala-azar, is produced by several subspecies of *L. donovani*. It occurs throughout the world but is especially prevalent in the Mediterranean area, Africa, Asia, and Latin America. This form of the disease is systemic, primarily affecting the liver, spleen, bone marrow, and other viscera. Symptoms, which include fever, weight loss, reduction in the number of white blood cells, and enlargement of the spleen and liver, usually appear two months or more after infection. The disease is usually fatal if not treated. Cutaneous leishmaniasis is caused by several *Leishmania* species. It is characterized by lesions that range from pimples to large ulcers located on the skin of the legs, feet, hands, and face, most of which heal spontaneously after many months. A distinction is made between cutaneous leishmaniasis of the Old World and of the New World. That of the Old World, also called Oriental sore, is endemic in areas around the Mediterranean, in central and northeast Africa, and in south and west Asia. It is caused primarily by *L. major*, *L. tropica*, and *L. aethiopica*. Cutaneous leishmaniasis of the New World, which is found in Central and South America and parts of the southern United States, is caused mainly by *L. mexicana* and *L. viannia braziliensis*. This infection may spread to the oral and nasal mucous membranes, a complication referred to as mucocutaneous leishmaniasis, or espundia. Destruction of the lips, throat, palate, and larynx can ensue. Mucocutaneous leishmaniasis may not appear until years after an initial cutaneous lesion has healed. All types of leishmaniasis are treated with compounds of antimony, such as sodium stibogluconate. Spread of the disease is prevented by controlling sand fly populations.

Sleeping Sickness

Sleeping sickness, or African trypanosomiasis, is an infection from the flagellate protozoan *Trypanosoma brucei gambiense* or the closely related subspecies *T. brucei rhodesiense*. These organisms are transmitted to humans by the tsetse fly. Sleeping sickness is characterized by fever, inflammation of the lymph nodes, and involvement of the brain and spinal cord leading to profound lethargy, frequently ending in death. Infections with *T. brucei gambiense* occur in an area extending from the west coast of Africa eastward to the East African lakes and southward to the Congo River basin. Cases caused by *T. brucei rhodesiense* are limited to the highlands of central East Africa.

The vast majority of human infections result from inoculation with the trypanosome by tsetse flies as they suck human blood. The flies have become infected while feeding on the blood of people or other mammals already infected. Usually 12 to 15 days elapse before such a fly becomes infective toward humans. During this time the trypanosomes multiply by binary division in the midgut of the fly, then migrate to the salivary glands, and pass out of the fly's proboscis in droplets of saliva during the fly's bloodsucking.

After an incubation period in humans lasting one to two weeks, the trypanosomes are found in significant numbers in the circulating blood. Next the lymph nodes and spleen are invaded, becoming swollen, soft, and tender. The marked enlargement of the lymph nodes at the back of the neck (known as Winterbottom's sign) is a common sign of the disease. Irregular fever and delayed sensation to pain are also characteristic symptoms at this stage. In the more severe Rhodesian, or East African, form of sleeping sickness, the toxemia becomes so profound that the patient soon dies. In the Gambian, or West African, type, by contrast, the trypanosomes proceed to invade the brain and spinal cord. The resulting neurological symptoms include severe headache, mental dullness and apathy, a weary shuffling gait, tremors, spastic or flaccid paralysis, chorea, and a profound sleepiness that develops during a meal or when the patient is standing or walking. These symptoms are followed by increasing emaciation, coma, and death. The Gambian form of sleeping sickness usually causes death in two or three years, but in some Africans a tolerance to the infection develops, and the patient may continue to live for many years as a carrier of the parasites.

The earlier sleeping sickness is diagnosed and treated, the greater are the chances for recovery. Diagnosis is made by microscopic examination of blood and lymph for the presence of trypanosomes and of cerebrospinal fluid for increased levels of white blood cells. Information obtained from these tests is then used to determine the stage of disease and course of treatment.

Suramin is effective for early stages of either form of sleeping sickness. Eflornithine is used for the early stages of the Gambian type, with pentamidine used as an alternative. For later stages involving the central nervous system, the Gambian form is treated with eflornithine, which replaced the highly toxic and less-effective organoarsenic agent melarsoprol. Suramin plus tryparsamide, a synthetic arsenical, may be used as an alternative to eflornithine. All treatment of *T. brucei rhodesiense* infection is useless once the fulminating toxemic stage has developed. Researchers have been investigating eflornithine-based combination therapies for Gambian sleeping sickness. The most effective combination has been eflornithine used in conjunction with nifurtimox, an agent used to treat Chagas' disease.

Sleeping sickness is still prevalent in parts of sub-Saharan Africa, and some regions that are heavily infested with tsetse flies are virtually uninhabitable because of the risks posed by the disease. Heroic efforts have been made to control sleeping sickness, including (1) isolation and proper treatment of all infected persons, including large numbers of asymptomatic chronic carriers, (2) protection of humans from bites of tsetse flies by the use of insecticides and by maintaining extensive clearings around villages and residence compounds, (3) prophylactic doses of suramin or of diamidine compounds once every 60 to 90 days for persons who must enter the jungle, so that they will not become infected from tsetse fly bites, and (4) occasional removal of entire villages from endemic to disease-free zones. Some have suggested that entire populations of wild animals be exterminated, because they tend to become reservoirs of the disease.

TOXOPLASMOSIS

Toxoplasmosis is an infection of tissue cells of the central nervous system, spleen, liver, and other organs by a parasite known as *Toxoplasma gondii*. Infection occurs in domestic and wild animals, birds, and humans and is worldwide in distribution. It is estimated that 30 to 50 percent of the world's human population carries demonstrable antibodies (indicating previous exposure), but overt symptoms are rare in adults. Swollen glands and fever are the most common findings in those who have any symptoms.

Organisms of the genus *Toxoplasma* reproduce by fission or internal budding. They move by a gliding motion, lacking either flagella or pseudopodia. The mode of transmission of the organisms is unknown, although they can be passed from mother to fetus through the placenta. Congenital toxoplasmosis may result in stillbirth or abortion. Infected infants may show various symptoms including jaundice, encephalitis, mental defects, and eye disease. Siblings of an infected infant are not usually affected.

CHAPTER 11

INFECTIOUS DISEASES: WORMS, PRIONS, AND FUNGI

Infectious diseases caused by worms, prions, and fungi tend to occur much less often in the global population than diseases caused by viruses, bacteria, and protozoans. But despite their relatively low prevalence, these conditions can cause severe and sometimes fatal illness in humans. Worms, prions, and fungi all infest particular animals, which often serve important roles in the organisms' life cycles and in their transmission to humans.

Prions are notably unique infectious agents. In contrast to worms and fungi, prions are not organisms. Rather, they are abnormal proteins that are found in the brain and that are capable of causing degeneration of nervous system function. Since the discovery of prions in the early 1980s, the diseases they cause have been the source of intense scientific study.

INFECTIOUS WORMS AND INTESTINAL DISEASE

Infectious worms often enter the body via contaminated food and water, and they typically burrow into cells and tissues. The different symptoms caused by infestation is a reflection of the different tissues the worms invade. In many cases, worms extract important nutrients from cells, leading to tissue degeneration, weight loss, and nutrient deficiencies. Examples of infectious diseases caused by worms include cestodiasis, filariasis, and onchocerciasis.

CESTODIASIS

Cestodiasis is an infestation with cestodes, a group of flattened and tapelike hermaphroditic worms that are intestinal parasites in humans and other animals, producing larvae that may invade body tissues. Because of the tapelike appearance of the worms, this disease is sometimes referred to as tapeworm infestation.

For humans there are two kinds of tapeworm infestations: (1) intestinal cestodiasis, in which the mature worm lives in the lumen of the intestine, producing eggs that are evacuated in the feces and develop further in other animal hosts, and (2) visceral and somatic cestodiasis, in which the larvae form lesions in body organs. Thirty or more species of tapeworms cause intestinal cestodiasis in humans. The more common ones include *Taenia saginata*, or beef tapeworm, about 4.5 to 6 metres (15 to 20 feet) long; *Taenia solium*, or pork tapeworm, about 2 to 3 metres (7 to 10 feet) long; and *Diphyllobothrium latum*, about 9 metres (30 feet) long, acquired by the eating of undercooked beef, pork, or fish that harbour larval forms of the worms. *Hymenolepis nana*, or dwarf tapeworm, only a few centimetres long, releases eggs that require no intermediate hosts. It is possibly the most common cestode found in humans, affecting chiefly children. Symptoms of intestinal cestodiasis include abdominal pain that may be relieved by eating and that may be associated with distention, flatulence, and nausea. Often, however, there are no symptoms, and first notice of infestation may occur only when segments of the worms are passed in the stools. Treatment may involve surgery or the use of antiparasitic drugs.

Visceral and somatic cestodiasis include the following infections: echinococcosis, or hydatic disease, and sparganosis. Echinococcosis is caused by the larval stage of *Echinoccocus granulosus* or *E. multilocularis*. In humans the first organism produces cystic, slowly expanding lesions principally involving the liver and lungs. The second organism produces an alveolar (pitted) type of lesion that progresses rapidly, may occasionally form lesions in the brain and bones, and is invariably fatal. The symptoms of echinococcosis are generally those of a slowly growing tumour and vary depending on the body structure involved. The adult worm lives mainly in dogs, and human infestation is contracted by the ingestion of eggs present in dog excreta. Surgical removal of the lesions is the only cure.

Sparganosis is caused by the *Spirometra mansoni* larva, which may be acquired by drinking water that contains water fleas harbouring the first larval stage. The larvae may grow to a length of 30 cm (12 inches) in the abdominal wall or in the region of the eye socket. Surgical removal of the larva is the current treatment.

TAPEWORM

A tapeworm, or cestode, is any member of the invertebrate class Cestoda (phylum Platyhelminthes), a group of parasitic flatworms containing about 5,000 species. Tapeworms, which occur worldwide and range in size from about 1 mm (0.04 inch) to more than 15 metres (50 feet), are internal parasites, affecting certain invertebrates and the liver or digestive tracts of all types of vertebrates—including humans, domestic animals, and other food animals, such as fish. Some attack a single host, others require one or two intermediate hosts as well as a final, or definitive, host during their life cycle. The disease caused by tapeworms is known as cestodiasis.

Tapeworms are bilaterally symmetrical (i.e., the right and left sides are similar). Some consist of one long segment, whereas others have a definite head, followed by a series of identical segments called proglottids. The head, or scolex, bears suckers and often hooks, which are used for attachment to the host. The body covering is a tough cuticle, through which food is absorbed. There is neither a mouth nor a digestive tract. Tapeworms also lack a circulatory system and an organ specialized for gas exchange.

Most tapeworms are hermaphroditic (i.e., functional reproductive organs of both sexes occur in the same individual). They are usually self-fertilizing, and gonads of both sexes also occur within a single proglottid. The life cycle is complex. The pork tapeworm (Taenia solium), found wherever raw pork is eaten, lives in the human intestine in its adult stage. Each proglottid, following fertilization, may contain as many as 40,000 embryos encased in separate capsules. If the embryos, which pass out with the host's feces, are eaten by a mammal such as a dog, camel, pig, monkey, or human, the larva emerges in the digestive tract. It bores through the intestinal wall into a blood vessel and is carried to muscle tissue in which it forms a protective capsule (encysts) and is called a cysticercus, or bladder worm. If the cysticercus is eaten alive in raw meat, it attaches itself to the host's intestine and develops directly into a mature adult.

The life cycle of the beef tapeworm (Taenia saginata), which occurs worldwide where beef is eaten raw or improperly cooked, is much like that of the pork tapeworm. Humans are the definitive host, and cattle serve as the intermediate host.

The fish tapeworm (Dibothriocephalus latus, or Diphyllobothrium latum), most common in waters of the Northern Hemisphere, infests humans and other mammals that eat fish, particularly bears and dogs. Fertilized eggs pass from the host's body in the feces. In a water medium they develop into a hairlike larva and are eaten by tiny crustaceans, which, in turn, are eaten by a fish. In the fish, the tapeworm larva encysts in muscle tissue. When the fish is eaten by a mammal, the larva attaches to the mammalian intestine and develops into a mature adult. Fish hosts of this tapeworm include trout, salmon, pike, and perch.

DRACUNCULIASIS

Dracunculiasis is an infestation with the guinea worm (*Dracunculus medinensis*; also called medina worm or dragon worm) of the phylum *Nematoda*. The guinea worm, a common parasite of humans in tropical regions of Asia and Africa, has also been introduced into the West Indies and tropical South America. A variety of other mammals are also parasitized by guinea worms.

The female worm grows to a length of 50 to 120 cm (about 20 to 48 inches), while the male (which is rarely found because it dies upon mating within a human or other host) measures only 12 to 29 mm (about 0.5 to 1.1 inches). Both sexes live in the connective tissue of various organs of the host. Females may live for 10 to 14 months. The female bores close to the skin surface, at which point a blister develops and finally bursts. Millions of larvae are released with the blister fluid. If the larvae are discharged into a watery medium and are eaten by *Cyclops*, an aquatic crustacean, they develop in the crustacean's body into larvae capable of infecting humans.

Humans become infected by drinking water containing the barely visible flealike crustacean containing the worm larvae. Gastric juices kill *Cyclops*, and the guinea worm larvae then bore from the human host's intestinal tract into blood vessels. They are carried to connective tissue areas, where they soon develop into adults. Adult worms slowly emerge from blisters, especially on the victim's legs or feet. When the victim enters a pond, stream, or other water, the released larvae are eaten by the crustaceans, to continue the cycle.

For humans the disease dracunculiasis can be extremely debilitating and painful, with worms slowly emerging from open blisters. The open blisters are also a common point of entry for other infections, such as tetanus. Several thousand people are currently infected by guinea worms each year, primarily in Ghana, Mali, the Sudan, and Ethiopia.

FILARIASIS

Filariasis is a group of infectious disorders caused by threadlike nematodes of the superfamily Filarioidea. These organisms invade the subcutaneous tissues and lymphatics of mammals, producing reactions varying from acute inflammation to chronic scarring. In the form of heartworm, it may be fatal to dogs and other mammals.

In the human body the female nematode gives birth to elongated embryos, the microfilariae, which migrate through the peripheral blood and skin, from which they are taken by bloodsucking insects. Within the insect carrier, the microfilariae grow into motile, infective larvae that, at the insect's next blood meal, are introduced into the human host, where they reach maturity in about a year. The term *filariasis* is commonly used to designate bancroftian filariasis, caused by *Wuchereria bancrofti*, organisms that are widely distributed in tropical and subtropical regions of the world and are transmitted to humans by mosquitoes, usually *Culex fatigans*. The nematode lives principally in the lymph nodes and lymph vessels, notably those draining the legs and genital area, where the adult worms induce allergic reactions in the sensitized tissues.

The initial inflammatory stage is characterized by granulomatous lesions, swelling, and impaired circulation. This stage is followed by enlargement of the lymph nodes and dilation of the lymph channels, which, over the years, harden and become infiltrated and clogged with fibrous tissue elements, resulting in some of the untreated cases in the condition known as elephantiasis, which is typically associated with the gross expansion of the tissues of the legs and scrotum. The most effective therapeutic drugs are diethylcarbamazine and sodium caparsolate, which kill the adult worms and microfilariae.

The form of filariasis known as filariasis malayi closely resembles bancroftian filariasis in its symptoms and pathological changes. It is caused by *Brugia malayi*, found chiefly in the Far East. Onchocerciasis (river blindness) is caused by *Onchocerca volvulus*, which is transmitted to humans by flies of the genus *Simulium*, which breed along fast-moving streams. Loiasis, prevalent in West and Central Africa, especially along the Congo River, is caused by *Loa loa* and transmitted by flies of the genus *Chrysops*. It is characterized by transient areas of allergic inflammation in the tissues beneath the skin, called calabar swellings. Adult worms may sometimes be visible beneath the conjunctiva (the delicate membrane lining the eyelids and covering the exposed surface of the eyeball). Loiasis produces irritation but seldom permanent damage. Treatment includes surgical removal of the worms from the conjunctiva and drug therapy. Other forms of filariasis are caused by *Acanthocheilonema perstans* and *Mansonella ozzardi* and are not in most cases associated with specific symptoms. The prevention of filariasis relies heavily on insecticides and insect repellents.

ONCHOCERCIASIS

Onchocerciasis, or river blindness, is a filarial disease caused by the helminth *Onchocerca volvulus*, which is transmitted to humans by the bite of the black fly *Simulium*. The disease is found chiefly in Mexico, Guatemala, and Venezuela in the Americas and in sub-Saharan Africa in a broad belt extending from Senegal on the west coast to Ethiopia on the east. In Africa its northern edge is about 15° N of the equator, and it extends as far south as Angola and Tanzania. It has also been reported in Colombia, northern Sudan, and Yemen.

Onchocerciasis is often called river blindness because the flies that transmit the disease breed on rivers and mostly affect riverine populations. Blindness is caused by dead microfilariae—the larvae that can be produced for some 15 to 18 years by adult worms—inside the eye.

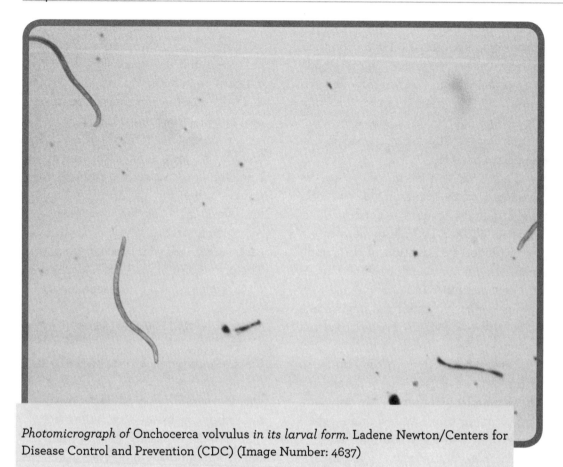

Photomicrograph of Onchocerca volvulus *in its larval form.* Ladene Newton/Centers for Disease Control and Prevention (CDC) (Image Number: 4637)

These disintegrating bodies damage surrounding tissue (often the cornea), and if the reproducing adult worms are not attacked, blindness will result. River blindness is common in savannah areas of Africa and in Guatemala and Mexico. In the forest areas (as opposed to the savannah), transmission of onchocerciasis is perennial rather than seasonal and blindness is rare.

Other symptoms of the disease include changes in skin pigmentation, dermal swelling, papules, and lichen-ification of the skin. In newly acquired infections severe itching is common. Nodules that may grow as large as a pigeon egg are found in the pelvic region or in the upper thorax and head region. In Yemen and northern Sudan a type of onchocerciasis called sowda, with infection localized in one leg, is the most common form.

The World Health Organization established a program to control the black fly in West Africa by spraying breeding sites with insecticides. In addition to spraying, a major goal of the

FILARIAL WORM

Filarial worms are parasitic worms of the family Filariidae (phylum Nematoda) that usually require two hosts, an arthropod (the intermediate host) and a vertebrate (the primary host), to complete the life cycle. The larval phase occurs within the body of a biting insect. The mature (reproductive) phase occurs in the body of an animal bitten by the insect.

The female worm produces large numbers of microscopic, active embryos called microfilariae that pass into the bloodstream of the primary host. The microfilariae may then enter the body of an insect as the insect bites the infected animal. The microfilariae grow into larvae in the insect's muscles and may then be passed to the primary host when the insect bites an animal. The larvae reach adulthood within the vertebrate host, and the cycle repeats. In mammals filarial worms cause a group of infectious disorders including heartworm, elephantiasis, and river blindness. These disorders are known collectively as filariasis. At present, more than 200 million people are infected with filarial parasites.

program was to make treatment available in all affected regions. A drug known as ivermectin, originally developed in the 1970s for use against livestock parasites, is the most effective drug available for river blindness. One dose each year is sufficient. Though it does not kill the adult parasite, it eliminates the microfilariae and is surprisingly safe and effective.

SCHISTOSOMIASIS

Schistosomiasis (also called bilharzia, or bilharziasis) is a group of chronic disorders caused by small, parasitic flatworms (family Schistosomatidae) commonly called blood flukes. Schistosomiasis is characterized by inflammation of the intestines, bladder, liver, and other organs. Next to malaria, it is probably humanity's most serious parasitic infection, being endemic to some 74 countries and affecting at least 200 million people yearly in Africa, Asia, South America, and the Caribbean. Schistosomiasis is most prevalent in rural communities where hygiene is poor because of poverty or the lack of infrastructure to support adequate health care services. The disease is ordinarily contracted by working, bathing, or swimming in water populated by snails that carry the worms. The parasites were first identified as a cause of the disease in the 1850s by Theodor Bilharz, a German pathologist working in Egypt.

There are three main types of schistosomiasis, caused by closely related organisms: (1) Japonica, or Eastern, schistosomiasis is caused by *Schistosoma japonicum*, found in Japan, southern China, the Philippines, Thailand, and Indonesia. (2) Manson's, or intestinal, schistosomiasis is caused by *S. mansoni*, found in Africa, the Middle East, the

Caribbean, and northern South America. (3) Vesical, or urinary, schistosomiasis is caused by *S. haematobium*, found throughout Africa and the Middle East.

Depending on the species of worm, the female fluke, 10 to 25 mm (0.4 to 1 inch) long, releases 300 to 3,500 eggs daily into the blood. The eggs find their way into the intestine or bladder and are evacuated in the feces or urine. On contact with freshwater, the eggs hatch, releasing ciliated larvae that swim about until they find an appropriate snail host, in which they develop further. Fork-tailed larvae, the cercariae, subsequently emerge from the snail into the water and, upon contact with the skin of a mammal, drop their tails and penetrate the tissues, getting into the blood circulation, where they feed.

The clinical course of schistosomiasis usually begins with an allergic reaction to the parasites and their by-products. Symptoms may include inflammation, cough, late-afternoon fever, skin eruption (giant urticaria), and swelling and tenderness of the liver. There may then be blood in the stools and urine in the more acute stage. The chronic stage of the disease is characterized by the gradual impactment of eggs into the walls of the body organs, leading to fibrous thickening and loss of elasticity. In the intestinal types there may be serious liver damage. In urinary schistosomiasis the eggs in the bladder may become focuses of stone formation. Fibrosis may extend to the pelvic organs, and there may be secondary bacterial infection of the urinary tract. Occasionally, eggs may also cause lesions of such organs as the brain and lungs. During autopsy, fluke eggs have been detected in almost all body structures. Unless exposure is overwhelming, however, early diagnosis and persistent treatment usually ensure recovery.

Diagnosis is established by a history of residence in or travel to areas where schistosomiasis is endemic, by the presence of blood in the stool or urine, and by the presence of the fluke in a blood smear. Treatment is by drugs aimed at killing the adult worms, which, if undisturbed, can live for 20 years and continue to cause damage. Several drugs have been used, but praziquantel, delivered orally, is the drug of choice. In efforts to control snail populations, such molluscicides as sodium pentachlorophenate, dinitro-o-cyclohexylphenol, and copper sulfate have been used extensively but with uneven success.

In 2009 the genomes of *S. japonicum* and *S. mansoni* were sequenced in their entirety. These sequences revealed new details about the basic biology of the parasites, as well as about the various factors that underlie parasite infectiousness. The findings derived from *Schistosoma* genomics studies are being used to guide the development of new treatments for the disease.

PRIONS

A prion is an abnormal form of a normally harmless protein found in the brain that is responsible for a variety of fatal neurodegenerative diseases of both animals and humans called transmissible spongiform encephalopathies. In the early 1980s the American neurologist Stanley B. Prusiner and colleagues identified the "proteinaceous infectious particle," a name that was shortened to "prion" (pronounced "pree-on"). Prions can enter the brain through infection, or they can arise from mutations in the gene that encodes the protein. Once present in the brain prions multiply by inducing benign proteins to refold into the abnormal shape. This mechanism is not fully understood, but another protein normally found in the body may also be involved. The normal protein structure is thought to consist of a number of flexible coils called alpha helices. In the prion protein some of these helices are stretched into flat structures called beta strands. The normal protein conformation can be degraded rather easily by cellular enzymes called proteases, but the prion protein shape is more resistant to this enzymatic activity. Thus, as prion proteins multiply they are not broken down by proteases and instead accumulate within nerve cells, destroying them. Progressive nerve cell destruction eventually causes brain tissue to become filled with holes in a spongelike, or spongiform, pattern.

Diseases caused by prions that affect humans include: Creutzfeldt-Jakob disease, Gerstmann-Sträussler-Scheinker disease, fatal familial insomnia, and kuru. Prion diseases affecting animals include scrapie, bovine spongiform

encephalopathy (commonly called mad cow disease), and chronic wasting disease of mule deer and elk. For decades physicians thought that these diseases resulted from infection with slow-acting viruses, so-called because of the lengthy incubation times required for the illnesses to develop. These diseases were, and sometimes still are, referred to as slow infections. The pathogenic agent of these diseases does have certain viral attributes, such as extremely small size and strain variation, but other properties are atypical of viruses. In particular, the agent is resistant to ultraviolet radiation, which normally inactivates viruses by destroying their nucleic acid.

Prions are unlike all other known disease-causing agents in that they appear to lack nucleic acid (i.e., DNA or RNA) which is the genetic material that all other organisms contain. Another unusual characteristic of prions is that they can cause hereditary, infectious, and sporadic forms of disease—for example, Creutzfeldt-Jakob disease manifests in all three ways, with sporadic cases being the most common. Prion proteins can act as infectious agents, spreading disease when transmitted to another organism, or they can arise from an inherited mutation. Prion diseases also show a sporadic pattern of incidence, meaning that they seem to appear in the population at random. The underlying molecular process that causes the prion protein to form in these cases is unknown. Other neurodegenerative disorders, such as Alzheimer disease or Parkinson disease, may arise from molecular mechanisms similar to those that cause the prion diseases.

BOVINE SPONGIFORM ENCEPHALOPATHY

Bovine spongiform encephalopathy (BSE; or mad cow disease) is a fatal neurodegenerative disease of cattle. BSE is caused by an infectious agent that has a long incubation period, between two and five years. Signs of the disease include behavioral changes, such as agitation and nervousness, and a progressive loss of muscular coordination and locomotive function. In advanced stages the animal frequently loses weight, shows fine muscular contractions over its neck and body, walks in an abnormal and exaggerated manner, and may isolate itself from the herd. Death usually follows within a year of the onset of symptoms. No treatment or palliative measures are known.

First recognized in cattle in the United Kingdom in 1986, BSE became epidemic there, particularly in southern England. Cases also were reported in other parts of Europe and in Canada. The disease is similar to the neurodegenerative disease of sheep called scrapie. It is thought to have arisen when cattle were fed high-protein supplements made from ruminant carcasses and offal (the trimmings of butchered animals). Although animal remains had been used as a source of dietary supplements for several decades without problems, modifications to the rendering process—specifically, reduction in the temperatures used and discontinuance of certain solvents—in the early 1980s were followed by the outbreak of BSE. The timing of events suggested that the modified process no longer incapacitated the infectious agent. In 1988, on the basis of this inferred connection, the British government banned the use of animal-derived protein supplements. The following year the U.S. Department of Agriculture banned the import of live ruminants from countries known to have BSE, and in 1997 both the United States and Canada implemented bans on the use of animal-derived proteins in ruminant feed. From 1986 to 2008 nearly 185,000 cases of BSE were confirmed in the United Kingdom. In contrast, through February 2008 a total of just 16 cases of BSE were confirmed in North America, with the majority of cases occurring in Canadian-born cattle. Because of heightened awareness of increasing prevalence of BSE in Canadian cattle, Canada enhanced its feed ban in 2007 to prohibit the inclusion of "specified risk materials," as well as animal proteins, from all animal feeds.

BSE, scrapie, and similar diseases in other species, such as Creutzfeldt-Jakob disease and kuru in humans, are categorized as transmissible spongiform encephalopathies. They are so named because the brain tissue of organisms with the disease becomes pitted with holes in a spongelike pattern. The cause of these diseases is attributed to an unusual infectious agent called a prion. The prion is a modified form of a normally harmless protein found in the brain of mammals and birds. In its aberrant form, however, the prion protein builds up in nerve cells as it multiplies. This accumulation somehow damages these cells and leads to the characteristic neurodegeneration. It is suspected that there also exists an atypical strain of BSE, which arises spontaneously (as opposed to orally through the ingestion of contaminated feed) and leads to a distinct prion disease characterized by a lack of pitted holes in the brain.

After the emergence of BSE, concern grew over a possible relationship between the animal disease and the occurrence of Creutzfeldt-Jakob disease in people. Beginning in the mid-1990s a new variant form of Creutzfeldt-Jakob disease (nvCJD) took the lives of dozens of people in Europe. In experiments with mice, researchers found that prions from human cases of nvCJD caused a disease pattern similar to that caused by prions from cows with BSE. The result suggested that the human infection is linked to BSE.

CREUTZFELDT-JAKOB DISEASE

Creutzfeldt-Jakob disease is a rare fatal degenerative disease of the central nervous system. Creutzfeldt-Jakob disease occurs throughout the world at an incidence of one person in a million. However, among certain populations, such as Libyan Jews, rates are somewhat higher. The disease most often occurs in adults between the ages of 40 and 70, although some young adults have been stricken with the disease. Both men and women are affected equally. The onset of the disease is usually characterized by vague psychiatric or behavioral changes, which are followed within weeks or months by a progressive dementia that is often accompanied by abnormal vision and involuntary movements. There is no known cure for the disease, which is usually fatal within a year of the onset of symptoms.

The disease was first described in the 1920s by the German neurologists Hans Gerhard Creutzfeldt and Alfons Maria Jakob. Creutzfeldt-Jakob disease is similar to other neurodegenerative diseases such as kuru, a human disorder, and scrapie, which occurs in sheep and goats. All three diseases are types of transmissible spongiform encephalopathies, so called because of the characteristic sponge-like pattern of neuronal destruction that leaves brain tissue filled with holes.

Although Creutzfeldt-Jakob disease can be acquired through infection with the prion protein, all but 1 percent of cases are either inherited or sporadic (i.e., occurring at random). Sporadic forms account for the majority of cases of the disease—between 85 and 90 percent. In these cases it is unclear what molecular process causes the prion protein to appear in the first place. The protein may arise from a mutation incurred as the body ages or as a result of a spontaneous conversion in the protein's shape. The remaining 10 to 15 percent of cases show a familial pattern of inheritance. In these inherited cases a mutation in the prion protein gene (designated *PRNP*), which

STANLEY B. PRUSINER

(b. May 28, 1942, Des Moines, Iowa, U.S.)

American biochemist and neurologist Stanley B. Prusiner discovered in 1982 the disease-causing proteins called prions. His discovery won him the 1997 Nobel Prize for Physiology or Medicine.

Prusiner grew up in Cincinnati, Ohio, and was educated at the University of Pennsylvania (A.B., 1964; M.D., 1968). After spending four years in biochemical research, he became (1972) a resident in neurology at the University of California, San Francisco, School of Medicine. He joined the faculty there in 1974 and became a professor of neurology and biochemistry. While a neurology resident, he was in charge of a patient who died of a rare fatal degenerative disorder of the brain called Creutzfeldt-Jakob disease. Prusiner became intrigued by this little-known class of neurodegenerative disorders—the spongiform encephalopathies—that caused progressive dementia and death in humans and animals. In 1974 he set up a laboratory to study scrapie, a related disorder of sheep, and in 1982 he claimed to have isolated the scrapie-causing agent. He claimed that this pathogenic agent, which he named "prion," was unlike any other known pathogen, such as a virus or bacterium, because it consisted only of protein and lacked the genetic material contained within all life-forms that is necessary for replication.

When first published, the prion theory met with much criticism but became widely accepted by the mid-1990s. In 1996, when a new variant of Creutzfeldt-Jakob disease emerged in Great Britain, Prusiner's research was the focus of national attention. Fears abounded that the new variant of the disease might be linked to "mad cow" disease, a brain disorder that first appeared in British cattle a decade earlier. Some evidence suggested that the mad cow prion may have jumped species, infecting humans who consumed beef contaminated with the infectious agent. Because mad cow disease was believed to have been caused when the agent that causes scrapie in sheep was transmitted to cattle in feed, there was precedent for species-jumping events to occur. Prusiner's research also could have significant implications for such disorders as Alzheimer disease and Parkinson disease, which seemed to share certain characteristics with the diseases caused by prions.

Prusiner received the Albert Lasker Basic Medical Research Award (1994) and the Louisa Gross Horowitz Prize (1997) for his discoveries pertaining to neurodegenerative disease. After he was appointed director of the Institute for Neurodegenerative Diseases at the University of California, San Francisco, he founded InPro Biotechnology, Inc. (2001). The company was designed to further develop and commercialize discoveries and technologies conceived in his laboratory at the university. Among the technologies promoted by InPro was a test to detect bovine spongiform encephalopathy in cattle and sheep, chronic wasting disease in deer and elk, and Creutzfeldt-Jakob disease in humans. Prusiner also wrote several books during his career, including Slow Transmissible Diseases of the Nervous System (1979; cowritten by William Hadlow) and Prion Biology and Diseases (2004).

encodes the protein, is passed from parent to child in a dominant fashion (i.e., only one of the two copies of the gene that are inherited—one from each parent—need be mutated for disease to occur). More than 30 different mutations in *PRNP* that give rise to prion proteins have been identified. While some of these mutations cause Creutzfeldt-Jakob disease, others cause Gerstmann-Sträussler-Scheinker syndrome and fatal familial insomnia. In addition, mutations have been identified that do not cause disease but may render individuals more susceptible to infection with the prion. These latter mutations may be involved in some of the sporadic incidences of the disease.

There is no evidence that a person with Creutzfeldt-Jakob disease is contagious. The rare cases of Creutzfeldt-Jakob disease that arise from human-to-human transmission have resulted only from exposure to the prion during medical procedures. This form of the disease is known as iatrogenic Creutzfeldt-Jakob disease (iCJD). Such accidental transmission has occurred in corneal transplants, through the use of contaminated medical or surgical instruments, and through the transfusion of contaminated blood products, including prion-infected plasma. Transmission also may have occurred through the injection of growth hormone derived from human pituitary glands.

Although human-to-animal prion transmission has been demonstrated in the laboratory, researchers are not sure whether prions that cause disease in one species can give rise to a prion disease in humans. Concern about this type of transmission increased in the mid-1990s when a number of young adults in Great Britain developed a new variant form of Creutzfeldt-Jakob disease (nvCJD). There is increasing evidence that these cases resulted from the consumption of tissues (notably nerve tissue) contaminated with the prion that causes bovine spongiform encephalopathy, or mad cow disease. Chronic wasting disease, which is caused by a prion that occurs in elk and deer, is similar in nature to bovine spongiform encephalopathy. Although there have been no cases of animal-to-human transmission of this prion, researchers suspect that eating contaminated tissues of deer and elk could give rise to another variant form of Creutzfeldt-Jakob disease. As a result, scientists have been monitoring cases of Creuztfeldt-Jakob disease in areas where chronic wasting disease is endemic.

KURU

Kuru is an infectious, fatal degenerative disorder of the central nervous system that occurs primarily among the Fore people of Papua New Guinea. Initial symptoms of kuru (a Fore word for "trembling," or "shivering") include joint pain and headaches, which typically are followed by loss of coordination, tremor, and dementia. After the onset of symptoms the disease progresses steadily, and death occurs within two years. The transmission of kuru is attributed to Fore cannibalistic rituals of mourning in which the brain of the dead was eaten, especially by women and children. The disease has virtually disappeared with the discontinuance of this practice.

The American physician D. Carleton Gajdusek established the infectious nature of the disease. The infectious agent responsible for kuru is a prion. The accumulation of prions within nerve cells damages the nerves and causes the characteristic neurodegeneration of the disease.

FUNGAL DISEASES

Fungal diseases, or mycoses, are caused by any fungus that invades the tissues, resulting in superficial, subcutaneous, or systemic disease. Superficial fungal infections, also called dermatophytosis, are confined to the skin and are caused by *Microsporum*, *Trichophyton*, or *Epidermophyton*. Athlete's foot, for example, is caused by *Trichophyton* or *Epidermophyton*. Subcutaneous infections, which extend into tissues and sometimes into adjacent structures such as bone and organs, are rare and often chronic. Candidiasis (*Candida*) may be a superficial infection (thrush, vaginitis) or a disseminated infection affecting certain target organs, such as the eyes or kidneys. Painful ulcerations and nodules appear in subcutaneous tissues in sporotrichosis (*Sporothrix*). In systemic fungal infections fungi may invade normal hosts or immunosuppressed hosts (opportunistic

infections). Cryptococcosis (*Cryptococcus*) and histoplasmosis (*Histoplasma*) are marked by respiratory distress.

Effective therapy against the invasive fungi is limited because the same antibiotics that interfere with fungi also attack the host's cells. Griseofulvin has met with some success in the treatment of superficial mycoses. Amphotericin B and flucytosine have also been used in treating the subcutaneous and systemic mycoses.

BLASTOMYCOSIS

Blastomycosis is an infection of the skin and viscera caused by fungal organisms of the genus *Blastomyces*. There are two major types of blastomycosis: the North American type, caused by *B. dermatitidis*, and the South American type, caused by *B. brasiliensis*. In North American blastomycosis, skin and lung lesions are most common: pulmonary lesions vary in size from granulomatous nodules to confluent, diffuse areas of pus-forming inflammation involving the entire lobe of the lung. In the skin, micro-abscesses lie just beneath the epidermis, the outermost layer of the skin, and are associated with a granulomatous appearance of the surrounding skin.

In South American blastomycosis, the portal of entry is usually the nasopharynx (the part of the alimentary canal between the cavity of the mouth and the esophagus that is continuous with the nasal passages). Swelling and ulceration of the mouth or nose may cause the infection to spread to the nearby lymph nodes. Primary lesions may also occur in the lymphoid tissues in the lower abdomen. In both North and South American varieties, the infection may spread not only to the lymph nodes but also to such organs as the brain, bones, liver, spleen, and adrenals. Treatment includes the use of antibiotics, antifungal agents, and sulfonamide drugs.

CRYPTOCOCCOSIS

Cryptococcosis (also known as European blastomycosis, or torulosis) is a chronic fungal infection of humans caused by *Cryptococcocus neoformans* and *C. bacillispora*. The organism may be present in soil or dust and is often found in pigeon droppings, with resulting high concentrations on window ledges and around other nesting places. How humans become infected is uncertain, but it is probably by inhalation of fungus-bearing dust. A large number of pulmonary infections caused by cryptococcosis may go unreported. Its symptoms include fever, malaise, and a dry cough. Nine-tenths of those cases of infection that are reported are of the more serious type known as disseminated cryptococcosis. In such cases, the fungus can spread from the respiratory system to the central nervous system, causing meningitis (inflammation of the membranes surrounding the brain). The principal symptoms of the meningitis are headache, blurred vision, and confusion, lethargy, or personality change. The *Cryptococcus* fungus can also spread to and cause lesions in the skin, bones, and visceral organs. Immunocompromised patients (e.g., those infected with HIV/AIDS or those receiving immunosuppressive drugs) are at particularly high risk of cryptococcosis.

All forms of cryptococcosis respond to amphotericin B, the survival rate of patients treated being approximately 80–90 percent. Before this therapy was available, there were few reported survivors of cryptococcal meningitis.

HISTOPLASMOSIS

Histoplasmosis is an infection with the fungus *Histoplasma capsulatum* that occurs in humans and other animals. The disease is contracted by the inhalation of dust containing spores of the fungus. *H. capsulatum* prefers moist, shady conditions and is found in woods, caves, cellars, silos, and old chicken houses. The last seem to be especially important because chickens often are infected and pass enormous numbers of organisms in their droppings. The use of chicken manure in gardens may lead to histoplasmosis in humans. Dogs, rats, mice, bats, pigeons, skunks, and probably many other animals become infected and may help to spread the disease. The chief site of infection is the lungs, though the fungus can spread through the bloodstream to other organs, such as the liver, and bone marrow.

There are three forms of the disease. The primary acute form involves only the lungs and causes symptoms of fever, coughing, and chest pain. The infection may be slight and is often asymptomatic. In the progressive disseminated form of histoplasmosis, the infection spreads to the liver, spleen, or adrenal glands, where it causes lesions and damages those organs. In the third form, chronic cavitary disease, the infection remains in the lungs but damages them more seriously, causing coughing and severe shortness of breath. All three forms can produce symptoms that are indistinguishable from those caused by other acute respiratory infections such as pneumonia and pneumonitis (i.e., coughing, chest pain, difficulty in breathing, fever, chills, and fatigue). X-ray examination of the lungs may show a localized shadow or a more diffuse mottling of the lungs. In most cases, however, infection with *H. capsulatum* causes no symptoms or discomfort at all. Diagnosis is made by serological tests or by culture of the organism. Most cases do not require treatment, but patients with widespread disease can be treated with the antibiotic amphotericin B.

Histoplasmosis is worldwide in distribution and is endemic in parts of the east-central United States and the Mississippi River valley. Infants and men past middle age show the least resistance to symptomatic infection, but 50 to 80 percent of the total population of endemic areas show positive skin tests.

RINGWORM

Ringworm is a disease characterized by superficial skin lesions arising from infection with a highly specialized group of fungi called dermatophytes. These organisms live and multiply on the surface of the skin and feed on keratin, the horny protein constituting the major part of the outermost layer of the skin and of the hair and nails. The fungi produce responses in the skin that vary from slight scaling to blistering and marked disruption of the keratin layer. The lesions are usually round or ring shaped and can be either dry and scaly or moist and covered with vesicles (blisters), depending on the body area and the type of fungus involved.

Ringworm is also referred to as tinea, both names referring to the round shape of most of the lesions, similar to the larva of the clothes moth, genus *Tinea*. In specifying the condition, *tinea* is usually followed by a modifying term indicating the body area or characteristics of the lesions. Thus, ringworm of the scalp, beard, and nails is also referred to as tinea capitis, tinea barbae or tinea sycosis, and tinea unguium (also called onychomycosis), respectively; ringworm of the body, groin, hands, and feet, as tinea corporis, tinea cruris (also called jock itch), tinea manuum, and tinea pedis, respectively. Tinea pedis is commonly referred to as athlete's foot, which may be of either the dry or inflammatory type. In the latter type, the infection may lie dormant much of the time and undergo occasional acute exacerbations, with the development of vesicles (blisters) affecting chiefly the skin folds between the toes. The dry type is a chronic process marked by slight redness of the skin and dry scaling that may

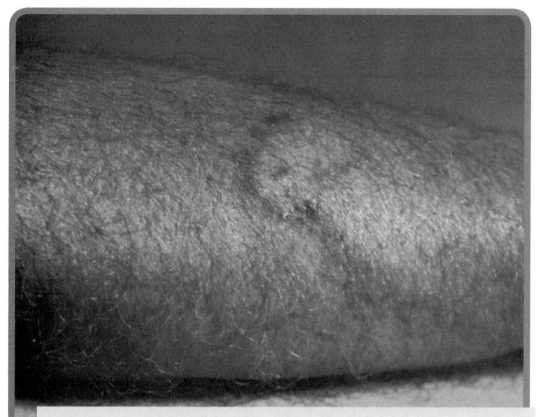

Ringworm, or tinea, is a fungus that infects the skin and causes skin lesions that are usually round or ring-shaped. CDC

involves the sole and sides of the foot as well as the toenails, which become thick and brittle.

Varieties of ringworm characterized by specific skin lesions include: Oriental ringworm, Tokelau ringworm, or tinea imbricata (Latin: "overlapping like tiles"), so called because it occurs chiefly in tropical climates and consists of concentric rings of overlapping scales; crusted, or honeycomb, ringworm, also called favus, a ringworm of the scalp, characterized by the formation of yellow, cup-shaped crusts that enlarge to form honeycomb-like masses; and black dot ringworm, also a ringworm of the scalp, deriving its distinctive appearance and name from the breaking of the hairs at the scalp surface. Except for ringworm of the scalp, which tends to be highly contagious, the contraction of ringworm depends to a large extent on individual susceptibility and predisposing factors, such as excessive perspiration.

Diagnosis of ringworm is made by observation and by microscopic examination. Treatment with topical or oral antifungal agents may be effective. Limited exposure to ultraviolet radiation may also be helpful.

CONCLUSION

Large-scale outbreaks of infectious disease, which have long plagued human societies, continue to rank among humanity's most-feared disasters in the modern era. The threat of epidemics and pandemics persists particularly because of increasing global population, increasing passenger travel, and lagging development of health care infrastructure in areas of the world where disease risk is highest. The speed with which infectious diseases can spread through a world both densely populated and connected by expedient travel systems was demonstrated by two notably dangerous outbreaks in the early 2000s: the SARS outbreak in 2003 and the H1N1 flu pandemic in 2009.

Efforts to speed national and international responses to emerging infectious diseases have played a vital role in preventing many small outbreaks from escalating into epidemics and pandemics. In the 20th century, many countries established national organizations to oversee disease control and to ensure preparedness in the event of an outbreak. Today, however, because of the rapid pace with which infectious diseases can spread, these national organizations

depend heavily on international support. This support is provided in large part by the World Health Organization's Global Alert and Response (GAR) system, a disease surveillance program designed for the rapid communication of information about outbreaks worldwide. GAR plays a particularly important role in monitoring emerging diseases and sending alerts to national health centres when these diseases migrate across national borders.

Efforts such as GAR have been strengthened by basic scientific investigation into the causes, pathology, and treatment of infectious diseases. Research projects aimed at understanding the origins and evolution of infectious agents have been pivotal in broadening global disease control from basic outbreak response to integrated outbreak prevention. One such project is the Global Viral Forecasting Initiative, which is designed to monitor the transmission of viruses from animals to humans in countries worldwide. The integration of disease forecasting and outbreak prediction with the work of biomedical researchers, epidemiologists, statisticians, pharmaceutical companies, and communications experts has become increasingly important. Indeed, in the 21st century, with the world's population growing at an unprecedented rate, the global fight against infectious disease relies on the effective unification of prevention, preparedness, and international collaboration.

GLOSSARY

aerobe An organism able to live and reproduce only in the presence of free oxygen (e.g., certain bacteria and certain yeasts).

anaerobe Living, active, occurring, or existing in the absence of free oxygen.

antibody Molecule in the immune system that circulates in blood and lymph in response to invasion by an antigen.

antigen Foreign substance in the body that induces an immune response.

antigenic drift Random genetic mutation of an infectious agent resulting in minor changes in proteins called antigens, which stimulate the production of antibodies by the immune systems of humans and animals.

attenuate To reduce the severity of (a disease) or the virulence or vitality of (a pathogenic agent); weaken.

bacillus Any of the rod-shaped, gram-positive bacteria (gram stain) that make up the genus Bacillus, widely found in soil and water.

chemotaxis Orientation or movement of cells or organisms in relation to chemical agents.

congenital Existing at or dating from birth.

enzootic Present in an animal population at all times but affecting only a few animals.

epidemic An occurrence of disease that is temporarily of high prevalence.

fomite An object (as a dish or an article of clothing) that may be contaminated with infectious organisms and serve in their transmission.

granulocyte A cell with granule-containing cytoplasm; specifically, a polymorphonuclear leukocyte.

iatrogenic Induced by a physician.

inoculation Process of producing immunity and method of vaccination that consists of introduction of the infectious agent onto an abraded or absorptive skin surface.

lentivirus Any of a group of retroviruses that cause slowly progressive often fatal animal and human diseases (as equine infectious anemia and AIDS).

mutation Alteration in the genetic material of a cell that is transmitted to the cell's offspring.

opsonin A constituent of blood serum that makes foreign cells (as invading pathogenic bacteria) more susceptible to the action of the phagocytes.

pandemic An epidemic of unusual extent and severity occurring over a wide geographic area and affecting an exceptionally high proportion of the population.

parasite An organism living in or on another living organism, obtaining from it part or all of its organic nutriment, and commonly exhibiting some degree of adaptive structural modification.

pathogen A specific cause of disease (as a bacterium or virus).

remission A temporary abatement of the symptoms of a disease.

serotype A group of intimately related microorganisms distinguished by the possession of a common set of antigens.

spirochete Any of an order (Spirochaetales) of spiral-shaped bacteria.

spore Reproductive cell capable of developing into a new individual without fusing with another reproductive cell.

sputum The matter discharged from the air passages in diseases of the lungs, bronchi, or upper respiratory tract that contains mucus and often pus, blood, fibrin, or bacterial products.

subclinical Marked by only slight abnormality and not being such as to give rise to overt symptoms; not detectable by the usual clinical tests.

vaccine Preparation containing either killed or weakened live microorganisms or their toxins, introduced by mouth, by injection, or by nasal spray to stimulate production of antibodies against an infectious agent.

viscus (plural viscera) An internal organ of the body; especially one (as the heart, liver, or intestine) located in the great cavity of the trunk proper.

zoonosis Any infectious disease transmitted between humans and other vertebrate animals.

BIBLIOGRAPHY

Gerald L. Mandell, John E. Bennett, and Raphael Dolin (eds.), *Mandell, Douglas, and Bennett's Principles and Practice of Infectious Diseases*, 7th ed. (2010), is a modern textbook that the general reader may find informative and useful. Ronald T.D. Emond, H.A.K. Rowland, and Philip D. Welsby, *A Color Atlas of Infectious Diseases*, 4th ed. (2003), uses colour photographs to reveal the actual clinical features associated with various infectious diseases. Laurie Garrett, *The Coming Plague: Newly Emerging Diseases in a World Out of Balance* (1994), is a Pulitzer Prize-winning account that focuses on emerging infectious diseases. Richard M. Krause (ed.), *Emerging Infections: Biomedical Research Reports* (1998, reissued 2000), is an excellent collection of articles edited by the former director of the U.S. National Institute of Allergy and Infectious Diseases. King K. Holmes (ed.), *Sexually Transmitted Diseases*, 4th ed. (2008), is a well-written text on a facet of infectious disease that is assuming increasing importance in society. Paul W. Ewald, *Evolution of Infectious Disease* (1993, reissued 1996), an accessible work, was the first to present a Darwinian perspective on infectious disease.

André Siegfried, *Routes of Contagion* (also published as *Germs and Ideas: Routes of Epidemics and Ideologies*, 1965; originally published in French, 1960); and Henry E. Sigerist, *Civilization and Disease* (1943, reissued 1970), deal with the effect of disease on human life and history; both are nontechnical. William H. McNeill, *Plagues and Peoples* (1976, reissued 1998), is a modern classic that looks at the role of epidemics in human history from an interdisciplinary perspective. Two other excellent books on the history of infectious disease are Charles-Edward Amory Winslow, *The Conquest of Epidemic Disease: A Chapter in the History of Ideas* (1943, reprinted 1980); and H. Zinsser, *Rats, Lice, and History* (1935, reissued 2000).

Basic information on the political, demographic, and scientific aspects of HIV/AIDS is provided by Alan Whiteside, *HIV/AIDS: A Very Short Introduction* (2008). Comprehensive coverage of the virus and disease is provided by Hung Fan, Ross F. Conner, and Luis P. Villarreal, *AIDS: Science and Society*, 5th ed. (2007). The effects of social and economic issues in Africa on epidemiological and biomedical research of AIDS are discussed in Ezekiel Kalipeni et al. (eds.), *HIV and AIDS in Africa: Beyond Epidemiology* (2003).

An informative documentary covering progress in both the sociopolitical and the scientific realms of HIV/AIDS is *The Age of AIDS* (2006), a PBS Home Video written and produced by Renata Simone, William Cran, and Greg Barker and narrated by Will Lyman. A critically acclaimed documentary about the AIDS pandemic and its impact on people worldwide is *A Closer Walk* (2006), a Worldwide Documentaries film, produced and directed by Robert Bilheimer and narrated by Glenn Close and Will Smith.

INDEX